Addiction and Responsibility

Philosophical Psychopathology: Disorders of the Mind

Jeffrey Poland and Jennifer Radden, Series Editors

Addiction and Responsibility Edited by Jeffrey S. Poland and George Graham (2011)

Psychiatry in the Scientific Image Dominic Murphy (2006)

Brain Fiction: Self-Deception and the Riddle of Confabulation William Hirstein (2004)

Imagination and Its Pathologies Edited by James Phillips and James Morley (2003)

Imagination and the Meaningful Brain Arnold H. Modell (2003)

When Self-Consciousness Breaks: Alien Voices and Inserted Thoughts G. Lynn Stephens and George Graham (2000)

The Myth of Pain Valerie Gray Hardcastle (1999)

Divided Minds and Successive Selves: Ethical Issues in Disorders of Identity and Personality Jennifer Radden (1996)

Addiction and Responsibility

edited by Jeffrey Poland and George Graham

The MIT Press
Cambridge, Massachusetts
London, England

© 2011 Massachusetts Institute of Technology

For information about special quantity discounts, please email special_sales @mitpress.mit.edu

This book was set in Stone Sans and Stone Serif by Toppan Best-set Premedia Limited. Printed and bound in the United States of America.

Library of Congress Cataloging-in-Publication Data

Society for Philosophy and Psychology. Meeting (34th : 2008 : University of Pennsylvania)
Addiction and responsibility / edited by Jeffrey Poland and George Graham.
    p. cm. — (Philosophical psychopathology)
Includes bibliographical references and index.
ISBN 978-0-262-01550-9 (hardcover : alk. paper)
1. Self-control—Congresses. 2. Responsibility—Congresses. 3. Psychology, Pathological—Philosophy—Congresses. 4. Dependency (Psychology)—Congresses. 5. Compulsive behavior—Psychological aspects—Congresses. 6. Psychology and philosophy—Congresses. I. Poland, Jeffrey Stephen. II. Graham, George, 1945– III. Title.
BJ1533.D49S67 2008
178—dc22

                                                                2010040931

10 9 8 7 6 5 4 3 2 1

To Barbara and to Patricia

Contents

Series Foreword

The Philosophical Psychopathology series publishes interdisciplinary work that is broadly concerned with psychopathology and that has significance for conceptual, methodological, scientific, ethical, and social issues related to contemporary mental health practices, as well as for more traditional philosophical issues such as the nature of mind, rationality, agency, and responsibility. In providing a philosophical examination of the forms, limits, and lessons of mental disorder as well as its study and treatment, the broader goal is to foster an interdisciplinary community focusing on issues in mental health and illness.

The present volume brings together scholars from a wide range of disciplines to address scientific, clinical, social, legal, and philosophical questions concerning the nature of addiction and its bearing on questions of individual responsibility. The disciplines represented include philosophy, psychiatry, psychology, neuroscience, and law. In addition, several authors expand the focus by addressing first-person experiences and perspectives that complement the understanding derived from the more formal disciplines. From this collection of perspectives, authors produce a range of views on such issues as how best to conceive of addictive behavior, the nature of addiction-related impairments, and whether those suffering from addictions are responsible for becoming addicted, for their addiction-related behavior, or for overcoming their addictions. As such, the volume furthers the aims of the series by promoting a rich discussion from a variety of scholarly disciplines and from diverse and divergent points of view.

Jeffrey Poland and Jennifer Radden, Series Editors

Preface

A perennial problem in the theory of human action and agency is how best to understand self-control, how we should describe the processes that constitute self-directed or self-governed behavior. Theorists sometimes say that we can understand self-control best if we understand its failure or absence and then compare and contrast its presence with its absence. Addictive behaviors are often assumed to be prototypical instances of behaviors that are not truly self-controlled and in which self-governance is absent. People may say, "I wasn't really in control when I gambled or took drugs." "I was addicted." "I could not help myself." Is there any validity in that manner of speech? Are we responsible for our addictions? Do we somehow make and direct them? If not, why or when not?

In 2007 we began thinking that this would be a good set of questions to pursue in a special session or colloquium of the Society for Philosophy and Psychology (SPP) at its annual meeting in 2008. The SPP is a robustly interdisciplinary group, and with the right mix of participants we believed that it would offer a stimulating venue. We proposed such a colloquium to the program chair. A colloquium on the eventual topic of this book then took place, under our direction, at the University of Pennsylvania, where the Society met in 2008. The participants were to include George Ainslie, Louis Charland, Owen Flanagan, and Nancy Petry. Louis and Nancy were (at the last minute) unable to attend, although their presentations were complete. So the two of us substituted for them. When the lively session was complete, we thought "This would make a good topic for a collection with the MIT Press." We proposed it to Tom Stone, who then was philosophy editor for the Press. The project had Tom's immediate and enthusiastic endorsement, for which we are grateful. The current book began to take shape.

We asked the invited participants for the session to publish versions of their papers in the book. We also wanted representation from several additional key theorists. Inviting all those who appear here went remarkably well. The questions raised and discussed in this book struck a responsive chord with everyone who was invited to participate and met with continued enthusiastic support from the Press. At the Press the project was welcomed by Phil Laughlin, Marc Lowenthal, and Gita Manaktala. We are appreciative of the support of both the Press and the SPP. We also wish to express our gratitude to the RISD Liberal Arts Humanities Fund for generous support for the creation of the index, and to Tracy Yonemoto for creating it.

There is no special way in which to read a book like this. One can browse through it. One can, we hope, teach from it. One can identify certain papers as potentially contributory to one's own research. One can learn from it. One does not have to be an academic or mental health or legal professional to read the book. Students in different disciplines and at different university or professional educational levels should be able to read the contributions.

We have ordered or arranged the contributions in a manner that we find helpful in thinking about addiction and responsibility, and this is discussed in our introduction. There is nothing inescapably linear in this ordering, however, and no single topic that is the subject of both an evolving and sharpening focus. It is a book with multiple subjects, diverse perspectives, and contributions from several distinct fields.

Each of us has written elsewhere on some of its topics. But this book is not about our own personal work. It is about new work of others. Except for some stage setting in our introduction, the authors speak for themselves.

1 Introduction: The Makings of a Responsible Addict

Jeffrey Poland and George Graham

A person drinks a glass of wine. Suppose this is an instance of recreational behavior. It is a minor part of dinner in a fancy restaurant with family and friends. If someone gave the person a good reason for not drinking that glass of wine, such as that it would interfere with her ability to drive home, the person would refrain.

Suppose a person sitting at a table next to the wine drinker is consuming a fifth glass of scotch within an hour. Suppose that because of this behavior, heavy drinking, which he engages in imprudently and often, he has lost his job, and his spouse has divorced him. Suppose also that the person cannot be persuaded to stop drinking the scotch. He has an "unhealthy" preference for the scotch. He is, in fact, addicted to alcohol. To his obvious detriment, he depends on it.

Consuming the scotch is not like shivering when one gets cold or grinding one's teeth when one is asleep. It is in some manner voluntary, deliberate, or intentional. But it is not as voluntary, deliberate, or reflectively intentional as the behavior of drinking the wine. Some causal responsibility on the part of the addict is present. But it is not of the paradigmatic sort exhibited in enjoying wine with family and friends.

This volume is focused on the scotch, as it were, not on the wine. It is focused on addiction. It is also focused on the role or roles of responsibility in and for addiction. It explores how best to understand the nature of addiction and the responsibility of an addict, as well as of other persons, including those who care for or treat an addict. Our intention in this editorial introduction is to engage in some conceptual stage setting: to describe the various topics examined in the book, the multiple perspectives offered herein, and the profound significance that the book's topics have for individuals and society. To encourage this fusion of multiplicity and significance, the contributors to the volume reflect a variety of disciplinary orientations and have been given substantial freedom or latitude with respect to the focal orientation of each chapter. Each essay also is new and original with this volume.

Background: Issues and Themes

What Is Addiction?

There is, of course, no simple answer to this question, no definitive definition of the very idea of addiction. By themselves, of course, abstract definitions provide no substantial level of understanding; rather, what is required is a complex theoretical framework that encompasses many facets of the phenomena labeled "addiction." To begin, an adequate theoretical framework will need to make distinctions among the types of objects to which an individual might become addicted. Not all addictions are to substances, since a variety of so-called "process addictions" are also widely recognized (e.g., eating, sex, gambling, self-injury, the Internet). Whether there is a unitary phenomenon that takes multiple objects of various sorts or whether there are as many types of addiction as there are objects of addiction is an open question. Further, an adequate theory should clarify what is meant by "addicted" drug seeking or dependency and use. Does such a term refer to patterns of behavior or to the character of the causes of behavior or both? And, in any event, which patterns and which causes are involved? Perhaps more important than explicating the very notion of addiction are delineations of the phases and time course of addiction and differentiations among the processes associated with becoming addicted, addiction-related seeking and use, struggling to overcome an addiction, remission, and recovery. Such theoretical complexities are of major significance for research, clinical practice, and, most importantly, the personal experience of the individual addict.

Another related limitation of abstract definitions of "addiction" is that they mask a considerable amount of causal ambiguity, that is, the fact that superficially similar patterns of behavior are associated with considerable heterogeneity of causal and constitutive structures and processes. To resolve such ambiguity requires recognition and study of multiple perspectives, multiple levels of analysis, and multiple dimensions of the phenomena labeled as "addiction." Specifically, the first-, second-, and third-person perspectives are all potentially relevant to understanding addiction, where each has its own particular modes of access to information of certain proprietary sorts. And, insofar as each perspective, while having access to its proprietary sorts of information, does not have access to information available from the other perspectives, how can any provide a complete understanding of addiction? How, for example, could a portrait of addiction that lays out one or another causal mechanism that explains patterns of addictive behavior provide any understanding of the experience of being an addict (or, of course, vice versa)? Authors in this volume vary considerably with respect to their focus on one or another of these broad types of perspective, although all are aware of the importance of each. A few have even been addicts themselves.

Further, the resolution of causal and constitutive ambiguity associated with addiction depends crucially on investigation at distinct levels of analysis, including genetic, neurophysiological, neurocognitive, neuroaffective, higher-level cognitive, phenomenological, behavioral, social, and cultural levels. And as research is making abundantly clear, the relationships among variables at the same and different levels of such analysis are typically dynamic and nonlinear, making research and the models and findings they produce more and more complicated. Authors in this volume have collectively succeeded in laying out a variety of (partial) models of addiction-related phenomena. These include the incentive-sensitization theory (Berridge & Robinson), the ego-depletion theory (Levy), behavioral learning theories (Petry, Alessi, & Rash), pathological affect theory (Charland), a learning-impairment theory (Yaffe), and a theory based on hyperbolic discounting and recursive self-prediction (Ainslie). Such theories and models do perhaps conflict in certain individual ways, but they also may be better seen as potentially complementary forms of causal analysis that may or may not be integrated into a unified framework. Further, the dual questions of how such causal analyses are related to the subjective experience of the individual addict and whether such analyses are compatible with a more or less robust conception of human agency and responsibility loom large for anyone attempting to develop an integrated theory of addiction.

The multiple levels of investigation involved in addiction research raise and potentially address a number of traditional philosophical problems. Most notably the following problems are touched on in one way or another in this volume: the mind-body problem, the problem of other minds, the free will problem, and problems both of human agency and responsibility. That any of these problems is "solved" is unlikely, although interesting observations and suggestions are presented in the chapters by Ainslie (free will and agency), Flanagan (mind-body and other minds), Morse (agency and free will), Levy (agency and responsibility), Yaffe (agency and responsibility), Charland (agency and responsibility), and Berridge and Robinson (mind body, free will, agency and responsibility). Those who come at the issues from the framework of the sciences are typically involved in problems of integrating findings from disparate research programs at different levels of analysis, and this inevitably brings them into contact with questions concerning relations between the mental and the physical. Those who are focused more on issues arising from within a first-person perspective, but who also take the third-person perspective of the sciences very seriously, are further engaged in how to integrate the findings of a phenomenological description or analysis and the findings of the sciences. In his chapter, for instance, Owen Flanagan brings to bear what he calls the "expanded natural method" to provide a framework for research into such integration. As alluded to above, that the various models and findings gleaned from various research programs and perspectives do not fit neatly and coherently into a single unifying framework is also a possibility, but it is one that does not necessarily compromise the value of each.

A further complication in comprehending and studying addiction-related phenomena concerns what may be described as the metaphysical status of addiction. Is addiction a brain disease, a moral failing, or something else, perhaps some sort of rational preference? The limited and evidently false dichotomy, brain disease or moral failing, fuels many ill-conceived debates, raises very difficult-to-resolve controversies over the proper analysis of the concepts of disease and moral failing, and masks deep-seated interests unrelated to the substance of questions concerning the nature of addiction (e.g., such interests may concern issues of access to health care or proprietary guild interests). As Morse discusses in his chapter, "status" questions are typically not probative in questions of legal responsibility, and we would add that they are not clearly probative with respect to most scientific and philosophical questions concerning addiction either.

This is especially the case with respect to whether addiction is a "mental disorder," perhaps as conceived within the *Diagnostic and Statistical Manual of Mental Disorders* (DSM). Putting aside the widely recognized problems with psychiatric classification as presented in the DSM, the lack of clarity concerning how to conceive of "mental disorder" that is manifest in the field of psychiatry creates suspicion over the value of categorizing addiction as a mental disorder. In addition, a variety of "disease"-related inferences are highly suspect, although also quite prevalent. Here are three:

1. The brains of addicted individuals are different from the brains of nonaddicted individuals; therefore, addiction to a substance is a brain disease.

2. X has difficulty controlling certain types of harmful behavior; therefore, X has a brain disease.

3. X has a brain disease; therefore, X is not responsible for behavior related to that disease.

Under close critical scrutiny such patterns of inference are clearly unsound, and they obscure important issues and confuse numerous discussions of addiction. Each is enthymematic, and when they are fleshed out, highly questionable premises come into view. For example, with respect to inference 3, candidate-intervening premises might be: if X has a brain disease, then X cannot control X's behavior, and if X cannot control X's behavior then X is not responsible for that behavior. But, the former premise is questionable, as Morse discusses in his chapter.

In lieu of substantial progress on such matters concerning the concepts of disease and disorder, it is probably best to focus on particular questions of interest concerning individuals in specific contexts (e.g., Was X responsible for committing a crime? or Should X be permitted access to health care resources? or Why does X exhibit certain patterns of behavior?). In all such cases disease or disorder status masks the genuinely relevant considerations and clouds engagement with the real issues of consequence.

Another issue is raised by the possibility that addiction is not anything at all: there is no "it" that is an addiction to some substance or activity; there is no objectively real status that one has as an addict or as someone with a disease, and so forth. Rather, there are only narratives or stories, with no reliable ways of constraining their content, that we tell about ourselves or that others tell about us or that attach to us as we enter into some institution. Such narratives might include that of "the chronic relapsing brain disease" or that of "the morally weak person who, although able to, does not resist temptation" or that of "one who has a bad habit that is difficult to break" or that of "the person who has lost control over his behavior and his life" or. . . . Such narratives bear directly not just on providing an understanding of how a person arrived at his current condition and situation but on how to understand those current conditions and situations, as well as what the future is likely to hold in store. All such attributions about the past, present, and future can have a decidedly powerful impact on what future course the person actually follows.

These issues of attributions and their impact arise acutely in the context of widely endorsed efforts at *destigmatizing* addiction and mental illness by advocating and teaching the idea that such conditions are brain diseases beyond a person's voluntary control and, hence, that they are conditions for which the person should not be blamed. In addition to its not being clearly the case that a brain disease is involved, such attributions are not clearly effective in reducing social stigma, and they pose a serious likelihood of introducing toxic first-person self-pathologizing or medicalizing attributions that may undermine a person's efforts to overcome her problems. There is much allure to medicalization, and it may well be appropriate to "medicalize" some conditions and, thereby, enable access for individuals to healthcare resources and insurance reimbursement, attract funding for research, and engender appropriate reactive attitudes in others. However, not all conditions warrant a "sick role," and, in some cases adopting such a stance is harmful to the interests and rights of the individual who is inappropriately cast into such a role.

In her chapter, Potter draws special attention to the variety of narratives that can be constructed concerning an individual, the ways in which such narratives can serve various interests and purposes, and the likelihood that some narratives might better serve the interests of particular individuals in their particular life context than others, which might, for example, be narratives informed by institutional authorities or conventional forms of understanding. Here the tension between first-person and third-person perspectives is manifest when the "best" narrative from the point of view of an individual might conflict with an institutional or conventional social narrative designed to serve other interests or to promote stigmatizing social stereotypes. Along these lines it is important to keep in mind that there are many "truths" concerning a particular person (addicted or otherwise) in his particular context, and which truths should be selected and identified as relevant in understanding that person will depend on a variety of pragmatic considerations (e.g., goals, interests, purposes, saliencies). If there is but one Ultimate Truth about us as persons, it embraces a multiplicity of contrasting aspects; if there are many truths about us, the set of them all is only very loosely "One." And in any event, different bodies of truth can have very different types of significance.

One special case concerning types of narrative is related to the focal issue of responsibility. Certainly an imaginative story teller can tell a story of a rock or a rat. But unlike the story of a human being, these tales are not narratives in a proper sense; rocks and rats harbor no responsibility for the "dramatic" episodes of their existence. They do not sculpt or author the conditions of their persistence, and, of course, they harbor neither moral nor legal responsibility for their circumstances or behavior. As we see below, there are various plausible ways of specifying the concepts of responsibility appropriate in discussions of addiction, and different conceptions will be more or less well suited to the demands of various contexts.

Another special case in which the choice among possible truths to focus on and narratives to tell arises in the context of what we will call "coping with addiction," something that can be understood from the first-person perspective of a person struggling with and attempting to overcome her addiction (with or without help) or from the third-person perspective of a clinician or other party concerned to help an individual overcome her addiction through some form of intervention. Certainly one important aspect of understanding what addiction is comes from an understanding of what might be involved in coping with addiction from either of these perspectives. Whether it is pharmacology-based therapy or behavioral rehabilitation or will power or a 12-step program or some other form of cognitive restructuring or social support, the question of which approach to overcoming and intervening is optimal presupposes important facts and values that may vary widely from case to case and from perspective to perspective.

Several authors in this volume have focused on just such questions about narrativity and coping, each from a somewhat different perspective. Whereas Potter focuses on the importance of the narrative that an individual embraces as her own, Petry and colleagues place heavy emphasis on the demonstrated efficacy of empirically grounded contingency-management techniques based on learning theory. And whereas both Garrett and Flanagan depict the exquisitely detailed individual character of their respective struggles with addiction, Garrett articulates and endorses the value of a framework of cognitive-affective restructuring grounded in ideas drawn from a variety of moral and religious traditions, whereas Flanagan emphasizes the importance of identifying "zones of control" and of social support that were of value to him. In the context of the present volume such approaches to understanding how addiction might be overcome bear directly on certain questions of responsibility, as the authors bring out, and we now touch on briefly.

What Is Responsibility?
Of primary importance for addressing the question of how addiction might bear on responsibility is to clarify how responsibility is to be conceived. In addition to "moral responsibility," which is generally conceived of as applying in all contexts of human activity, there are several more specific contexts in which questions concerning responsibility arise; and such contexts carry with them different standards and criteria for understanding and making determinations about the specific forms of responsibility appropriate to those contexts. Each of these more specific conceptions is tuned to the purposes, values, interests, relevant truths, limitations, and traditions of the corresponding context. Thus, as Morse outlines in detail in his chapter, "legal responsibility" reflects standards operating within the judicial system and involves such conditions as rationality and freedom from compulsion and duress. Charland, on the other hand, is concerned with questions of responsibility arising in health care and research contexts; the idea of responsibility for making health care decisions or decisions to participate in research is tightly associated with the requirements of informed consent and the types of condition that are required for giving such consent (e.g., factual understanding and adequate decision-making capacity).

Necessary conditions for moral responsibility have been conceptualized in various ways; possibilities include, X is responsible for A only if:

• A is an action that is intentional, voluntary, and free.
• A is an action that is rational and not the result of compulsion or duress.
• A is an action that is the result of X's capacity for "guidance control."

This latter conception of "guidance control" is a widely accepted concept developed by John Fisher and Mark Ravizza and concerns a certain sort of counterfactual sensitivity to reasons, understood partly in terms of the notions of "reasons responsiveness" and "reasons reactivity":

Reasons responsiveness Were X presented with a sufficient reason to act in a different way (from A), X would be capable of recognizing it as a sufficient reason.

Reasons reactivity X's mechanism that produces A would actually cause X to act otherwise in response to at least some sufficient reasons to do otherwise, if it is allowed to act unhindered.

In their chapters, Yaffe and Levy deploy this approach to understanding moral responsibility in their arguments.

Closely affiliated with conceptions of responsibility, whether they are general conceptions of moral responsibility or more context-specific conceptions, are conceptions of excuse from responsibility or of diminished responsibility. An excuse is, roughly, some condition that drives a wedge between a person and the wrongfulness (or rightfulness) of his act and is often associated with matters of knowledge, control, influence, and cognitive process. A person might be eligible for an excuse from responsibility (or a diminution of responsibility) if his act were a result of any of the following: loss of motor control, coercion, duress, ignorance, accident, mistake, lack of appreciation, irrationality of belief or of reasoning process. Several authors in this volume (Morse, Yaffee, Levy, Charland, Berridge and Robinson, Ainslie) discuss various features of addiction that are candidates for being excusing conditions, although these authors vary in the conclusions that they draw. Whereas some demur from reaching a definitive conclusion, others address directly the question of whether those suffering from an addiction are appropriately viewed as having diminished responsibility at least some of the time.

Other issues concerning responsibility come into view when we shift attention away from the person who may or may not be excused from responsibility for a wrongful act and toward other people who are in the person's life or who are part of the social landscape in which the person lives. Wrongful acts do not occur in a social vacuum, so it is appropriate to ask what roles and responsibilities others might have with respect to either the actions themselves or the agents who commit them. For example, do other people or institutions share in the responsibility for a person's addiction-related wrongful actions? Or, if not, do other people or institutions have responsibilities to change the social landscape in which such wrongful actions occur in order to make them less likely? Or, do other people or institutions have responsibilities to treat or rehabilitate, or to show compassion for, those who engage in such wrongful acts? In this volume, although the primary focus of attention is on the individual responsibility of those who suffer from an addiction, some attention is given to these broader questions concerning the responsibilities of others.

How Does Addiction Bear on Questions of Responsibility?

With respect to the question of how addiction bears on individual responsibility, many of the distinctions surveyed above must be deployed: What context and conception of responsibility is involved (moral, legal, clinical, research)? What are the specifics concerning the individual's addiction, and what impact do they have on processes or conditions related to a person's responsibility for some condition or act? What specifically is an individual supposed to be responsible for? With respect to this last question, an individual might be responsible for (1) becoming addicted to some object of addiction, (2) seeking and using his specific object of addiction, (3) other behavior or consequences related to his addiction (e.g., criminal activity, impact on family, friends, or community, harm to himself, consent to participate in research or treatment), or (4) overcoming his addiction. Several of the authors in this volume deploy such distinctions to specifically address questions of moral responsibility (Levy, Yaffe, and Garrett), legal responsibility (Morse), and responsibility in health care and research settings (Charland) and reach definitive conclusions, one way or another.

In each case the strategy of argument is to identify a relevant standard for determining responsibility in the identified context, to identify critical features of addictive processes, and to assess, given the relevant standard, whether or not those features are sufficient for a determination of responsibility for some sort of behavior or condition (from among 1–4). Other authors (Ainslie, Berridge and Robinson, Petry et al., Flanagan, and Potter) identify important considerations relevant to such questions, but they do not reach definitive conclusions on specific questions of responsibility. Rather, they identify important dimensions of the scientific, personal, cultural, and clinical background for addressing such questions.

With respect to the responsibilities of other individuals or institutions, there are at least three important areas to consider. First, in the context of health care, providers who are bound by standards of professional ethics have duties to secure informed consent before providing care or pursuing a research protocol, and this requires that they make determinations of whether an individual is capable of giving such consent. When clinicians fail in giving due diligence with respect to such determinations (either by ignoring a legitimate refusal or accepting an illegitimate consent), they fall short of their ethical obligations. In addition health care providers and institutions that are bound by standards of "evidence-based practice" and "best practice" have duties to identify and make available the best available therapies or rehabilitation interventions for those suffering from health problems; when such interventions exist but are ignored because of cognitive or interest-based biases, such providers and institutions again fall short of their ethical obligations. Social, professional, and institutional biases and stigmata associated with addiction and those who are addicted may lead to unethical conduct and inferior health care services that are not appropriately responsive to the health care needs of addicts and may ultimately promote addiction and its harmful consequences.

Second, with respect to the administration of the law and the meting out of punishment for criminal activity, the core question of whether addiction bears upon determinations of individual legal responsibility is addressed against a backdrop of law and social policy that may be relevant to the substantial prevalence of addiction and addiction-related criminal activity. As Morse argues in his chapter, the legal system is bound to administer the law as it is written, although he allows that current laws may be defective and that responsibilities might exist to replace such laws with better ones. Further, in the administration of the law, judges might show compassion during sentencing for those suffering from addiction, even as those individuals have been found guilty of criminal conduct. Whether such compassion rises to the level of a judicial responsibility is not clear, although such compassion might be the mark of a superior form of justice. Thus, a context constituted by legal or health care policies and practices that are harmfully flawed or biased raises the question of who is responsible for improving those policies and practices.

Finally, although not specifically addressed in this volume, a further feature of the cultural context in which questions of addiction and responsibility arise concerns business practices that may promote addictions of various sorts. Visible examples concern the practices of casino owners and the developers of casino gaming technologies, the manufacturers of tobacco products, and the manufacturers of legal drugs advertised for use in health care contexts. To the extent that such practices are designed to manipulate users of the related products in a way that leads to addiction in many cases, the question arises concerning whether such business entities or the individuals within them have obligations to reform such practices (e.g., by warning consumers or by ceasing in a deceptive and manipulative practice). Here again, the question of responsibility concerns those who are part of the context in which addiction occurs rather than the persons who suffer addictions.

Overview of the Chapters

We would now like to turn to each of the chapters in this volume. We will not highlight connections among the chapters; to some extent, we have already done that. Nor will we try to smooth over differences of perspectives that may exist among the chapters. As noted, differences among perspectives animate the heart of the contemporary literature on addiction and responsibility.

In "Drug Addiction as Incentive Sensitization," Kent Berridge and Terry Robinson lay out the main claims and implications of their "incentive sensitization" model of addiction. In so doing they outline evidence for the model as well as argue for its superiority relative to dual-process learning-theoretic approaches. They further identify various implications of the model for cognition, motivation, evaluation of behavioral outcomes, decision making, and behavior choice that are potentially relevant to determinations of responsibility. For example, they identify biases in attention, a distinction between wanting and liking, compulsive wanting/desire, irrational desire, unconscious desire, nonintentional desire, and impairments of executive control over behavior. Indeed, they take the core of addiction to be the combination of an impairment of executive control with incentive sensitization. Their research represents an example of integrative research that brings together behavioral, cognitive, and neuroscientific findings in a coherent model that explains a substantial portion of the phenomena labeled "addiction." And, it provides a significant factual backdrop for the assessment of responsibility in various contexts.

In "Free Will as Recursive Self-Prediction: Does a Deterministic Mechanism Reduce Responsibility?," George Ainslie embeds a discussion of addiction and responsibility in the larger philosophical context of the classical problem of free will; he navigates toward a compatibilist approach in which ascriptions of freedom and responsibility do not require a rejection of strictly deterministic mechanisms as the causes of behavior. He further rejects cultural assumptions of the self as a unitary governor and the will as the self's organ of selection. Rather, Ainslie develops a view of free will as involving unpredictability, initiative, and responsibility, a view of the self as a population of partially conflicting interests, and a view of the will as a property that emerges from these conflicts. Ainslie builds on research establishing the existence of a hyperbolic discounting function with respect to preferences in humans and the effectiveness of various strategies (e.g., early commitment, bundling of choices, recursive self-prediction) for managing the distortions this function introduces into human decision making (e.g., impulsiveness and preference reversals over time). He proposes a "marketplace model" of decision making in which the process of choice is analogous to an economic marketplace trading in a limited resource (viz., access to a limited channel of behavior) and in which self-control is an emergent property not requiring a central organ of the will.

In laying out the model, Ainslie identifies "recursive self-prediction" as a vital process by which current commitments and choices impact future commitments and choices; this process involves the building of cognitive resources that enable individuals to exercise self-control (e.g., keep to current commitments in the face of temptations to defect). In addiction, these resources become diminished in the context of numerous defections (e.g., from a commitment to abstinence); this is a form of psychological damage that he refers to as "motivational bankruptcy." Although he rejects the idea that diseases (or other abnormal causes) ipso facto provide an excuse, Ainslie allows that some addicts might be excused from responsibility when they reach this bankrupt condition. However, the setting of criteria for when bankruptcy occurs is a culture-bound matter, and there may well be no practical way of determining whether such a condition exists in individual cases; hence, the model may have limited pragmatic value with respect to determinations of responsibility and excuse. Within this framework Ainslie also provides an understanding of self-blame and social blame, and he notes that regeneration of the will can occur as addicts reframe their choices.

In "Addiction, Responsibility, and Ego Depletion," Neil Levy explicates and deploys the ego-depletion hypothesis of addiction, according to which a certain form of loss of control over mental life is a significant feature in addictions. After rejecting both the medical model and the moral model of addiction, he argues further that strength of craving and aversiveness of withdrawal are not sufficient for making either proximal or distal addictive behavior compulsive and hence not reactive to reasons. Rather, he suggests that addictive behavior is similar to much of "normal" behavior and that both can be produced by mechanisms that render it not responsible. According to the ego-depletion hypothesis, addiction involves periodic failures of self-control due to vacillations in the individual's self-control reserves: when such reserves are strong, a preference for abstinence may result; whereas when they are weakened, the individual may experience a judgment shift and proceed to engage in drug-seeking or drug-consuming behavior. As a consequence, Levy contends that standard accounts of moral responsibility must be amended to add ego depletion (failure of control over one's mental life) to failures of reasons responsiveness and reactivity as conditions that undermine responsibility. He concludes that, although addicts are moderately reasons responsive, they cannot be expected to exercise greater self-control over their mental life than they do, and hence they are not to blame for their failures.

In "Lowering the Bar for Addicts," Gideon Yaffe argues that addicts should be excused from certain things but not others, and he bases his argument on the claim that addicts should be excused, when they are, not because they are disabled but because they should not be expected to comply with a norm when it demands too high a cost. Specifically, he argues that, when the burdens of compensation for a deficit are too high, the person cannot be expected to carry them in order to comply with some relevant norm of conduct. In the case of addiction the deficit is a learning deficit that makes addicted individuals relatively ineffective in learning from their own mistakes about the values of actions and outcomes in a way that guides their behavior, and the burden of compensation is to have their behavior guided by a mechanism that does not involve the individual's appreciating the reasons for the behavior (i.e., the burden is an abdication of individual autonomy). The hypothesized deficit (for which there is substantial evidence) is one that not only is associated with active use of a substance but also is present even when the addict is not using a substance. The bottom line is that addicts are responsible for whichever of their behavior is such that they could have avoided doing it without giving up their autonomy.

In "Decision-Making Capacity and Responsibility in Addiction," Louis Charland addresses the question of whether severely heroin-dependent individuals are responsible for their decision to consent to therapy or research protocols involving their drug of choice. By challenging the presumption of capacity when consent is provided and focusing on impairments of decision-making capacity found in many heroin-addicted individuals, he argues that such individuals are not fully responsible for their decisions to consent in these circumstances. The argument is premised on the hypothesis that pathological processes of valuation at the core of addiction-related cognition lead to a failure to appreciate the significance of various options and to a vacillation in the evaluation of options over time. Such vacillation and lack of appreciation diminish an individual's capacity to provide informed consent to participate in treatment and research protocols involving his drug of choice.

In "Addiction and Criminal Responsibility," Stephen Morse argues that addicts are, for the most part, responsible for becoming addicted and for their further drug-related activity. Specifically, those who are addicted are, most of the time, legally responsible for their drug-related criminal activity (e.g., behavior related to drug seeking and drug consumption). This is so, according to Morse, because most of the time addicts have sufficient capacity for action that is neither irrational nor compelled nor grounded in a hard choice (i.e., none of the relevant and recognized legal excuses are present). In the course of his discussion, he clears away a variety of false claims about addiction and responsibility and argues that metaphysical determinism is irrelevant to legal responsibility, that status as an addict or as mentally disordered is not an excuse, and that those who argue that addictive behavior is excused because it is caused by genetic, neurophysiological, social, or other nonintentional causal variables are guilty of what he calls "the fundamental psycholegal error." Addiction, disease, or any other causal variables are relevant to questions of responsibility only to the extent that they cause a genuine excusing condition such as lack of rational capacity or compulsion. Nonetheless, despite contending that addicts are responsible agents most of the time, Morse suggests that contemporary law and public policy concerning addiction fail to measure up to the standards of a just society; vastly more treatment options for addicts should be available to help reduce their risk for criminal behavior; and doctrines of mitigation should be expanded to cover cases where addicts commit crimes that are not part of criminal use itself.

In "Grounding for Understanding Self-Injury as Addiction or (Bad) Habit," Nancy Potter explores the question of whether self-injurious behavior (SIB) is best understood as a form of addictive behavior and argues that it is not. More deeply, she also examines why this is an important question, raising issues about the nature of addiction as well as about habitual self-injury. Potter frames her discussion around the notion of a narrative (i.e., stories that are told about ourselves and each other to make sense of some event, state, activity, or condition and to guide responses to such events), and she notes that different narratives can be constructed from different perspectives and designed for various purposes. Conventional and culturally prevalent narratives (e.g., a medical disease model, a moral model) may capture some features of a condition, but they tend to lose a grip on the particularity of a person's identity and life context; and such conventional narratives may serve interests not aligned well with those of the individual. Other narratives generated by individual addicts may be toxic because of heavy emphasis on guilt, blame, and helplessness or because of the influence of prevalent cultural narrative themes. The question of which narrative is best for given purposes depends on pragmatic considerations that are sensitive to perspective and context, and, given the limitations of any perspective, multiple narratives may be necessary for an understanding of SIB and other patterns of addictive behavior. Potter advocates the importance of opening up space for alternative, patient-generated, and patient-friendly narratives tied to particular persons and their (frequently invisible to others) perspectives.

In "Contingency Management Treatments of Drug and Alcohol Use Disorders," Nancy Petry, Sheila Alessi, and Carla Rash emphasize the importance of theoretical models of addiction for designing effective strategies and techniques for clinical intervention. After calling into question both disease and moral models, they suggest that behavioral models, focusing on the role of environmental contingencies in establishing and maintaining addictive patterns of behavior, provide the basis for a useful clinical approach. Although such approaches have demonstrated efficacy, they are nevertheless not often employed in clinical settings as a result of practical barriers and philosophical biases and disputes. This discrepancy obviously raises questions about the responsibility of clinicians to provide evidence-based therapies as part of best practice. After outlining considerable clinical evidence establishing the clinical superiority of voucher-based and prize-based contingency management approaches over standard approaches, and the cost effectiveness of prize-based approaches, Petry et al. strongly suggest that obstacles and biases should be overcome and that such approaches ought to be in more widespread use.

In "Addiction, Paradox, and the Good That I Would," Richard Garrett is concerned with the question of what is necessary or at least helpful for overcoming addiction, and he addresses his own addiction to food and his personal struggle to overcome it. Conceiving of this struggle as a fundamentally moral and spiritual matter concerning what kind of life to live and what kind of person to be, Garrett approaches it as a process of cognitive-affective-behavioral restructuring, a process that is grounded in fundamental ethical principles (e.g., the Golden Principle, Buddha's Eightfold Path). Such restructuring consists, in part, in embracing certain attitudes and commitments to oneself and to others (e.g., the recognition of the dignity and worth of all persons, including oneself; an attitude of self-love and love of others; and a commitment to the welfare and well-being of oneself and all other persons). Further, the core strategy for overcoming addiction consists in identifying and engaging in behavior that is under the control of reason ("what one can do") for the purpose of bringing under such control behavior that is (currently) beyond the control of reason ("what one would do"). In laying out this framework, Garrett demonstrates the importance of the first-person perspective and associated narratives for understanding addiction, and he shows that a moral model need not consist of toxic and naive moralizing or of associated (and highly prevalent) guilt and blame narratives. Rather, a sophisticated moral understanding grasps the struggle with addiction in the context of an individual's particular life project and identifies key issues that all persons face and key normative principles that constitute a way to live a life and face life's struggles.

In "What Is It Like to Be an Addict?," Owen Flanagan provides a personal narrative of his struggles with addiction as a basis for exploring issues ranging from the integration of forms of understanding developed from a variety of phenomenological and scientific perspectives to issues related to the nature of recovery from addiction. His phenomenological read out of what it is like to be an addict sets the stage for discussions of the limits of knowledge characteristic of both phenomenological and scientific perspectives, the importance of the particularity of an individual addict's experience and situation, and the distinction between talking of an addiction as an entity and talking of an addict as a person living a life in the world. Further, emphasizing the distinction between two kinds of epistemic "capture" (i.e., one concerning explanation of cause and constitution of addictive brains, psychology, and behavior; another concerning first-person experience uniquely accessible to the individual), he outlines an "expanded natural method" that recognizes the importance of multiple phenomenological and scientific perspectives, gives priority to none, emphasizes a process of mutual coordination and constraint, and provides a context for moving among different levels and perspectives as required in particular contexts.

With respect to recovery, as comprehended via the phenomenology of agency, control, and responsibility, Flanagan allows that there are multiple narratives available to addicts that may be more or less useful to individuals at different stages of their addiction. In his own case, recovery was based on a view of addiction as a deep moral problem of who, what, and how he wanted to be in his life and on a process of establishing and leveraging zones of control that promoted a goal of reintegration and that was grounded in social support.

Concluding Comments

Besides drinking a fifth glass of scotch even knowing the damage it may do to him, our second restaurant patron may regret drinking the scotch, lamenting his weakness in consuming it. *That* is not the way he wants to behave. That is not the way he *should* have behaved.

The interplay between forward-looking and backward-looking beliefs, desires, and feelings in addiction is a complex process. Surely, though, the development of more consistent and prudent beliefs, desires, and feelings may require (and certainly may encourage) the associated development of understanding the sources of addicted behavior and the modes, manners, and dimensions of responsibility for behavior. There is no point in regretting drinking the libation in the restaurant if one cannot refrain the next time one tries. A person has to identify the signs, learn the *why, when,* and *how* if change is to be produced in his very being. And that is precisely the sort of result we hope this collection encourages. In terms of associated phenomena, what else, other than addiction itself, is necessary for understanding the conundrum of addiction but the very multimodal responsibility for addiction—for when and why it occurs and for how it may be overcome or avoided.

2 Drug Addiction as Incentive Sensitization

Kent C. Berridge and Terry E. Robinson

In this chapter we present a brief overview of the incentive-sensitization theory of addiction. This description is excerpted from our previous articles on the topic (Robinson & Berridge, 1993, 2003, 2008). We then offer a few additional comments on related issues that we hope might be relevant to philosophical analyses, some excerpted from essays on the concept of incentive salience for philosophers and psychologists (Berridge, 2009; Berridge & Aldridge, 2008).

Addiction and Incentive Sensitization

At some time in their lives most people try a potentially addictive drug—for example, alcohol. However, few become addicts. Even relatively few people who try "hard drugs," such as cocaine or heroin, go on to become addicts. Addiction refers specifically to a pathological and arguably compulsive pattern of drug-seeking and drug-taking behavior, which occupies an inordinate amount of an individual's time and thoughts, and persists despite adverse consequences. Addicts also find it difficult to quit taking drugs, even when they express a strong desire to do so. Finally, if they do manage to abstain, addicts remain highly vulnerable to relapse for long periods of time, well after symptoms of withdrawal have disappeared.

Presumably people initially experiment with drugs because of their pleasant consequences, but what is responsible for the transition from casual or experimental drug use to drug abuse and, eventually, the symptoms of addiction? Over the last 20 years or so there has been increasing recognition that drugs themselves can change the brains of susceptible individuals in complex ways and that these drug-induced changes in the brain contribute to the transition to addiction. Furthermore, some of these brain changes, especially those related to mesolimbic sensitization, are very persistent and far outlast other changes associated with tolerance and withdrawal (Hyman, Malenka, & Nestler, 2006; Kalivas & Volkow, 2005; Robinson & Berridge, 2003).

Drug-induced changes in the brain alter a number of different psychological processes in parallel, contributing to multiple symptoms of addiction. We suggested in the *Incentive-Sensitization Theory of Addiction*, originally published in 1993, that the most important of these psychological changes is a persistent *"sensitization" or hypersensitivity to the incentive motivational effects of drugs and drug-associated stimuli* (Robinson & Berridge, 1993). *Incentive sensitization* produces a bias of attentional processing toward drug-associated stimuli; it also produces pathological motivation for drugs themselves (compulsive "wanting"). The intensified "wanting" or incentive salience is especially focused on drugs in addicts, in part by Pavlovian associative mechanisms, because an addictive drug is a stimulus that both potently activates the mesolimbic brain system and initiates neurobiological events that enduringly sensitize that system. Importantly, the intensified "wanting" for drugs is not matched by an intensification of "liking" for the same drugs. The dissociation occurs because brain "liking" mechanisms are somewhat separable from "wanting" mechanisms, even for the same reward (Berridge, 2007; Berridge & Robinson, 1998). Only "wanting" systems sensitize, and so "wanting" can increase and become quite intense due to sensitization, regardless of whether a drug still remains "liked" after many repeated uses.

After sensitization of brain mesolimbic systems, excessive "wanting" can be triggered by drug-associated cues or their mental representations, especially in contexts where drugs have been taken before, or in other specific situations such as when one is under stress and similar circumstances. Specific contexts, stimuli, or mood states can facilitate the expression of a sensitized "wanting" response. When combined with impaired executive control over behavior, perhaps due to drug-induced prefrontal cortex dysfunction, incentive sensitization culminates in the core symptoms of addiction (Robinson & Berridge, 1993, 2000, 2003). The concept of incentive sensitization has drawn considerable interest in the past 15 years as an explanation of addiction. Here we summarize this view of addiction, based on past articles, and raise some current issues.

What Is Drug Sensitization?

In its most generic sense, a pharmacologist would define sensitization as simply any increase in a drug effect that occurs after repeated exposures to the drug. However, in both neurobiological and psychological terms, a more specific form of drug sensitization is central to the incentive-sensitization theory. Incentive sensitization refers to particular neurobiological changes in brain mesolimbic dopamine systems and in related structures belonging to the same larger brain circuit that mediate the psychological function of incentive salience ("wanting"). Measured neurobiologically, sensitization is associated with an increase in the ability of drugs to elevate dopamine neurotransmission in brain regions that receive dopamine inputs, such as the nucleus accumbens, and with changes in the physical structure of neurons in the dopamine-related circuits (Boileau et al., 2006; Robinson & Kolb, 1999). Measured psychologically, incentive sensitization is associated with increases in "wanting" for specific rewards triggered especially when the sensitized individual encounters cues related to those rewards and is expressed in behavioral seeking and sometimes in subjective ratings of rewards (Tindell, Berridge, Zhang, Peciña, S., & Aldridge, 2005; Vezina, 2004; Vezina & Leyton, 2009; Volkow et al., 2008; Wyvell & Berridge, 2001). In a nutshell, we think that the core features of addiction result from sensitization of brain systems that mediate the incentive motivational effects of drug rewards and drug cues—which leads to pathological motivation for drugs in addicts.

Why do only some drug users become addicts? Not all individuals are equally susceptible to sensitization—some are much more vulnerable than others. Individual susceptibility to sensitization is determined by many factors: genetic factors, hormonal factors, gender differences, previous drug experiences, and previous experiences with major stresses in life (Robinson & Becker, 1986; Robinson & Kolb, 2004; Samaha, Yau, Yang, & Robinson, 2005). Sensitization is also influenced by factors related to the drug itself. Drugs such as heroin, cocaine, amphetamine, alcohol, and nicotine can all induce sensitization, although not necessarily to the same degree. Once induced, sensitization to one drug often crosses to other drugs too. More sensitization is produced by exposure to high doses of drug than to low doses. The repeated but intermittent use of drugs induces greater sensitization than a single dose or even continuous exposure to a drug, and sensitization is further facilitated if periods of use are interspersed with periods of abstinence—as is typically the case during the development of addiction. For example, the induction of sensitization would presumably be facilitated in someone who regularly indulged in drug parties of high consumption on weekends but abstained during the week. Sensitization is also influenced by the speed with which drugs reach the brain (related to route of administration) and is facilitated by having extended access to drugs that leads to increased intake.

Once neural sensitization occurs, the brain's mesolimbic dopamine system becomes hyperreactive to drugs. The system is not *constantly* hyperactive in a stable fashion, but it can be put temporarily into a hyperactive state by exposure to the drug again or by exposure to drug-related cues: that is, it is hyperreactive to particular stimuli. Furthermore, the effects of drug cues and drugs themselves can interact, such that a small amount of drug can potentiate the influence of drug cues (Caggiula, Donny, Palmatier, Liu, Chaudhri, & Sved, 2009).

Thus, our theory suggests that sensitization of mesolimbic systems may create unusually strong (compulsive) levels of "wanting" for drugs or other addictive incentives. A sensitized brain responds with extra incentive salience to reward cues just as a brain that has been drugged with amphetamine does—even if the sensitized brain has no drug on board at that moment (Leyton, 2007; Tindell et al., 2005; Vezina, 2004; Wyvell & Berridge, 2001). An addict, on encountering the right drug cue, would "want" the cued reward at that moment because of excessive incentive salience—even if the person cognitively expected not to like it very much and eventually did not like it much in the end. And crucially, sensitization may last years after an individual stops taking any drugs (Boileau et al., 2006; Paulson, Camp, & Robinson, 1991; Vezina & Leyton, 2009).

Traditional Withdrawal-Based Explanations of Addiction

How does incentive sensitization compare to other explanations for addiction? The most intuitive explanation for addiction has long been simply the traditional view that drugs are taken first because they are pleasant and then that after repeated drug use, drugs are then taken also to avoid the unpleasant withdrawal symptoms that would ensue upon the cessation of use (Koob & Le Moal, 2006). Compulsive drug taking is maintained, by this view, to avoid unpleasant withdrawal symptoms. This two-sided hedonic hypothesis has gone by many different names: pleasure-pain; positive-negative reinforcement; opponent processes; hedonic homeostasis; hedonic dysregulation; reward allostasis, and others (Koob & Le Moal, 2006; Solomon, 1977). No matter what the name, these hypotheses posit the same basic explanatory logic: addictive drugs are taken initially simply to achieve pleasant drug "highs," and after addiction, to escape withdrawal "lows."

We believe that drug pleasure and withdrawal, which no one doubts contribute to reasons why people take drugs, are unlikely to be a complete explanation of addiction. Everyone agrees that addicts sometimes take drugs chiefly for pleasure and sometimes to escape withdrawal or other dysphoric states (e.g., life stresses). However, there are several major problems with hedonic/withdrawal theories as full explanations of drug addiction. One of the most striking problems is that drug withdrawal actually may be much less powerful at motivating drug-taking behavior than people generally think. Relative to positive incentive processes caused directly by drugs themselves and by their cues, withdrawal states are not especially potent in motivating drug-seeking behavior (Stewart, 2004). For example, in animal studies Stewart and colleagues examined what causes rats to "relapse" into drug-seeking behavior if they previously were dependent on cocaine or heroin but have been drug-free for some time (Shalev, Grimm, & Shaham, 2002; Stewart, 2004). Stewart, Shaham, and colleagues measured lever-pressing to obtain drug infusions under extinction conditions after activating brain mesolimbic systems or instead by inducing an aversive withdrawal state. To activate mesolimbic systems (to produce, we suggest, a resurgence of incentive salience), the rats were simply given a small injection of their old drug prior to the test (called a priming injection). To induce the negative withdrawal state, the rats where given naltrexone (an opioid antagonist drug that blocks opioid receptors in the brain and that induces "precipitated withdrawal" symptoms in the relatively fragile brain of an individual who was recently heroin dependent). Precipitated withdrawal is clearly a negative state, and so it would be expected by any withdrawal-based hypothesis of addiction that was predicated on escape from unpleasant distress to be a very powerful cause for reactivating drug-seeking behavior (Koob & Le Moal, 2006; Solomon, 1977).

But in fact a priming cocaine or heroin injection turns out to be far more effective at reinstating drug-seeking behavior than naltrexone administration (Shalev et al., 2002; Stewart, 1992, 2004). The free cocaine-heroin injection would have been mostly pleasant in valence, rather than aversive, making reinstatement harder to explain in terms of escape from distress. Withdrawal was relatively ineffective at directly motivating drug taking, and further studies have shown that withdrawal remains ineffective unless individuals have already learned before that they can escape withdrawal by taking the drug (Hellemans, Dickinson, & Everitt, 2006). That is, withdrawal is a state individuals can learn to avoid (Kenny, Chen, Kitamura, Markou, & Koob, 2006), but withdrawal may not be very powerful at directly motivating drug taking without that previous learning. Furthermore, withdrawal symptoms are maximal within a few days after the cessation of drug use, but the susceptibility to reinstatement continues to grow for weeks to months (Grimm, Hope, Wise, & Shaham, 2001). The finding that drug withdrawal can be relatively weak at motivating drug seeking is counterintuitive to many and is a direct contradiction of the opponent-process prediction. But the laboratory finding fits with the reports of some human addicts who say that their sick feelings of withdrawal are quite different from their most intense feelings of drug craving. As one heroin addict explained to a researcher studying craving, "No doc, craving is when you want it—want it so bad you can almost taste it . . . but you ain't sick . . . sick is, well sick" (Childress, McLellan, Ehrman, & O'Brien, 1988).

Another major problem for withdrawal theories is explaining why addicts so often relapse into drug taking again even after they have long been free from withdrawal symptoms. After only a few weeks of drug abstinence the symptoms of withdrawal dissipate, and they therefore can no longer be a powerful motivating factor, whether learned or direct. Yet elimination of withdrawal symptoms does not protect against future relapse, as the many recidivist graduates of detoxification programs can attest. One reply by withdrawal theorists to explain this comes from *conditioned* opponent theories, which suggest that associative conditioning causes predictive drug cues to elicit conditioned tolerance and conditioned withdrawal symptoms (Kenny et al., 2006; Schull, 1979). Conditioned withdrawal effects have sometimes been found in studies of human drug addicts as well as in animal studies, and in principle these could prompt relapse long after unconditioned withdrawal symptoms have subsided. However, many human addicts report that cues often fail to elicit conditioned withdrawal. Plus, drug cues often elicit quite different effects, such as conditioned feelings of a drug high or feelings of drug craving by themselves (O'Brien, Childress, McLellan, Ehrman, & Ternes, 1988). Indeed, one report found that only 27.5% of heroin addicts experienced conditioned withdrawal, and of these, only 5% indicated this was a reason for relapse (McAuliffe, 1982). In conclusion, neither unconditioned withdrawal nor conditioned feelings of withdrawal seems to be sufficiently strong or reliable to serve as the principal explanation for relapse.

We think that a better explanation for such anomalies comes from a distinction between "liking" and "wanting" that is posited by the incentive-sensitization theory but overlooked by traditional pleasure and withdrawal accounts of addiction. Many potentially addictive drugs initially produce feelings of pleasure (euphoria), encouraging users to take these drugs again. However, with the transition to addiction there sometimes appears to be a decrease in the role of drug pleasure. Some people would argue that the hedonic impact of the drugs undergoes tolerance, so that a stable drug dose induces less of a high. How can it be that drugs come to be "wanted" more and more even if they become "liked" less and less? According to incentive-sensitization theory the reason for this paradox is because repeated drug use sensitizes only the neural systems that mediate the motivational process of incentive salience ("wanting"), but not neural systems that mediate the pleasurable effects of drugs ("liking"). Thus, with repeated drug use the degree to which drugs are "wanted" increases disproportionately to the degree to which they are "liked," and with the development of addiction, this dissociation between "wanting" and "liking" gets progressively greater (figure 2.1). The dissociation between "wanting" and "liking" solves the puzzle that otherwise has led some neuroscientists to conclude that, "one prominent prediction of an incentive-sensitization view would be that with repeated use, addicts would take less drug" (Koob & Le Moal, 2006). Of course, incentive sensitization actually predicts that "wanting" drugs more intensely should make addicts take more drug—not less.

In a related but opposite way the separation of "wanting" from "liking" also frees the control of addiction from being driven solely by the negative affective dysphoria that often follows cessation of drug use, at least for a

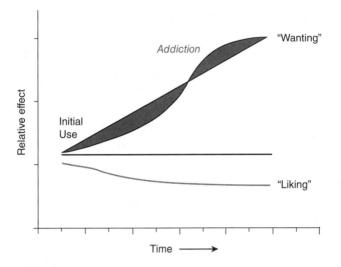

Figure 2.1
Incentive-sensitization model of addiction. Schematic model of how "wanting" to take drugs may grow over time independently of "liking" for drug pleasure as an individual becomes an addict, due to sensitization of brain mesolimbic systems. Modified from Robinson and Berridge (1993).

few days or weeks. Withdrawal states may well contribute to drug taking while they last (Koob & Le Moal, 2006). But addiction typically persists long after withdrawal states dissipate. Sensitization-related changes in the brain, which can persist long after withdrawal ends, provide a mechanism to explain why addicts continue to "want" drugs and are liable to relapse even after long periods of abstinence and even in the absence of a negative affective state.

Aberrant Learning as an Explanation of Addiction?

There is now considerable evidence that in both animals and humans the brain's nucleus accumbens (NAcc) and dopamine-related circuitry are involved in some aspect of reward learning, which has prompted the speculation that in addicts *drugs may alter learning processes* to somehow cause the transition to addiction (Hyman et al., 2006; Robbins, Everitt, & Nutt, 2008; Schultz, 2006). For example, cues that *predict* the availability of rewards can powerfully activate NAcc-related circuitry (Childress et al.,

2008; Day & Carelli, 2007; Tindell et al., 2005; Volkow et al., 2006), some-times even better than the reward itself (Schultz, 2006). Further, repeated exposure to drugs of abuse facilitates some forms of learning (Nelson & Killcross, 2006; Phillips, Harmer, & Hitchcott, 2002) and triggers some of the same types of neuroadaptations in reward-related neurons as seen in learning (Hyman et al., 2006). Several researchers have hypothesized, therefore, that the transition to addiction results from the ability of drugs to promote *aberrant learning* (Hyman et al., 2006; Redish, 2004; Robbins, Everitt, et al., 2008; Schultz, 2006).

How Does Incentive-Sensitization Theory Contrast to Learning Accounts of Addiction?

Everyone agrees that learning plays a role to guide aspects of addicted behavior, but it has become popular among some to actually refer to addic-tion as a "learning disorder" (Hyman, 2005). Is aberrant learning per se a chief cause of addiction? We suggest that thinking about addiction as a disorder of learning may not be quite accurate. Learning is only one part of the reward process—and probably not the one that contributes most to the pathological pursuit of drugs in addicts.

Perhaps the most influential type of "learning hypothesis" suggests that compulsivity arises in addiction because drugs facilitate the learning of especially strong automatic stimulus-response (S-R) *habits* and that by their nature S-R habits confer compulsivity to behavior (Belin, Jonkman, Dick-inson, Robbins, & Everitt, 2009; Berke & Hyman, 2000; Everitt, Dickinson, & Robbins, 2001; Hyman et al., 2006; Robbins, Everitt, et al., 2008; Tiffany, 1990). After all, some would argue, is an automatic habit not a compulsion if it is performed independently of a person's intentions? We think not. Instead we think a confusion may be involved in calling a pure habit "compulsive" (Robinson & Berridge, 2003). Automatic S-R habits do not become compulsive merely by virtue of being extremely well learned. The defining feature of habits is that they tend to be performed autonomously when one is thinking of something else, without having to think about them. However, habits do not intrude and impose themselves when one is consciously trying to do something else—at worst, they slip in only when one's attention wanders. That is, automatic habits appear only when there is no countervailing purpose to act otherwise. In a classic example of habit at work, William James wrote of going upstairs to his bedroom to dress formally for dinner and removing his clothes while thinking about one of his intellectual projects. Suddenly he found that he had put on his pajamas and nearly climbed into bed (James, 1890). "Oops, silly me!" A habit explanation of addiction must rely on similar absentmindedness to create that cognitive vacuum. "Oops, silly me, I took drugs again!" is how the habit theory must construe an addict's experience of relapse. But absentminded drug taking followed by surprise is surely not an accurate account of most instances of addictive relapse.

And no matter how many times an action is repeated, repetition or "stamping in" cannot by itself make a habit compulsive. Strong S-R habits do not necessarily lead to compulsive behavior: tying your shoe, brushing your teeth, and similar acts are not performed compulsively by most people, even after having been performed more than 10,000 times. Few people think obsessively or compulsively about doing one of these things again. For an action to acquire compulsive properties requires something motivational. A compulsive psychological trait is characterized by patho-logical motivation—that is, something like incentive salience (Robinson & Berridge, 2003). A similar point has been made concerning the compulsive feature of rituals in obsessive-compulsive disorder (OCD). For example, Boyer and Lienard argue that in OCD compulsiveness and automaticity are quite different and, in fact, nearly opposites (Boyer & Lienard, 2008). They write: "Note that [compulsive OCD] ritualized behavior in the sense used here is the opposite of routinized behavior, which people can accom-plish 'without thinking'" (293). We agree, and think the same distinction can be applied to compulsive drug use versus drug habits performed "without thinking."

Beyond compulsion, addictive behavior also displays a high degree of targeted flexibility, which requires a completely different explanatory mechanism from S-R habits, and which again suggests a motivational component. Habit cannot explain why an addict waking up in the morning with no drug spends the day engaging in a complex series of behaviors that may never have been performed in quite the same way before—scamming, stealing, negotiating—all seemingly motivated to procure drug. Addicts do what they have to do and go where they have to go to get drugs, even if actions and routes that never have been performed before are required. Such focused yet flexible behavior in addiction shows pathological motivation for drugs that cannot be explained by evoking S-R habits, which by their nature consist of stereotyped inflexible actions triggered by specific stimuli. Indeed, a strict S-R habit theory would require the addict, on waking up in the morning with no drug available, to engage *automatically* in exactly the same old sequence of habitual actions he used previously to get drugs, whether the actions were currently effective or not. Yet addicts in the real world are not S-R automatons; they are, if nothing else, quite resourceful.

On the other hand, everyone must agree that S-R associations involved in habits are responsible for the automatized habits and rituals involved in *consuming* drugs once they have been obtained, and we also agree that treatment with drugs facilitates the development of S-R habits in animals (Miles, Everitt, & Dickinson, 2003; Nelson & Killcross, 2006), perhaps via recruitment of the dorsal striatum (Everitt et al., 2008; Robbins, Ersche, & Everitt, 2008). We further agree that habits may be especially prominent in standard self-administration animal models, where only a single response is available to be performed (e.g., press a lever) thousands of times in a very impoverished environment to earn injections of drugs. Thus we applaud efforts to understand the neural basis of habits that are a prominent feature of *drug consumption behavior* in addicts.

How Does Learning Interact with Incentive Sensitization?

As we reject aberrant learning as an explanation of addiction, it is incumbent on us to explain how learning might interact with incentive sensitization. The central thesis of the incentive-sensitization theory of addiction (Robinson & Berridge, 1993) is that repeated exposure to potentially addictive drugs can, in a way that is not reducible to learning, persistently change brain cells and circuits in susceptible individuals and under particular circumstances. After it has developed, there is no question that the *expression* of sensitization is powerfully *modulated* by learning—but sensitization is not caused by associative learning (Anagnostaras & Robinson, 1996; Anagnostaras, Schallert, & Robinson, 2002). The sensitized brain circuits normally regulate the attribution of incentive salience to stimuli, a psychological process involved in motivated behavior. The nature of these neuroadaptations is to render these brain circuits hypersensitive ("sensitized") in a way that results in pathological levels of incentive salience being attributed to drugs and drug-associated cues. Persistence of incentive sensitization makes pathological incentive motivation ("wanting") for drugs last for years, even after the discontinuation of drug use. Sensitized incentive salience can be manifest in behavior via either implicit (as unconscious "wanting") or explicit processes (as conscious craving), depending on circumstances.

Although learning is not identical to "wanting," learning is still an important contributor to the operation of incentive salience mechanisms. The specific *focus* on drugs in particular in addicts is produced by an interaction between incentive-salience mechanisms with associative learning mechanisms that normally direct motivation to specific and appropriate targets. Learning specifies the object of pathological desire via associations to that object gained from past experiences and also modulates the expression of neural sensitization at particular places or times (and not others). Yet it is important to note that learning per se is not enough for pathological motivation to take drugs. We argue that pathological motivation arises from the sensitized and nonassociative adaptations in brain circuits that mediate incentive-motivational processes (i.e., incentive sensitization). The fact that learning can modulate the expression of those changes is why neural sensitization is often expressed in behavior only in contexts in which drugs have been previously experienced (Badiani & Robinson, 2004; Vezina & Leyton, 2009). The exact nature of associative contextual control over the expression of sensitization needs further study, but we suggest this contextual control provides an additional mechanism for why addicts will "want" drugs most particularly when they are in drug-associated contexts.

As further testimony to the difference between learning and incentive salience, we note that by spreading beyond the learned focus of "wanting" on drug targets, incentive sensitization can also sometimes spill over in animals or humans to other targets such as food, sex, gambling, and others (Fiorino & Phillips, 1999; Mitchell & Stewart, 1990; Nocjar & Panksepp, 2002; Taylor & Horger, 1999). For example, treatment with dopaminergic medications in some patient populations can lead to a "dopamine dysregulation syndrome" (DDS) that is manifest not only by compulsive drug use but also sometimes by "pathological gambling, hypersexuality, food bingeing . . . and punding, a form of complex behavioral stereotypy" (Evans et al., 2006; Lawrence, Evans, & Lees, 2003).

Other Addictions?

Does incentive sensitization apply to any other form of addiction beyond drugs? This question remains difficult to answer. As indicated above, there is some reason to believe that overactivation of brain dopamine circuits can power certain human cases of excessive "wanting" to have sex, to binge eat, gamble, and so forth. The clearest cases involve use of drugs. What is not known so far is whether sensitization-type states ever emerge in any brains in the *absence* of the person having taken any drugs or medications (with the exception of repeated intermittent exposures to intense stress, for which there is some evidence for sensitization induction). Such emergence is within the realm of possibility, but it is not yet an established fact. In support of this possibility, for example, some researchers have suggested that when rats are exposed to patterns of alternating periods of dieting interspersed with access to sugary treats, their brains may undergo changes that overlap with drug sensitization (Avena & Hoebel, 2003). If so, some plausibility is gained by the hypothesis that excessive "wanting" might power episodes of binge eating in some people, to the extent that similar changes might occur in them either by related environmental exposures or even spontaneously in a gene-related fashion (Kessler, 2009).

It is conceivable then that sensitization or sensitization-like processes could contribute to cases of pathological motivation for gambling, sex, food, and other addictions. But it must be cautioned that to our knowledge at present no actual evidence exists that such sensitization-like processes actually occur spontaneously in the brains of any particular individuals. Perhaps the closest cases so far in this direction come from suggestions that some obese binge eaters have inherited gene variants that may predispose their brains toward excessive mesolimbic activations, including stronger dopamine activation (Davis et al., 2009). Still, more evidence is needed. Until and unless such evidence does appear, the extension of incentive sensitization to other types of addiction remains essentially speculative.

Relation of Incentive Sensitization to Cognitive Dysfunction

The incentive-sensitization theory focuses on sensitization-induced changes in incentive-motivational processes and related changes in the brain, but it is important to also acknowledge that myriad other brain changes contribute to addiction as well, including damage or dysfunction in cortical mechanisms that underlie cognitive choice and decision making (Robinson & Berridge, 2000, 2003). Many important studies have documented that changes in executive functions, involving how alternative outcomes are evaluated and decisions and choices made, occur in both addicts and animals that take drugs (Bechara, 2005; Robbins, Ersche, et al., 2008; Schoenbaum & Shaham, 2008). We agree that impairment in executive control plays an important role in making bad choices about drugs, especially when combined with the pathological incentive motivation for drugs induced by incentive sensitization.

Unpacking Some Issues That Remain

Beyond addiction, there are a number of related issues that might be important to evaluation of our claims about the nature of "wanting," its relation to "liking," whether "wants" can be truly compulsive, and whether "wants" can be irrational. In the remainder of this chapter we briefly explore several of those additional issues that seem to us to be of potential interest to philosophers.

The Nature of Incentive Salience as a "Wanting" Module

Desire is not a unitary phenomenon but contains several neurological-psychological modules (figure 2.2). Incentive salience is a "wanting" module, that is, just one of several types of what is meant ordinarily by the word wanting (no quotes) (Berridge, 2007; Berridge & Aldridge, 2008; Robinson & Berridge, 1993). As a distinct module, incentive salience is psychologically most visible in its cue-triggered "wanting" and motivational magnet effects that cause individuals to be strongly attracted to particular reward stimuli. Importantly, "wanting" can occur even in the absence of conscious awareness of the reward. By comparison, cognitive wanting, in the more familiar sense of the word, is quite a different module of desire. If one has a cognitive want, one has a conscious desire for a specific reward—one knows what one wants. Cognitive wanting has declarative goals, involving explicit expectations of future outcomes. Incentive salience "wanting" has causes and targets but not explicit goals except to the degree that incentive salience can color cognitive desires. When the two forms of desire are congruent, "wanting" adds a visceral

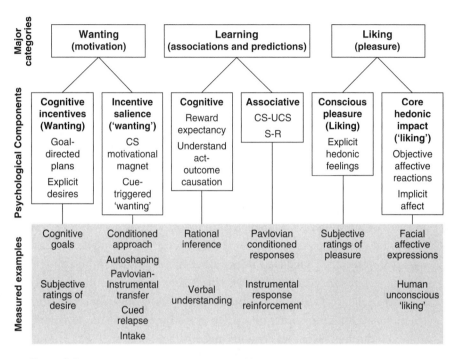

Figure 2.2
Components of liking, wanting, and learning in reward. The desire module of incentive salience is shown as a "wanting" module inside Wanting (motivation). The separate desire module of cognitive incentives (wanting without quotation marks) exists alongside, mediated by separable neural systems. The separate nature of these motivation modules underlies why a sensitized "want" can become compulsive. Modified from Berridge and Robinson (2003).

"oomph" to mental desires. Ordinarily "wanting" and wanting work together toward the same incentives, but in certain situations the two psychological processes can be momentarily dissociated. When this happens, "wanting" can manifest in seeking behavior that occurs somewhat irrationally and even in some cases unconsciously, as described further below.

Another way of distinguishing among modules of desire is through the concept of reward utility that stems from behavioral economics. Drawing on the terminology of Kahneman and colleagues, for example, utility comes in several forms: predicted, decision, experienced, and remembered (Kahneman, Wakker, & Sarin, 1997). Predicted utility is the expectation of how much a future reward will be liked. Decision utility is what we actually decide to do, manifest in choice and pursuit. Experienced utility is what most people think of the term reward, being the hedonic impact experienced when the reward is gained. Remembered utility is the memory of how good a previous reward was in the past and, typically, the chief determinant of predicted utility.

In this framework, incentive salience "wanting" is a pure form of decision utility, which is distinct from other forms of utility and in some conditions can decouple from all the others. That is, "wanting" for an outcome is distinguishable from experienced utility (hedonic impact or "liking" the outcome), remembered utility of how nice the outcome was in the past, and forecast or predicted utility of how nice it will be in the future. For cognitive wants, by contrast, decision utility essentially becomes joined to forecast or predicted utility. That is, one wants an outcome to the degree one expects it to be good. This difference is part of what makes incentive salience "wanting" a unique module and quite different from cognitive wanting (no quotation marks). It is why we put quotation marks around "wanting" when referring to incentive salience.

Incentive salience "wants" are bound closely to percepts: the sights, sounds, or smells of rewards and their associated cues, or vivid images of those stimuli. Incentive salience typically is triggered as a phasic pulse or relatively brief peak upon encountering a reward or a physical reminder of the reward (a cue) (Tindell et al., 2005; Wyvell & Berridge, 2001; Zhang, Berridge, Tindell, Smith, & Aldridge, 2009). Incentive salience does not require a clear cognition of what is wanted and does not even need to be consciously experienced as a feeling of wanting, at least in some cases (although on occasions when it is brought into consciousness by additional neural machinery, "wanting" can considerably intensify feelings of desire). Perhaps a reason for the difference is that incentive salience is mediated chiefly by subcortical brain mechanisms, whereas cognitive forms of desire are more dependent on higher cortex-based brain systems. Incentive salience may have initially evolved in animals as a distinct "wanting" module to facilitate the pursuit of particular innate incentives. Possibly it gave an elementary form of goal directedness, which could guide behavior in the right direction toward appropriate rewards and cues in advance of experiencing the goals.

Incentive salience as a module is not the form of desire we are most aware of in daily life nor the type of desire that has been the greatest focus of philosophers. But incentive salience is important in daily life, needed to color conscious desires with motivational power, to make them compelling spurs to action—even though its effects may be more implicit than explicit. Indeed, incentive salience may be a crucial component of our most intense and visceral desires, and especially important in the pathological intensity of some addictions and compulsive desires.

Incentive salience can be viewed as a motivational transform of a brain signal corresponding to the perceived object of desire or its mental representation. When attributed to a stimulus representation, incentive salience transforms mere sensory shapes, smells, or sounds into attractive and attention-riveting incentives. Once attributed with incentive salience a percept becomes difficult to avoid noticing: the eyes naturally move toward the incentive; it captures the gaze and becomes motivationally attractive; and the rest of the body may well follow to obtain it. It is what distinguishes a mere stimulus from an *incentive stimulus*.

How can one tell if a stimulus is attributed with incentive salience? It has several distinguishing psychological features that help it to be recognized even in animal experiments as well as in human daily life. First, incentive salience gives a "motivational magnet" property to stimuli it is attributed to and makes those stimuli attractive and potently able to elicit approach toward them. Second, stimuli attributed with incentive salience are "wanted." in the sense that animals and people will work to get them. Incentive stimuli even support the learning of new actions to get them (i.e., they act as what psychologists call *conditioned reinforcers*). Incentive cues typically predict the reward to follow, although it is worth noting that the predictive and incentive properties of cues are dissociable, and only the incentive properties are due to incentive salience attribution (Flagel, Akil, & Robinson, 2009; Robinson & Flagel, 2009; Tindell et al., 2005; Zhang et al., 2009). Third, incentive salience also triggers momentary peaks of intense motivation to obtain a cued reward, often manifest as a "surge" in the instrumental action required to obtain the reward. Such features (reward cues becoming motivational magnets, cues as objects of desire, peaks of cue-triggered "wanting" for the actual reward) allow us to determine if a stimulus is or is not attributed with incentive salience in behavioral neuroscience experiments with animals as well as in people.

Can "Wanting" Be Compulsive?

It may seem mistaken to some readers to claim that sensitized "wanting" in an addict ever creates an actual *compulsion* to take drugs. In an illuminating argument, for example, Stephens and Graham have taken issue with our claim (Stephens & Graham, 2009). Their argument is reasonable and helpful to consider here.

Stephens and Graham write that "a motive or want does not qualify as compulsive or addictive in character or purport unless it contravenes or violates a contrary" (Stephens & Graham, 2009, 32). Defining compulsive, they draw on Aristotle's sense of an external force, such as a strong wind or of one being forcefully carried by outside hands to compel an outcome contrary to desire. In that sense, a compulsive "want" or motive seems self-contradictory. The "want" is part of the internal desire and not outside the person.

We agree with the Stephens and Graham (2009) analysis of compulsion. Still, we suggest that the possibility of a compulsive "want" arises from the complex dissociation among components of desire discussed above. The difference between incentive salience "wanting" versus cognitive wanting allows a compulsion to arise internally from within the individual (via sensitized incentive salience), as well as from without. A person's most central desire, from the philosophical stance, must surely be what the person cognitively wants—the willed-for goal (even when the goal is abstinence). A person has some choice over the cognitively prized goal but not so much choice over the "wanted" target of incentive salience. If desire is not unitary, one can "want" one thing at the same time as one cognitively wants a different thing. For example, an addict may sincerely want to abstain from taking drugs and know full well that the drug on offer at that moment will not be worth the cost of taking it. The sincere recovered addict cognitively desires not to take the drug, and in the most extreme cases he may even be said to in no sense cognitively desire to take it (e.g., when the only drug available is known not to be particularly hedonic because of its type, poor quality, or low dose; when the consequences of relapse can be expected to be distressing; etc.). But if drug cues are dangled in the right context, by our theory, the sensitized addict will be seized by a sudden pulse of cue-triggered "wanting" for drugs (although we note that the expression of "wanting" is subject to top-down modulatory control, and this provides a way to win many battles over compulsions; however, a single loss may mean not winning the war). This would not be compulsive in Stephen and Graham's sense if the pulse of "wanting" always momentarily corrupted the dominant cognitive desire to produce a judgment shift, so that "wanting" and wanting became aligned together to thwart earlier precommitment and produce relapse (Holton, 2009). But we suggest that the dominant cognitive desire need not necessarily switch in every case and that sensitized "wanting" can act in the absence of a strong cognitive desire (described below under unconscious "wanting")—and sometimes even against the cognitive desire. "Wanting" can act against a dominant cognitive intention or desire. That is one reason why we say when "wanting" is strong enough, it can take on compulsive properties.

In practice it is admittedly difficult to prove that "wanting" actually competes with and wins out over a dominant cognitive desire. But we think there is at least some suggestive evidence. One piece of evidence comes from animal neuroscience studies regarding the difference in neuropharmacological substrates of cue-triggered "wanting" versus cognitive wanting. For example, administration of a dopamine-blocking drug to a rat prevents the occurrence of cue-triggered "wanting" but does not seem to have any effect on the rat's more cognitive wants involving experience-derived goal expectations and understandings of the relation between its acts and the outcome (Dickinson, Smith, & Mirenowicz, 2000).

Another piece of evidence comes from the highly transient nature of cue-triggered "wanting," which often seems to occur as a fleeting burst that rests on a stable and unchanging baseline of more cognitive wanting. For example, even when a rat's brain is in a constantly elevated state of dopamine activation due to having received a recent (painless) microinjection of amphetamine into its brain, its excessive hyper-"wanting" is still expressed only momentarily on encounters with reward cues (Wyvell & Berridge, 2000, 2001). Before the cue comes, the dopamine-activated brain of the rat simply wants sugar in the ordinary sense, without necessarily showing any indication of elevation over normal levels. The next moment, when the cue comes, the dopamine-activated brain transiently "wants" sugar to an exaggerated degree, as well as more stably wanting to the original degree, according to the incentive salience hypothesis. On the cue's arrival, the rat engages in a frenzied burst of efforts to obtain the sugary reward, far above normal levels. Yet just a few moments after the cue ends, the rat returns to its earlier and lower predominant level of wanting. Finally again, moments later still, the cue is reencountered once more, and excessive and irrational "wanting" again takes control. It seems unlikely that mesolimbic activation altered rats' dominant expectation or stable cognitive want because the intense enhancement of pursuit typically lasted only while the cue stimulus was actually present, although amphetamine was present in the nucleus accumbens throughout the entire session.

The neural mesolimbic mechanism for "wanting" seems to involve a synergy between dopamine levels and the external presence of a reward-related event or object. This seems separable from the cortex and other neural systems that mediate more stable cognitive goals and steady-state performance. Much more evidence is needed of course to convincingly resolve this issue, but we think such observations do seem compatible with the idea that cue-triggered bursts of "wanting" do not always lead to a shift in dominant cognitive desire but, rather, can overlay and override the stable desire at special moments.

Is Incentive Salience Intentional?

Intentionality seems to be an important part of many philosophical treatments of desire. Most cognitive desire has intentionality in the form of an explicit object of desire. Cognitive mental representations of a desired object can be imagined—its look or feel—and one can remember what it was like on previous occasions. Basically, one knows what one wants, and when one has a cognitive want, one always wants some goal in particular.

Incentive salience, by contrast, has a less stable relation to intentionality. We think "wanting" is intentional in some cases but not in others. At its most nonintentional, incentive salience may detach from the object of desire and be attributed too widely among stimuli, spewing indiscriminant "wanting" in directions that are inappropriate or completely general. The entire world can brighten up in a motivational sense on such occasions, taking on diffuse incentive properties. Thus, intentionality is not intrinsic to "wanting" but depends on mechanisms that focus the attribution of incentive salience to particular targets.

A special but odd form of intentionality seems involved when the cue for a reward becomes "wanted" as a motivational magnet, rather than only the pleasant reward itself (Flagel et al., 2008; Mahler & Berridge, 2009; Robinson & Flagel, 2009; Tomie, 1996). When cues become the focus of desire, there is a slight distortion in the targeting of intentionality. No *reason* exists to desire the cue, only a neural and psychological *cause* and a target in the form of an external stimulus that is transformed into a "wanted" incentive. There is merely a psychological associative history and a neural mechanism that makes it desired. In some addiction situations an individual may become obsessively focused on the attractive cue. For example crack cocaine addicts are known to "chase ghosts," which means to compulsively pick up pebbles on the ground that somewhat resemble crack rocks (Rosse, Fay-McCarthy, Collins, Risher-Flowers, Alim, & Deutsch, 1993). They may even put the inert pebbles in their crack-smoking pipe and try to smoke them. Similarly, in animal experiments rats eagerly sniff and nibble a stark piece of metal when its appearance predicts that a food pellet will soon follow (figure 2.3) (Mahler & Berridge, 2009; Robinson & Flagel, 2009), and quail copulate with a bird-sized terrycloth object that predicts a subsequent sex partner in a manner perhaps related to human sexual fetishes (Koksal et al., 2004).

Figure 2.3
A cue as motivational magnet. This rat is trying to "eat" a metal lever, simply because it is a cue for sugar reward. Whenever the lever has previously been inserted through the wall into the chamber, it has predicted a sugar pellet to follow. Now whenever the lever is inserted, the rat approaches and nibbles on the lever. From Mahler and Berridge (2009); Robinson and Flagel (2009).

Least intentional of all may be cases when incentive salience is attributed indiscriminately to more than one thing at once. This may happen under conditions of intense activation of mesolimbic systems, for example, by electrical brain stimulation or a drug microinjection in some limbic structures, or perhaps even as a function of neural sensitization in certain cases. In such instances pathological incentive salience may simultaneously disrupt associative mechanisms that usually focus "wanting" on a particular target. As a result, one may "want" many different stimuli at the same time. Essentially everything perceived at that moment might become more attractive and "wanted." For example, some people who have been implanted with stimulation electrodes in their brain mesolimbic systems have been reported to describe the entire room as "brightening" in a motivational sense, so that they perceive everyone present as more interesting, more socially attractive, and even more romantically or sexually attractive, and at that moment they feel motivated to do quite a number of activities (Green, Pareira, & Aziz, 2010; Heath, 1996). Such indiscriminate "wanting" is powerfully motivational, but when everything is "wanted," then nothing in particular is. Does such an unfocused desire have intentionality at all?

Finally, we note that "wanting" mechanisms may also share a perhaps surprising link to dread. For example, we have found evidence that NAcc circuits are organized as an affective keyboard in which generators for desire versus dread are anatomically arranged at opposite ends and that some of the generators in the middle can generate desire and/or dread depending on circumstances (Reynolds & Berridge, 2008). We and others have suggested that such a mesolimbic dread may reflect a negatively valenced form of motivational salience, and we have postulated that this fearful salience may contribute to the paranoia of drug psychosis or schizophrenia by making the environmental stimuli it is attributed to become perceived as frightening (Berridge & Robinson, 1998; Kapur, 2003; Robinson & Berridge, 1993). Potential flickering between desire and dread, sometimes even directed to the same external object, may perhaps raise some questions regarding whether the want possesses stable intentionality.

Can "Wanting" Be Unconscious?

Another way in which incentive salience diverges from cognitive desire and intentionality is that incentive salience need not always be conscious.

There exist examples of unconscious core "wanting" in people ranging from drug addicts to ordinary college students. For instance, when given opportunity to work (press a button) for an intravenous cocaine dose too low to produce detectable physiological or subjective effects, drug addicts have been reported to say that the injection feels empty and completely devoid of any cocaine at all, yet they still work more to receive more of the same "empty" dose—all the while denying that they are doing so (Fischman & Foltin, 1992).

Similarly even for ordinary college students, Winkielman and colleagues found that unconscious "wanting" and "liking" could intensify a person's motivation to drink a subsequently encountered beverage without ever emerging into conscious awareness as subjective pleasure or desire (Winkielman & Berridge, 2004). The unconscious "wanting" was triggered by flashing subliminally brief visual presentations of happy emotional facial expressions that might activate brain limbic systems, as brief facial flashes (1/60 sec each), which could not be consciously seen or recognized later and did not cause any change in the person's ratings of his or her own positive or negative mood. But when the students were asked to subsequently judge a "new fruit-flavored beverage that was under development by a beverage company" and given a pitcher of the drink to pour, taste, and evaluate, their reactions to the drink were powerfully altered. When presented with the beverage, students found it more attractive after seeing subliminal happy faces, pouring and drinking 50% more of it. Further, they expressed willingness to pay four times more for the drink if it were sold when asked after the subliminal happy faces than after subliminal angry faces instead. We hypothesize that the subliminal happy faces activated incentive mesolimbic circuits of "wanting" in the brains of students who viewed them, which persisted for some minutes undetected as students evaluated their own mood. The "wanting" surfaced only when an appropriate target was finally presented in the form of a hedonically laden sweet stimulus that they could taste and choose to ingest or not.

Applying a related logic to cocaine addicts, Childress and colleagues induced limbic brain activation and positive affective psychological reactions by subliminal photos of drugs or sex (Childress et al., 2008). Subliminally brief photographs of scenes such as cocaine preparation or of erotic sexual scenes were flashed to the addicts. Although not consciously perceived, the photos activated brain limbic structures, including dopamine targets. The degree of limbic brain activation predicted the strength of positive affective reaction the same photos would elicit when the addict viewed them consciously for longer periods on another day, and reactions were measured in an emotional-cognitive conscious recognition task. Childress and colleagues suggested that "[b]y *the time the motivational state is experienced and labeled as conscious desire, the ancient limbic reward circuitry already has a running start*" (Childress et al., 2008, 4).

Such instances of unconscious "wanting" suggest that incentive salience can at least sometimes operate underneath conscious awareness. Mesolimbic "wanting" may run in parallel with ordinary (and more cortex-mediated) wanting. Usually they point in the same direction, but in cases of unconscious "wanting," only one of the mechanisms seems to be in operation. These cases may lack recruitment of the additional brain and psychological mechanisms needed to translate the core "wanting" process into a cognitive and conscious desire. An unconscious "want" seems difficult to reconcile with intentionality in the usual sense. To the degree that an unconscious "want" can be assigned to a malleable target, it does not have an explicit object of desire. It has only a stimulus target, which may to some degree depend on chance in the form of what happens to turn up next.

Can "Wanting" Be Irrational?

Ordinarily in optimal decisions, all subtypes of reward utility will be maximized together. But sometimes a decision is less than optimal, and then subtypes of utility may diverge from each other. A major contribution of Kahneman's utility taxonomy mentioned above has been to identify cases where predicted or remembered utility diverges from actual experienced utility (Kahneman, Fredrickson, Schreiber, & Redelmeier, 1993; Kahneman et al., 1997). Such divergence can lead to bad decisions on the basis of wrong expectations, called miswanting by Gilbert and Wilson (Gilbert & Wilson, 2000; Morewedge, Gilbert, & Wilson, 2005). If one has a distorted remembered utility because of memory illusions of various sorts, one will have a distorted predicted utility. Decisions made on the basis of false predicted utility are likely to turn out to fail to maximize eventual experienced utility. Or if predicted utility is distorted for reasons other than faulty memory, such as by inappropriate cognitive theories about what rewards will be like in the future, then decisions will again turn out wrong. In either case predicted utility will fail to match actual experienced utility, and the decision is liable to be wrong.

Thus, if decisions are guided principally by predictions about future reward (if decision utility equals predicted utility), then faulty predictions consequently entail that wrong decisions will be made (decision utility does not equal experienced utility). People may thus choose outcomes that they turn out not to like when their predictions about them are wrong. People choose them because they wrongly expect to like them in such cases (and perhaps because they wrongly remember having liked them in the past)—but then turn out not to like them after all.

The previously described mismatch captures much of what is discussed under the label of miswanting and decisions that fail to maximize utility. But Kahneman's taxonomy has a further use for an even more intriguing form of miswanting that we point to here, regarding the potential *irrationality* of incentive salience in addiction. This might be called "irrational miswanting" because it can lead to an outcome being "wanted" even when an outcome value is correctly predicted to be less than desirable (Berridge & Aldridge, 2008; Robinson & Berridge, 1993, 2003).

An irrational decision, we suggest, is to choose what you expect not to like. That is, a decision is irrational when its decision utility does not equal predicted utility. When decision utility is greater than predicted utility, if that can happen, then one might be said to choose what one does not expect to like (not only what one mistakenly expects to like). To choose what one does not expect to like is to choose in a way that is distinctly irrational, as we define irrationality.

If decision utility exists as a distinct psychological variable (with a somewhat separate neurobiological mechanism), it might sometimes dissociate from predicted utility—just as decision utility (together with predicted utility) sometimes dissociates from experienced utility. If at any time decision utility could grow above predicted utility, that could mean choosing an outcome that we actually expected not to like at the moment of decision (and that we not only expected not to like but also turned out not to like in the end). The conditions we expect to produce such excessive "wanting" would include when a sensitized addict encounters drug-related cues in an appropriate context. In addition, the potency of irrational "wanting" triggered by those cues would be especially exacerbated if the addict tried to take "just one hit." The presence of drug on board can prime mesolimbic systems and can amplify the response to drug cues, creating a surge of incentive salience in a way that might well precipitate a compulsive binge of further drug taking.

Conclusion

According to the incentive-sensitization theory, addiction involves drug-induced changes in many different brain circuits, and incentive sensitization of mesolimbic circuits is the most prominent of these for producing the distinguishing features of addiction. Bolstered by the evidence that has accumulated over recent years, we remain confident in concluding,

> that at its heart, addiction is a disorder of aberrant incentive motivation due to drug-induced sensitization of neural systems that attribute salience to particular stimuli. It can be triggered by drug cues as a *learned motivational response* of the brain, but it is not a disorder of aberrant learning per se. Once it exists, sensitized "wanting" may compel drug pursuit whether or not an addict has any withdrawal symptoms at all. And because incentive salience is distinct from pleasure or "liking" processes, sensitization gives impulsive drug "wanting" an enduring life of its own. (Robinson & Berridge, 2003, 44)

Sensitized "wanting" in an addict may motivate behavior independent of drug "liking" or withdrawal and independent of cognitive desires and intentions. Incentive sensitization can produce addictive features that make drug taking more compulsive than mere habits could ever achieve, and it may rise above expectations of drug value to become "wanted" to a degree that might even be called irrational. Such an addictive "want" has truly gained a destructive "life of its own." These phenomena of desire seem intriguing topics for philosophers and psychologists trying to understand the mind.

Acknowledgment

The results from our labs described here were made possible by research grants from the National Institutes of Health.

References

Anagnostaras, S. G., & Robinson, T. E. (1996). Sensitization to the psychomotor stimulant effects of amphetamine: modulation by associative learning. *Behavioral Neuroscience, 110*(6), 1397–1414.

Anagnostaras, S. G., Schallert, T., & Robinson, T. E. (2002). Memory processes governing amphetamine-induced psychomotor sensitization. *Neuropsychopharmacology*, *26*(6), 703–715.

Avena, N. M., & Hoebel, B. G. (2003). A diet promoting sugar dependency causes behavioral cross-sensitization to a low dose of amphetamine. *Neuroscience*, *122*(1), 17–20.

Badiani, A., & Robinson, T. E. (2004). Drug-induced neurobehavioral plasticity: the role of environmental context. *Behavioural Pharmacology*, *15*(5–6), 327–339.

Bechara, A. (2005). Decision making, impulse control and loss of willpower to resist drugs: a neurocognitive perspective. *Nature Neuroscience*, *8*(11), 1458–1463.

Belin, D., Jonkman, S., Dickinson, A., Robbins, T. W., & Everitt, B. J. (2009). Parallel and interactive learning processes within the basal ganglia: relevance for the understanding of addiction. *Behavioural Brain Research*, *199*(1), 89–102.

Berke, J. D., & Hyman, S. E. (2000). Addiction, dopamine, and the molecular mechanisms of memory. *Neuron*, *25*(3), 515–532.

Berridge, K. C. (2007). The debate over dopamine's role in reward: the case for incentive salience. *Psychopharmacology*, *191*(3), 391–431.

Berridge, K. C. (2009). Wanting and Liking: Observations from the Neuroscience and Psychology Laboratory. *Inquiry—an Interdisciplinary Journal of Philosophy*, *52*(4), 378–398.

Berridge, K. C., & Aldridge, J. W. (2008). Decision utility, the brain and pursuit of hedonic goals. *Social Cognition*, *26*(5), 621–646.

Berridge, K. C., & Robinson, T. E. (1998). What is the role of dopamine in reward: hedonic impact, reward learning, or incentive salience? *Brain Research. Brain Research Reviews*, *28*(3), 309–369.

Berridge, K. C., & Robinson, T. E. (2003). Parsing reward. *Trends in Neurosciences*, *26*(9), 507–513.

Boileau, I., Dagher, A., Leyton, M., Gunn, R. N., Baker, G. B., Diksic, M., et al. (2006). Modeling sensitization to stimulants in humans: an [^{11}C]raclopride/positron emission tomography study in healthy men. *Archives of General Psychiatry*, *63*(12), 1386–1395.

Boyer, P., & Lienard, P. (2008). Ritual behavior in obsessive and normal individuals. *Current Directions in Psychological Science*, *17*(4), 291–294.

Caggiula, A. R., Donny, E. C., Palmatier, M. I., Liu, X., Chaudhri, N., & Sved, A. F. (2009). The role of nicotine in smoking: a dual-reinforcement model. *Nebraska Symposium on Motivation*, *55*, 91–109.

Childress, A. R., Ehrman, R. N., Wang, Z., Li, Y., Sciortino, N., Hakun, J., et al. (2008). Prelude to passion: limbic activation by "unseen" drug and sexual cues. *PLoS ONE* *3*(1), e1506.

Childress, A. R., McLellan, A. T., Ehrman, R., & O'Brien, C. P. (1988). Classically conditioned responses in opioid and cocaine dependence: a role in relapse? *NIDA Research Monograph*, *84*, 25–43.

Davis, C. A., Levitan, R. D., Reid, C., Carter, J. C., Kaplan, A. S., Patte, K. A., et al. (2009). Dopamine for "wanting" and opioids for "liking": a comparison of obese adults with and without binge eating. *Obesity*, *17*(6), 1220–1225.

Day, J. J., & Carelli, R. M. (2007). The nucleus accumbens and Pavlovian reward learning. *Neuroscientist*, *13*(2), 148–159.

Dickinson, A., Smith, J., & Mirenowicz, J. (2000). Dissociation of Pavlovian and instrumental incentive learning under dopamine antagonists. *Behavioral Neuroscience*, *114*(3), 468–483.

Evans, A. H., Pavese, N., Lawrence, A. D., Tai, Y. F., Appel, S., Doder, M., et al. (2006). Compulsive drug use linked to sensitized ventral striatal dopamine transmission. *Annals of Neurology*, *59*(5), 852–858.

Everitt, B. J., Belin, D., Economidou, D., Pelloux, Y., Dalley, J. W., & Robbins, T. W. (2008). Review. Neural mechanisms underlying the vulnerability to develop compulsive drug-seeking habits and addiction. *Philosophical Transactions of the Royal Society of London. Series B, Biological Sciences*, *363*(1507), 3125–3135.

Everitt, B. J., Dickinson, A., & Robbins, T. W. (2001). The neuropsychological basis of addictive behaviour. *Brain Research. Brain Research Reviews*, *36*(2–3), 129–138.

Fiorino, D. F., & Phillips, A. G. (1999). Facilitation of sexual behavior and enhanced dopamine efflux in the nucleus accumbens of male rats after d-amphetamine-induced behavioral sensitization. *Journal of Neuroscience*, *19*(1), 456–463.

Fischman, M. W., & Foltin, R. W. (1992). Self-administration of cocaine by humans: a laboratory perspective. In G. R. Bock & J. Whelan (Eds.), *Cocaine: scientific and social dimensions, CIBA Foundation symposium No. 166* (pp. 165–180). Chichester, UK: Wiley.

Flagel, S. B., Akil, H., & Robinson, T. E. (2009). Individual differences in the attribution of incentive salience to reward-related cues: Implications for addiction. *Neuropharmacology*, *56*(Suppl. 1), 139–148.

Gilbert, D. G., & Wilson, T. D. (2000). Miswanting: Some problems in forecasting future affective states. In J. P. Forgas (Ed.), *Feeling and thinking: the role of affect in social cognition* (pp. 178–198). Cambridge: Cambridge University Press.

Green, A. L., Pereira, E. A., & Aziz, T. Z. (2010). Deep brain stimulation and pleasure. In M. L. Kringelbach & K. C. Berridge (Eds.), *Pleasures of the brain* (pp. 302–319). Oxford: Oxford University Press.

Grimm, J. W., Hope, B. T., Wise, R. A., & Shaham, Y. (2001). Neuroadaptation— Incubation of cocaine craving after withdrawal. *Nature, 412*(6843), 141–142.

Heath, R. G. (1996). *Exploring the mind-brain relationship.* Baton Rouge, LA: Moran Printing Inc.

Hellemans, K. G., Dickinson, A., & Everitt, B. J. (2006). Motivational control of heroin seeking by conditioned stimuli associated with withdrawal and heroin taking by rats. *Behavioral Neuroscience, 120*(1), 103–114.

Holton, R. (2009). *Willing, wanting, waiting.* Oxford: Oxford University Press.

Hyman, S. E. (2005). Addiction: a disease of learning and memory. *American Journal of Psychiatry, 162*(8), 1414–1422.

Hyman, S. E., Malenka, R. C., & Nestler, E. J. (2006). Neural mechanisms of addiction: the role of reward-related learning and memory. *Annual Review of Neuroscience, 29*, 565–598.

James, W. (1890). *Principles of Psychology.* New York: H. Holt and Company.

Kahneman, D., Fredrickson, B. L., Schreiber, C. A., & Redelmeier, D. A. (1993). When more pain is preferred to less: adding a better end. *Psychological Science, 4*, 401–405.

Kahneman, D., Wakker, P. P., & Sarin, R. (1997). Back to Bentham? Explorations of experienced utility. *Quarterly Journal of Economics, 112*, 375–405.

Kalivas, P. W., & Volkow, N. D. (2005). The neural basis of addiction: a pathology of motivation and choice. *American Journal of Psychiatry, 162*(8), 1403–1413.

Kapur, S. (2003). Psychosis as a state of aberrant salience: a framework linking biology, phenomenology, and pharmacology in schizophrenia. *American Journal of Psychiatry, 160*(1), 13–23.

Kenny, P. J., Chen, S. A., Kitamura, O., Markou, A., & Koob, G. F. (2006). Conditioned withdrawal drives heroin consumption and decreases reward sensitivity. *Journal of Neuroscience, 26*(22), 5894–5900.

Kessler, D. A. (2009). *The end of overeating: taking control of the insatiable American appetite.* New York: Rodale Press. Distributed to the trade by Macmillan.

Koksal, F., Domjan, M., Kurt, A., Sertel, O., Orung, S., Bowers, R., et al. (2004). An animal model of fetishism. *Behaviour Research and Therapy, 42*(12), 1421–1434.

Koob, G. F., & Le Moal, M. (2006). *Neurobiology of addiction.* New York: Academic Press.

Lawrence, A. D., Evans, A. H., & Lees, A. J. (2003). Compulsive use of dopamine replacement therapy in Parkinson's disease: reward systems gone awry? *Lancet Neurology, 2*(10), 595–604.

Leyton, M. (2007). Conditioned and sensitized responses to stimulant drugs in humans. *Progress in Neuro-Psychopharmacology & Biological Psychiatry, 31*(8), 1601–1613.

Mahler, S. V., & Berridge, K. C. (2009). Which cue to "want?" Central amygdala opioid activation enhances and focuses incentive salience on a prepotent reward cue. *Journal of Neuroscience, 29*(20), 6500–6513.

McAuliffe, W. E. (1982). A test of Wikler's theory of relapse: the frequency of relapse due to conditioned withdrawal sickness. *International Journal of the Addictions, 17*(1), 19–33.

Miles, F. J., Everitt, B. J., & Dickinson, A. (2003). Oral cocaine seeking by rats: action or habit? *Behavioral Neuroscience, 117*(5), 927–938.

Mitchell, J. B., & Stewart, J. (1990). Facilitation of sexual behaviors in the male rat associated with intra-VTA injections of opiates. *Pharmacology, Biochemistry, and Behavior, 35*(3), 643–650.

Morewedge, C. K., Gilbert, D. T., & Wilson, T. D. (2005). The least likely of times: how remembering the past biases forecasts of the future. *Psychological Science, 16*(8), 626–630.

Nelson, A., & Killcross, S. (2006). Amphetamine exposure enhances habit formation. *Journal of Neuroscience, 26*(14), 3805–3812.

Nocjar, C., & Panksepp, J. (2002). Chronic intermittent amphetamine pretreatment enhances future appetitive behavior for drug- and natural-reward: interaction with environmental variables. *Behavioural Brain Research, 128*(2), 189–203.

O'Brien, C. P., Childress, A. R., McLellan, A. T., Ehrman, R., & Ternes, J. W. (1988). Types of conditioning found in drug-dependent humans. *NIDA Research Monograph, 84*, 44–61.

Paulson, P. E., Camp, D. M., & Robinson, T. E. (1991). Time course of transient behavioral depression and persistent behavioral sensitization in relation to regional brain monoamine concentrations during amphetamine withdrawal in rats. *Psychopharmacology, 103*(4), 480–492.

Phillips, G. D., Harmer, C. J., & Hitchcott, P. K. (2002). Blockade of sensitisation-induced facilitation of appetitive conditioning by post-session intra-amygdala nafadotride. *Behavioural Brain Research, 134*(1–2), 249–257.

Redish, A. D. (2004). Addiction as a computational process gone awry. *Science, 306*(5703), 1944–1947.

Reynolds, S. M., & Berridge, K. C. (2008). Emotional environments retune the valence of appetitive versus fearful functions in nucleus accumbens. *Nature Neuroscience, 11*(4), 423–425.

Robbins, T. W., Ersche, K. D., & Everitt, B. J. (2008). Drug addiction and the memory systems of the brain. *Annals of the New York Academy of Sciences, 1141,* 1–21.

Robbins, T. W., Everitt, B. J., & Nutt, D. J. (2008). Introduction. The neurobiology of drug addiction: new vistas. *Philosophical Transactions of the Royal Society of London. Series B, Biological Sciences, 363*(1507), 3109–3111.

Robinson, T. E., & Becker, J. B. (1986). Enduring changes in brain and behavior produced by chronic amphetamine administration: a review and evaluation of animal models of amphetamine psychosis. *Brain Research, 396*(2), 157–198.

Robinson, T. E., & Berridge, K. C. (1993). The neural basis of drug craving: an incentive-sensitization theory of addiction. *Brain Research. Brain Research Reviews, 18*(3), 247–291.

Robinson, T. E., & Berridge, K. C. 2000. The psychology and neurobiology of addiction: an incentive-sensitization view. *Addiction, 95*(8 Suppl. 2), 91–117.

Robinson, T. E., & Berridge, K. C. (2003). Addiction. *Annual Review of Psychology, 54*(1), 25–53.

Robinson, T. E., & Berridge, K. C. (2008). Review. The incentive sensitization theory of addiction: some current issues. *Philosophical Transactions of the Royal Society of London. Series B, Biological Sciences, 363*(1507), 3137–3146.

Robinson, T. E., & Flagel, S. B. (2009). Dissociating the predictive and incentive motivational properties of reward-related cues through the study of individual differences. *Biological Psychiatry, 65*(10), 869–873.

Robinson, T. E., & Kolb, B. (1999). Alterations in the morphology of dendrites and dendritic spines in the nucleus accumbens and prefrontal cortex following repeated treatment with amphetamine or cocaine. *European Journal of Neuroscience, 11*(5), 1598–1604.

Robinson, T. E., & Kolb, B. (2004). Structural plasticity associated with exposure to drugs of abuse. *Neuropharmacology, 47,* 33–46.

Rosse, R. B., Fay-McCarthy, M., Collins, J., Jr., Risher-Flowers, D., Alim, T. N., & Deutsch, S. I. (1993). Transient compulsive foraging behavior associated with crack cocaine use. *American Journal of Psychiatry, 150*(1), 155–156.

Samaha, A. N., Yau, W. Y. W., Yang, P. W., & Robinson, T. E. (2005). Rapid delivery of nicotine promotes behavioral sensitization and alters its neurobiological impact. *Biological Psychiatry, 57*(4), 351–360.

Schoenbaum, G., & Shaham, Y. (2008). The role of orbitofrontal cortex in drug addiction: a review of preclinical studies. *Biological Psychiatry*, *63*(3), 256–262.

Schull, J. (1979). A conditioned opponent theory of Pavlovian conditioning and habituation. In G. H. Bower (Ed.), *The psychology of learning and motivation* (Vol. 13, pp. 57–90). New York: Academic Press.

Schultz, W. (2006). Behavioral theories and the neurophysiology of reward. *Annual Review of Psychology*, *57*, 87–115.

Shalev, U., Grimm, J. W., & Shaham, Y. (2002). Neurobiology of relapse to heroin and cocaine seeking: a review. *Pharmacological Reviews*, *54*(1), 1–42.

Solomon, R. L. 1977. Addiction: an opponent-process theory of acquired motivation: The affective dynamics of addiction. In M. E. P. S. Jack D. Maser (Ed.), *Psychopathology: experimental models* (pp. 66–103). San Francisco: W. H. Freeman & Co.

Stephens, G. L., & Graham, G. (2009). An addictive lesson: a case study in psychiatry as cognitive neuroscience. In M. Broome & L. Bortolotti (Eds.), *Psychiatry as cognitive neuroscience: philosophical perspectives* (pp. 203–222). Oxford: Oxford University Press.

Stewart, J. (1992). Neurobiology of conditioning to drugs of abuse. *Annals of the New York Academy of Sciences*, *654*, 335–346.

Stewart, J. (2004). Pathways to relapse: Factors controlling the reinitiation of drug seeking after abstinence. *Nebraska Symposium on Motivation*, *50*, 197–234.

Taylor, J. R., & Horger, B. A. (1999). Enhanced responding for conditioned reward produced by intra-accumbens amphetamine is potentiated after cocaine sensitization. *Psychopharmacology*, *142*(1), 31–40.

Tiffany, S. T. (1990). A cognitive model of drug urges and drug-use behavior: role of automatic and nonautomatic processes. *Psychological Review*, *97*, 147–168.

Tindell, A. J., Berridge, K. C., Zhang, J., Peciña, S., & Aldridge, J. W. (2005). Ventral pallidal neurons code incentive motivation: amplification by mesolimbic sensitization and amphetamine. *European Journal of Neuroscience*, *22*(10), 2617–2634.

Tomie, A. (1996). Locating reward cue at response manipulandum (CAM) induces symptoms of drug abuse. *Neuroscience and Biobehavioral Reviews*, *20*(3), 505–535.

Vezina, P. (2004). Sensitization of midbrain dopamine neuron reactivity and the self-administration of psychomotor stimulant drugs. *Neuroscience and Biobehavioral Reviews*, *27*(8), 827–839.

Vezina, P., & Leyton, M. (2009). Conditioned cues and the expression of stimulant sensitization in animals and humans. *Neuropharmacology*, *56*(Suppl 1), 160–168.

Volkow, N. D., Wang, G. J., Telang, F., Fowler, J. S., Logan, J., Childress, A. R., et al. (2006). Cocaine cues and dopamine in dorsal striatum: mechanism of craving in cocaine addiction. *Journal of Neuroscience, 26*(24), 6583–6588.

Volkow, N. D., Wang, G. J., Telang, F., Fowler, J. S., Logan, J., Childress, A. R., et al. (2008). Dopamine increases in striatum do not elicit craving in cocaine abusers unless they are coupled with cocaine cues. *NeuroImage, 39*(3), 1266–1273.

Winkielman, P., & Berridge, K. C. (2004). Unconscious emotion. *Current Directions in Psychological Science, 13*(3), 120–123.

Wyvell, C. L., & Berridge, K. C. (2000). Intra-accumbens amphetamine increases the conditioned incentive salience of sucrose reward: enhancement of reward "wanting" without enhanced "liking" or response reinforcement. *Journal of Neuroscience, 20*(21), 8122–8130.

Wyvell, C. L., & Berridge, K. C. (2001). Incentive-sensitization by previous amphetamine exposure: Increased cue-triggered "wanting" for sucrose reward. *Journal of Neuroscience, 21*(19), 7831–7840.

Zhang, J., Berridge, K. C., Tindell, A. J., Smith, K. S., & Aldridge, J. W. (2009). A neural computational model of incentive salience. *PLoS Computational Biology, 5*(7), e1000437.

3   Free Will as Recursive Self-Prediction: Does a Deterministic Mechanism Reduce Responsibility?

George Ainslie

Advances in brain imaging have revealed more and more about the physical basis of motivated behavior, making the age-old dispute about free will and moral responsibility increasingly salient. Science seems to be delineating chains of causality for feelings, choices, and even beliefs; but if all mental life is strictly caused by prior events, and those by still earlier events in a chain extending back before birth, how can individuals be held responsible for their actions? Most people feel that they originate their actions (Nadelhoffer, Morris, Nahmias, & Turner, 2005) and will readily give opinions about whether particular circumstances make an action blameworthy or not (Monterosso, Royzman, & Schwartz, 2005); but when philosophers take the chain of causality explicitly into account they generally distance themselves from these direct introspections, holding for instance that blame is just a way of assuaging instinctive resentment (Strawson, 1962/2003) or a threat to manipulate people's motives (Dennett, 1984, 131–172). I come to this subject with a behavioral science rather than a philosophy background, but the free-will dispute looks to this outsider like something that recent empirical findings might resolve.

The dispute is age old because of a fundamental conundrum. We insist on the truth of each of two propositions, the compatibility of which is far from obvious and perhaps even absurd:

1. that all events are fully caused by preexisting factors, and

2. that a person's choices are not always caused by preexisting factors.

David Hume was already testifying to the historical scope of the conundrum a quarter-millennium ago: "To proceed in this reconciling project with regard to the question of liberty and necessity—the most contentious question of metaphysics, the most contentious science—it will not require many words to prove, that all mankind have ever agreed in the doctrine of liberty as well as in that of necessity . . . " (Hume, 1748/1962, 104). Hume thought the dispute was "purely verbal" and sought to clear it up with a flourish, but over the years the failure of countless rewordings to produce a widely accepted reconciliation has revealed it to be substantive. There is something we have not understood, either in the operation of physical causality or in the nature of human will.

After first looking briefly at the chain of causality, I develop here a proposal that the will is not only deterministic but mechanistic—the outgrowth of a specifiable interaction of simpler processes. However, I argue that this mechanistic will fits compatibilists' requirements for being free, which are close to the intuitive conception of freedom. This conception is not just the illusion of freedom but the accurate introspection of a discrete natural process. Finally, I argue that fitting this mechanism to the intuitive understanding of responsibility, in the sense of blameworthiness, requires an additional step—a specific implication of the free will mechanism that reverses the conventional explanation.

A Misunderstanding of Causality?

The use of the word "indeterminacy" in atomic physics has led some authors to ascribe the conundrum to a false certainty about physical causality (e.g., Landé, 1961). From the discoveries in quantum mechanics in the 1920s, these authors have hoped for a way around strict determinism. However, it was soon pointed out that the random movement of particles translates into highly predictable averages at observable volumes—it matters little to the flow of a river that some water molecules are always moving upstream, for instance—and is unlikely to produce a sense of efficacy at either micro or macro levels (see Smart, 1961). In reply, there were suggestions, mostly by physical scientists, that made the brain into an analogue of Schroedinger's famous (but hypothetical) Geiger counter, which could kill a cat or not on the basis of a single particle emission. Physiologist John Eccles proposed that a nondetermined, spiritual self could interact with the brain by its effect on a single, strategically placed neuron (Eccles, 1994), and physicist Henry Stapp suggested that chaotic systems in the brain could be sensitively dependent on a few calcium ions determining neurotransmissions (Stapp, 1998). Such models fail to predict a sense of responsibility, as opposed to happenstance, unless the particles are endowed with mystical properties that supply the real responsibility, properties that would have to be miniaturized to an astounding degree. How many angels can dance on a subatomic particle?

Despite this problem, indeterminacy at the subatomic level continues to be put forward as a mechanism. When physicist Gerard t'Hooft recently constructed a model in which subatomic activity is deterministic, another physicist, Antoine Suarez, retorted: "If t'Hooft is really correct then the work for which he is famed was not carried out as a result of his free will. Rather, he was destined to do it from the beginning of time . . . Maybe his Nobel prize should rightfully have been presented to the big bang instead" (Merali, 2007). Physicists seem fascinated by this approach and continue to look for the flaw in our understanding of physical causality. However, a failure to recognize atomic happenstance seems unlikely to have concealed a freedom of will that could be the basis for moral responsibility.

Early concepts of freedom were easy to accept. Hume, calling it "liberty," said it was "a power of acting or not according to the determinations of the will" (Hume, 1748/1962, 104). It was just the ability to do what you wanted, leaving alone the question of whether what you wanted was subject to a chain of causality. By the time of William James, that question had become unavoidable, and the answers had hardened: "The juice has ages ago been pressed out of the free-will controversy" (James, 1884/1896). To keep moral responsibility, his main concern, from being crushed by determinism, James felt the need to postulate some wiggle room: "Indeterminism . . . says that the parts have a certain amount of loose play on one another, so that the laying down of one of them does not necessarily determine what the others shall be" (James, 1884/1896). But attempts to specify what that "loose play" might consist of led inexorably to Eccles's microscopic indeterminism. An examination of our idea of human will seems more promising.

A Misunderstanding of Will?

There has always been antipathy to the notion of strict determinism because it seems to imply a loss of our humanity—of the subtle balance we experience in facing close choices, of our pride in feats of self-control, and of our outrage at people who do harm through losses of self-control.

Even stronger has been antipathy to one implication of determinism, that we are assemblages of component parts that function and combine according to material laws. The idea that our choices occur entirely through physical mechanisms dates back at least to Hobbes (1651/1996, ch. 6, 37–46) and has caused repeated scandals through concrete interpretations of what it implies. In the Enlightenment it was carried furthest by La Mettrie, who declared that man was a machine and that since the machine was driven by pleasure and pain, rational behavior consisted of finding ways to intensify pleasure (La Mettrie, 1748/1999), research that was undertaken by the Marquis de Sade among others. At the time the threat to received religion seemed even greater than the risks of dissipation, and 18th-century orthodox opinion lumped the new physiocratic philosophy together with pornography (Darnton, 1995, 3–21). In the next century social Darwinists seized on evolution to equate rationality with biologically driven dog-eat-dog competitiveness, which became synonymous with social irresponsibility. In the 1920s the behaviorism popularized by John B. Watson asserted that choice consisted of habits conditioned to external stimuli (Watson, 1924, 207–210), an opinion that attracted both admiration and revulsion before it was shown to be a misinterpretation of early experimental evidence (e.g., Rescorla, 1988). Suspicions about determinism are still founded especially on the fear that it is incompatible with morality.

Determinists have felt a need to defend their view largely by explaining how it can preserve personal responsibility, or, in the case of "hard" determinism, the *illusion* of personal responsibility (Smilansky, 2002; Strawson, 1962/2003). There have been many formulations of the properties needed for a subjectively free will. These properties seem to boil down to three: unpredictability, initiative, and moral responsibility (summarized in Haji, 2002). A brief look at discussions of these properties in the philosophical literature reveals some useful suggestions, especially on the topic of initiative, but no basis for a synthesis.

Unpredictability

To be experienced as free a choice cannot be a foregone conclusion even for someone who knows all the preexisting incentives that bear on it, and even if it is the person herself who is trying to predict the choice. This condition is often expressed as, "I could have done otherwise." William

James famously pointed out to his lecture audience that he could walk home either by Oxford Street or Divinity Avenue, and either choice was possible; thus looking back on whichever choice he made, he would not be able to say that the other choice was impossible (James, 1884/1967). The possibility of alternatives continues to be put forward as a test for freedom of choice (e.g., Broad, 1966); but as a subjective experience, possibility of alternatives means no more than unpredictability of choice—"*for all I know* I can take/could have taken Oxford Street.*" James was using an example of near indifference, but a similar test for freedom can be applied to great motivational struggles: "For all I know, my effort to resist the urge to get drunk will succeed/might have succeeded." Tomis Kapitan is unusual in characterizing unpredictability of choice not as "could have done otherwise" but in the person's inability to consciously add up her motives (Kapitan, 1986). This suggestion points us toward a valuable insight, as we will see.

Unpredictability by itself should feel the same as indeterminacy—as Dennett has pointed out, the pseudorandom numbers generated by a computer cannot be distinguished from the (truly?) random numbers generated by radium emissions (Dennett, 1984, 144–152)—but this is not enough to create what feels like free will. Many authors have pointed out that simple unpredictability, even to the person herself, could not make choices seem free. Indeed, one argument against subatomic indeterminacy as a mechanism for freedom has been that the resulting choices would not feel *made* but just encountered (Strawson, 1986). The same problem would attach to any other model based entirely on unpredictability. However, any explanation of free will needs to account for the *introspective opacity* that keeps you from reading your impending choices from your perceived incentives. The quality of unpredictability is necessary but not sufficient for the experience of freedom.

Initiative

In a free choice you add something beyond identifying and aggregating the existing incentives. Some authors have proposed that the addition comes from the assignment of weights to motives (Nozick, 1981, 294–309) or "a second-order capacity to reflect critically upon one's first-order preferences" (Dworkin, 1988, 108). Aside from the obvious problem of causal regression—what are your motives to reflect upon your motives?—this mechanism seems to involve a setting up of motives in advance, not part of initiation in the moment. As Richard Holton has put it, "Action is experienced as something that the agent instigates, rather than something that just happens to the agent as the result of the state that they were antecedently in" (Holton, 2009). However, it is unclear where such instigation would come from. What keeps a person from being simply a throughput that translates discerned incentives of the first, second, or nth degrees into actions?

One answer to this question is implicit in Cartesian dualism, which, although no longer viable as a theory, has a suggestive variant in Kant's proposal that the human faculty he called reason could cause phenomena in the physical world without itself being caused by them (Kant, 1781/1966, 369–384). The part of Kant's proposal that is of continuing interest is that he saw reason as structured by moral law, so its power in initiating actions would come from its capacity to inhibit urges that violated a categorical imperative. For Kant, the important function of (and theoretical need for) this reasoned initiation would be what we would call self-control. Recent authors have also pointed out the close relationship of freedom and strength of will (Dennett, 1984, 51–73; Holton, 2009; Mele, 1995, 32–143).[1] The relationship of freedom and strength will be important to our discussion presently.

James Garson has proposed a mechanism for the introspective opacity that makes choices unpredictable from a knowledge of their motives. He suggests that this opacity is the result of a chaotic choice-making process, in the technical sense—that it is modulated by ongoing feedback (Garson, 1995). Certainly we are aware of cybernetic systems in ourselves, which let us follow a moving target with a finger or keep ourselves from getting too hot or cold. But these, too, feel like assigned tasks, not the sites of true initiative. Garson was not thinking of negative feedback, as in a thermostat—or exactly positive feedback, as in an atomic reaction, either—but offsetting feedback, in which one output could knock the next output onto a radically different course, an idea he got from chaos theory. In chaos final outcomes are *sensitively dependent* on small differences in input. However, this suggestion alone does not explain a sense of initiative. Why would choosing chaotically not feel like being swept about by the weather, or even overtaken by epileptic fits (Kane, 1989, 231)? As Sappington put it, "If chaos-type data can be used to justify the existence of free will in humans, they can also be used to justify the existence of free will in chaotic pendulums, weather systems, leaf distribution, and mathematical equations" (Sappington, 1990). Furthermore, conventional physiology and psychology do not suggest a process that would behave in this way—plenty of homeostatic processes, but nothing chaotic. However, this suggestion, too, supplies a root from which an adequate explanation can grow.

Moral Responsibility

Compatibilist analyses of unpredictability and initiative have tried to spot these processes in the introspection of moments of choice—"What does free choice feel like?" Analyses of moral responsibility, by contrast, start with the necessity of preserving it and look for justifications. These discussions are largely based on examples that distinguish intuitively between behaviors for which we would assign responsibility and behaviors we would excuse (Haji, 2002). Those authors who have tried to connect this approach with causality have generally concluded that blame is just another psychological phenomenon that arises from our natures. Peter Strawson, for instance, holds that moral "reactive attitudes" are ingrained and could not be given up on the basis of philosophical argument (Strawson, 1962/2003). Paul Russell does make a proposal like Kant's by pointing out that such attitudes can be modified, like any emotion, by the dictates of reason (Russell, 1992); however, it is not clear why such modification is caused any differently than the attitudes themselves.

Similarly, an empirical search for brain locations of moral reasoning has led to the conclusion that a sense of free will is merely one of the experiences our brains are wired to have. After a thorough and generally insightful examination of the problem in the light of modern neuroscience, psychologists Joshua Greene and Jonathan Cohen conclude that a rather despairing form of compatibilism is inevitable: hard determinism is true and "every decision is a thoroughly mechanical process" (Greene & Cohen, 2004, 1781), but there are also "mechanisms that underlie our sense of free will" (1781). Hardwired human "folk psychology" makes us ascribe responsibility to some agents, in such a way that "seeing something as an uncaused causer is a *necessary but not sufficient* condition for seeing something as a moral agent" (Greene & Cohen, 2004, 1782; their italics). As a result, "the problem of free will and determinism will never find an intuitively satisfying solution because it arises out of a conflict between two distinct cognitive subsystems that speak different cognitive 'languages' and that may ultimately be incapable of negotiation" (Greene & Cohen, 2004, 1783). We are left with a sorry dualism, not between spirit and flesh but between two differently programmed areas of brain, an obedient motivation-follower and a somewhat deluded introspector.

I propose that these three properties—unpredictability, initiative, and responsibility—have remained elusive because our understanding of human will has been inadequate:

• that there is good reason within strict determinism that people cannot predict their own choices with certainty;

• that there is a strictly determined mechanism by which people take genuine initiative in their choices; and

• that ascription of personal responsibility for actions does not require denial of (or other inattention to) the strict determination of those actions.

My method is to abandon cultural assumptions of the self as a unitary governor and of the will as this self's organ of selection. Rather, I present evidence that the self is a population of partially conflicting interests, and the will is a property that emerges from these conflicts. A sense of responsibility comes in turn from personal experience with this emergence.

Recasting the Choice-Maker: Hyperbolic Discounting

Freedom of choice has always been considered at single moments, without regard to how the person's expectations for her own choices at future moments bear upon her current choice. This has not seemed to be an important limitation, since people are conventionally assumed to expect that they will keep following their current choice in the absence of new information about its likely consequences. However, a great deal of research over the last 40 years has shown that all reward-seeking organisms devalue delayed prospects according to a function that often leads them to change preferences as time elapses, without getting any new information. Humans are the only species hampered by this phenomenon, since, with minor exceptions (deWaal, 2007, 184–187; Henderson, 2009), we are the only one that makes future plans, as opposed to just obeying the promptings of current instincts that have evolved to protect future welfare—hoarding, dam building, migrating, and so on. To some extent we can learn to compensate for this *dynamic inconsistency—akrasia* is the popular term in philosophy—but the most powerful kind of compensation makes our choosing a different operation than has been conventionally assumed. I have developed this argument elsewhere (Ainslie, 2001, 27–104, 2005) but will present the essentials here.

Future prospects are usually thought of as devalued, or *discounted*, according to the only function that would make preference stable over time, the exponential curve. Exponential curves describe a prospect's loss of value by a constant percentage of the value it has at a given time, for every unit of time that it is delayed:

Present value = Value$_0$ × δ^{Delay}

where *Value$_0$* = value if immediate, and δ = (1 – discount rate). However, controlled experiments with both humans choosing spontaneously and nonhumans have shown that delayed options are discounted in a fairly simple inverse proportion of their expected delay. The formula was given its most-cited form by Mazur (1987):

Present value = Value$_0$/[1 + (k × Delay)]

where *Value$_0$* = value if immediate, and *k* is degree of impatience. This function predicts that, for some cases where smaller rewards precede larger alternatives, subjects will prefer the larger, later (LL) reward when both are distant but change to preferring the smaller, sooner (SS) reward as time elapses. Inverse proportionality also describes how tall a building appears on your retina as you walk toward it, so a shorter, closer building may loom larger than a taller, more distant one as you get close to it. We are used to ignoring this effect without a second thought when it occurs on our retinas. However, if it occurs in the centers where we evaluate prospective rewards, it may have a direct influence on our motives, of the kind Homer described for the Sirens on Ulysses. We cannot reason away distortions arising from the hyperbolic function; we must deal with them strategically.

It might seem that an evaluation process that regularly led to preference reversals as a function of time would have been selected against in evolution. However, this process is only one aspect of a general perceptual organization, described by the Weber-Fechner law (Gibbon, 1977), in which changes in any psychophysical quantity are perceived in proportion to the baseline quantity—that is, hyperbolically. It is problematic only in humans—animals that do not plan are best off trying to gratify their instinctive urges as quickly as possible—and the few hundred thousand years of human evolution may not have been enough to change such basic apparatus. Evolution may be seen instead in compensatory processes such as the larger prefrontal cortices, which seem to be crucial for the process of self-control, in *Homo sapiens* than in *Homo heidelbergensis* (DuBreuil, 2009).

Whatever the evolutionary rationale, hyperbolic discount functions have been well demonstrated. Parametric experiments on the devaluation (discounting) of prospective events in animal and human subjects have repeatedly found that an exponential shape does not describe spontaneous choice as accurately as a hyperbolic shape (reviewed in Green & Myerson, 2004; Kirby, 1997; Mazur, 2001). Three implications of hyperbolic discounting have also been found experimentally—preference reversal toward SS rewards as a function of time (impulsiveness), early choice of committing devices to forestall impulsiveness, and decreased impulsiveness when choices are made in whole series rather than singly (Ainslie, 1992, 125–142, and 2001, 73–78).

These findings suggest a model for the choice-making process: Mental processes are learned to the extent that they are rewarded. Hyperbolic discount curves predict that mental processes based on incompatible rewards available at different delays do not simply win or lose acceptance but interact over time. Processes that are congenial to each other cohere into the same process. Contradictory processes treat each other as strategic enemies. Ineffective ones cease to compete at all. Thus hyperbolically discounted reward creates what is in effect a population of reward-seeking processes that group themselves loosely into *interests* on the basis of common goals, just as economic interests arise in market economies (compare the "constituencies" that vie to elect governments in a self that has been analogized to a democracy—Humphrey & Dennett, 1989/2002). The choice-making self will have many of the properties of an economic marketplace, with a scarce resource—access to the individual's limited channel of behavior—bid for with a common currency—reward.[2] The competition of interests creates regularities within the internal marketplace, including support for those farsighted processes that can forestall or foster future behaviors whose rewards are not yet highly valued.

The finding that making choices in series increases patience is a key to how an autonomous self, one which initiates choices and is morally responsible for them, can arise from the interaction of elementary mechanisms. Standing alone, hyperbolic discounting depicts the opposite of such responsibility: a person at different moments is in a state of *limited warfare* with herself at other moments, sharing with herself at those moments some long-range goals but also motivated to shift resources away from these goals for current gratification. The self of one moment is helpless against what future selves may momentarily prefer and can influence their choices only by literal commitment (think of Ulysses) or negotiation. But with no overriding government to appeal to, what does the present self have with which to negotiate?

We can get a hint from the advice that philosophers and psychologists have given about the will over the centuries. Beginning with Aristotle they have discerned a source of strength based in choosing according to principle rather than according to the particulars of the current circumstance. The power of abstract principle to reduce actual impulsiveness is problematic for an exponential discounting model, which depicts people as naturally consistent to begin with; but it is predicted by the hyperbolic discount function, given only two conditions: that the cumulative discounted value of a series of expected rewards is roughly additive (figure. 3.1a,b), and that a person's expectation of getting the whole series can be made contingent on her current choice without physical commitment. The additivity condition has been verified experimentally (Mazur, 2001; Kirby, 2006). So has its implication that subjects will show greater preference for LL over SS rewards when choosing a whole series at once than they do when choosing singly. This increase in patience has been found in students choosing between amounts of money and of pizza (Kirby & Guastello, 2001) and in rats choosing amounts of sugar water (Ainslie & Monterosso, 2003). The replication of this finding in animals shows that the increase in patience comes from the properties of the elementary discount function rather than dependence on cultural suggestion or on other effects seen only in humans (e.g., the "magnitude effect"; Green, Myerson, Holt, Slevin, & Estle, 2004).

The second condition— that mere self-prediction can create binding commitments to bundle series of choices together—does not lend itself to direct experimental test, since the subject's awareness of being in an experiment would itself create an exception to what she would require herself

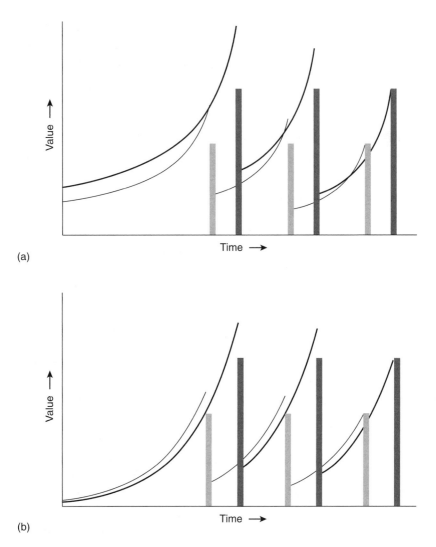

(a)

(b)

Figure 3.1
(a) The effect of bundling three pairs of larger, later (LL) rewards and smaller, sooner (SS) alternatives. Each *hyperbolic* curve shows the cumulated expected value of all similar rewards still to come. At the beginning of the series there is no temporary preference for the SS rewards. The curves from the last pair show what such a temporary preference would be if there were no bundle. (b) Absence of a bundling effect with cumulative *exponential* curves, from the same series of alternative reward pairs as in (a). Cumulation still increases the values of the prospective series over those of a single pair (e.g., the last pair), but the values of LL and SS rewards keep the same proportionality to each other.

to do in everyday life. However, the dependence of large expectations on current test cases is a common intuition. The cost to a dieter of eating a piece of chocolate is clearly not a detectable gain in weight, but the loss of her expectation that she will stick to her diet. It is as if she were playing a variety of *repeated prisoner's dilemma* with her future selves, with a personal rule such as her diet serving as the criterion for which moves are cooperations (serving the common interest in slimness) and which moves are defections (abandoning the common interest for momentary pleasure). Uncontrolled observations of several kinds support this intuition: the lore on willpower mentions the disproportionate effect of a single lapse in reducing willpower (e.g., Bain, 1859/1886, 440), and disproportionate damage done by single defections has been observed in interpersonal prisoner's dilemmas (Monterosso, Ainslie, Toppi-Mullen, & Gault, 2002). Furthermore, when Kirby and Guastello added a condition to the repeated-choice experiment just mentioned, in which they suggested to freely choosing subjects that their current choice predicted future ones, the subjects increased their preference for LL alternatives while still choosing between single pairs (Kirby & Guastello, 2001). Even more significant is the finding that when smokers and nonsmokers are run in a design similar to that of Kirby and Guastello, the smokers' initial preferences are less patient than those of the nonsmokers, but they increase their patience in both the forced bundling and the suggested bundling conditions (Hofmeyr, Ainslie, Charlton, & Ross, in press). The nonsmokers do not further increase their patience. It seems that they are already avoiding *akrasia*, but the smokers are open to improvement from strategic methods.

Perhaps the best way to test the longstanding cultural intuition about choosing according to principle is to sharpen it by a device popular in the philosophy of mind, the thought experiment. I have argued that a small number of selected thought experiments yield a valid rejection of the null hypothesis—the hypothesis that volition affects choices but is not affected by them in turn (Ainslie, 2001, 126–129; 2007). Most illustrative is Gregory Kavka's problem (Kavka, 1983), here redescribed so as not to rely on his magical brain scanner: You are a mediocre movie actor, and a director casts you, with some misgivings, to play a pipsqueak who gets sent down a terrifying toboggan run. You do not have to go down the run yourself—the director is happy to have a stunt man do it—but you have to play a big scene beforehand in which you are frightened out of your wits at the prospect. You realize that you cannot fake the necessary emotion, but also that you are genuinely terrified of the toboggan run. The role is your big break, but if you cannot do it convincingly the director will fire you. Under these circumstances, you think it is worth signing up to do the run yourself in order to ace the preceding fright scene. But if, after playing this scene you can still chicken out of the toboggan run, is it rational to do so? And if you realize in advance that you will find this rational, will not this realization undermine your intention and thus spoil your acting in the fright scene?

Conventional utility theory says that it would be rational to chicken out, as do members of the lecture audiences who have been given this problem. Neither can say how *intending* to go down the toboggan run would be possible when aware of this rationality. I interpret this finding as showing that there is a conceptual piece missing in the common-sense theory of how people intend difficult behaviors. The null hypothesis is wrong. It is not possible to intend to toboggan if you expect to renege, and it is rational not to renege so as to preserve the credibility of your intentions for future challenges.

How can you commit yourself not to renege? The relatively high tails of hyperbolic discount curves make it possible (see figure 3.1a). You do this by putting up a pledge of sufficient value; and the only pledge available to put up irrevocably in this situation is the credibility of your pledges in difficult situations in the future. This kind of pledge is *recursive*: the more you believe that you will keep it, the more you *can* keep it, and the more you will subsequently believe; the less you believe you will keep it, the less you can keep it, and so on. The current pledge need not put all future pledges at risk, but if you intend it to include only choices involving toboggan runs, you will probably expect it to be inadequate from the start and have to throw in more collateral, as it were, such as the credibility of your intentions to face major fears in general, if you are to play that scene with conviction. You expect to follow through with the toboggan run to the extent you are aware of caring that the credibility of future resolutions is at stake. Whether or not you actually go, the substantive impact of perceiving your choices in bundles is clear: Your present choice affects and is affected by the choices you expect to make in the future. This *recursive self-prediction* fulfills the second condition of our hypothesis about self-control without a central organ of will—binding commitment from self-prediction alone.

Now we can extend our model of choice making. Maintenance and change of choice will be governed by intertemporal bargaining, the activity in which reward-seeking processes that share some goals (e.g., long-term sobriety) but not others (the pleasure of having some drinks now) maximize their individual expected rewards, discounted hyperbolically to the current moment. This limited warfare relationship is familiar in interpersonal situations (Schelling, 1960, 21–80), where it often gives rise to "self-enforcing contracts" (Klein & Leffler, 1981) such as nations' avoidance of using a nuclear weapon lest nuclear warfare become general. In interpersonal bargaining, stability is achieved in the absence of an overarching government by the parties' recognition of repeated prisoner's dilemma incentives. In intertemporal bargaining, personal rules arise through a similar recognition by an individual in successive motivational states, with the difference that in a future state she is not motivated to retaliate, as it were, against herself in the past states where she has defected. In the intertemporal case, her fear of a loss of confidence in the success of her personal rule during future states, and of her consequent defection in favor of short-term interests during those states, will present the same threat as a fear of actual retaliation. These contingencies can create a will without an organ, serving a self without a seat, just as the "will" of nations not to use nuclear weapons seems to be guided by an invisible hand.

It might seem incredible that intertemporal bargaining was not described in so many words a long time ago. However, even at the interpersonal level negotiations ranging in importance from ordinary courtesy to whether wars will be escalated have long had the form of repeated prisoner's dilemmas, but the formal game was described only in 1950 (Poundstone, 1992)-- despite the fact that interpersonal prisoner's dilemma contingencies always made sense in terms of conventional utility theory. By contrast, without the limited warfare relationship among successive selves that hyperbolic discount curves predict, there would be no reason to suppose that intertemporal prisoner's dilemmas would arise in the first place. As with interpersonal prisoner's dilemmas, intertemporal ones are apt to be perceived intuitively, without deliberation. If you notice that the toboggan choice is similar to other choices where you face major fears, you have the sense that you will lose something of larger importance if you intend and then renege. At various degrees of awareness, you evaluate current choices partly as test cases predicting bundles of those similar future choices, bundles that hyperbolic discounting predicts will increase your patience.

Diets and other resolutions are examples of consciously constructed personal rules, with clearly defined conditions as to what kinds of choice are members of the relevant bundle and criteria for which choices are cooperations and which are defections. However, once you have discovered that your current choice gives you predictive information about your future choices, even choices that are not governed by actual resolutions are apt to be influenced by this information to a greater or lesser extent. This influence will be largely nameless, or be hidden in seemingly disparate processes with names like force of habit, being true to yourself, following your intuition, or even responding to some external necessity. After repeated experiences with resolutions, an individual with foresight who notices the predictiveness of present choices should develop by experience alone processes that look very much like a will. She will not usually need explicit resolutions, much less a faculty supplied *ex machina* by an intrinsically unitary self.

At this point someone is apt to object that strength of will often feels more like the direction of attention, for instance avoidance of reconsidering a prior resolution (Bratman, 1999, 58–90; McClennen, 1990, 200–218). I agree that avoiding reconsideration is one tactic of impulse control, and it is often the "effort of will" of which people are most aware. However, it is a limited tactic, apt to be unstable over time, "holding your breath." You can avoid considering a potential reward for only so long, especially when the activity of considering that reward offers some pleasure in its own right. The systematic direction of attention itself requires willpower, although perhaps less than would resistance to the index temptation itself. Willpower in my sense is William James's kind in which "both alternatives are steadily held in view, and in the very act of murdering the vanquished possibility the chooser realizes how much in that instant he is making himself lose" (James, 1890, 534). The amorous teenager who is advised to avoid intercourse by avoiding sexual thoughts or play needs to make some use of will to employ this tactic; if he wants to have sex play and still not have intercourse, then will is his sole weapon, and accordingly it must be stronger. Diversion of attention and the related control of emotion are ancillary tactics that are distinct from willpower itself (Ainslie, 1992, 133–142).[3]

The Experience of Free Will: Unpredictability and Initiative

With intertemporal bargaining, will can grow from the bottom up, through the selection by elementary motivations of increasingly sophisticated processes. In many depictions from Descartes onward the will has the appearance of a canoeist steering through rapids—using skill and foresight to ride forces much stronger than itself, but still something made of different stuff, a spirit, a homunculus. The intertemporal bargaining process can generate the canoeist from the stuff of the rapids, different in skill and foresight but subject to the same motivational forces and, in fact, developed by those forces. It is when the "canoeist" learns to include its own future tendencies as part of the currents it must anticipate that a pattern recognizable as a self develops. There are many implications of this learning, but here I focus just on the way that recursive self-prediction permits the leap from current to canoeist, that is, from strict causality to the experience of free will.

When the incentives for alternatives are closely balanced, small changes in the prospects for future cooperation swing the decision between cooperation and defection. In that case an expectation about the direction of the present choice will be a major factor in estimating future outcomes. But this estimate in turn affects the probability that the present choice will be in that direction. Such a recursive decision process is not tautological but continuously fed back like the output of a transistor to its own input. Where the person's predictions about her propensity to make the choice in question are at all in doubt, this feedback process may play a bigger role in her decision than any preexisting incentive, external or internal. For instance, a dieter faces a tempting food, guesses that she will be able to resist it, experiences this guess as an increase in the likelihood that she will reap the benefits of her diet, and thus has more prospective reward to stake against the temptation. Then she notices a possible excuse. Her guess that she will try the excuse and not get away with it—that is, that she will subsequently judge her choice to have been a lapse—will reduce her expectation of a successful diet and thereby her stake against lapses. This fall may be so great as to make the expected values of eating this tempting food versus trying to diet about equal, until some other consideration tips her self-prediction one way or the other.

Sometimes, of course, the alternative choices may not seem to be closely balanced at all. When recursive self-prediction puts at stake a major element of self-esteem, a remarkable degree of leverage can result (discussed by Bodner & Prelec, 2001, as "self-signaling"). David Premack described the example of a father who put off picking up his children in the rain to get a pack of cigarettes, and, when he noticed what this meant about his character, gave up smoking on the spot (Premack, 1970, 115; quoted in Miller, 2003, 63). The sensitive dependence of strongly motivated decisions on interpretation of such small observations, or of thoughts without any new observation at all, lends itself to theories of an overarching ego (which was Miller's purpose in quoting this example); but it can be fully derived from intertemporal bargaining. The power of symbolic acts that so impressed Freud and his followers needs no more explanation than their salience to aggregate expectations of prospective reward. Self-signaling is not subtle conceptually, but it lets choice elude any prediction based only on the contingencies of reward, and it insulates the person's decision from coercive contingencies such as addictive cravings and looming toboggan runs. Thus it can be argued to generate the experience of free will (also in Ainslie, 2001, 129–134). Furthermore, such an explanation allows us to characterize free choices better than by saying that they are too close to predict. After all, many behaviors are quite predictable in practice and are still experienced as free. What becomes crucial is the person's belief that a given choice is subject to this self-prediction process, in whatever way she has come to represent this process to herself.

I am thus proposing that freedom of will comes from the same chaotic mechanism that generates strength of will. I hypothesize that the sensitive dependence of choices on the perception of bundles of reward supplies the experience of unpredictability, and that the siting of recursiveness within the process of will itself supplies the missing sense of initiative. Although we can only guess at our future choices, the fact that these guesses change the incentives that govern those choices creates, I would argue, the "self-forming actions" that libertarian Robert Kane locates at the root of free will (Kane, 1989). By our vigilance about those choices we are actively participating in the choice process, all the more so because of our genuine suspense as to the outcome.

Returning to the pair of conflicting propositions that I listed at the beginning of this chapter, identification of an unsuspected assumption makes this conundrum solvable. We have commonly assumed the first proposition to mean: all events are always fully caused *in linear fashion* by preexisting factors. This proposition is false; we have not understood something about the nature of human will. Choices by self-aware humans are subject to recursive self-prediction. The truth of the second proposition, that a person's choices are not always caused by preexisting factors, depends on what we take "preexisting" to mean. Choices are still completely predetermined; but I have argued that the process of recursive self-prediction removes the sting from determinism by providing both unpredictability and the experience of initiation. The ultimate causes preexist, but they have by no means completed their activity when they have entered the person's motivational process. Their dynamic interaction during intertemporal bargaining is what initiates choices. To demand more of initiation, such as being a true first cause, is to add a layer of cosmological fantasy to a perfectly adequate interpretation of the subjective event.

The Experience of Free Will: Responsibility

So far we have a proposal about the unpredictability of choices and people's sense of initiating them. Up to this point it is still not clear whether people can be held morally responsible for them, given that this proposal preserves a line of strict causality from before birth. The question of responsibility is what gives the free will controversy its urgency. To analyze it we will need to move beyond the nature of human will to the nature of blame. Given determinism, the only justification for blame has seemed to be as a threat to provide an incentive for good behavior (e.g., Dennett, 1984, 131–172). However, it has been objected that blame as a tool of deterrence does not capture the common understanding of the term, and might not even be practical once people saw it as cynical manipulation (Railton, 1984; Smilansky, 2000; Strawson ,1962/2003). We would prefer a model in which blame reflects the perception of an intrinsic deservingness in the person's conduct. However, that would seem to require that the conduct is freely chosen, that is, not predetermined.

There is a way out of this dilemma, too. The literature on responsibility is concerned with social blame; self-blame, if mentioned at all, is a subsidiary process. If your choices spring entirely from causes that existed before you were born, the common argument goes, you cannot help them. Society cannot hold you responsible. You cannot hold yourself responsible, either, but that implication has seemed relatively unimportant. Given conventional theories of motivation, the subordination of self-blame makes sense, but I will argue that it is backward. The way to understand social blame is to understand self-blame.

People are said to learn self-blame from their parents—first the learning of their rules and then an "internalization" of those rules by a process that is still a matter of debate, often said to be something like classical conditioning. Initially your motivation is to win praise or escape blame, but after you have internalized the rules your motivation is to achieve pride or escape guilt, with guilt said perhaps to be the conditioned expectation of blame that now occurs whether or not it is realistic. In this view internalization is somewhat magical, unrealistic, perhaps the product of social deception or self-deception.

Hyperbolic discounting, and the recursive process of deliberate choice that can be derived from it, suggest a different motivational picture. Parental authority is still the original source of behavioral control, but obedience serves two purposes: to make your choices fit your parents' wishes, and to protect you from temporary preferences that you yourself would later regret (including damage to whatever quantum of other people's welfare you value for its own sake). To the extent that you become aware of the latter function you have two prospects at stake in obeying rules—your expectation of avoiding external blame and your expectation of containing impulses that would be harmful in their own right. As you become able to escape the scrutiny of parents and others, the second kind of stake becomes a separate incentive that has to stand on its own if the "internalization" is to endure. In the intertemporal bargaining game between your present and future selves, you risk a loss in addition both to the larger, later reward that is literally available and to your reputation in society, but your sense of this additional risk may not have a name—an unaccountable reverence for some received wisdom, perhaps, or just a nagging intuition. When you catch yourself violating your diet, what do you call the cost? Functionally it is the credibility of your intentions, regarding this diet and to some extent other diets and perhaps even more general kinds of self-control, but you are apt to call it just guilt or chagrin or self-reproach. If you have found it helpful to maintain your original sense of being watched by your parents, you may have cultivated a sense of ongoing presence in the form of an ancestor or god or saint, or even a living other, who somehow knows what you did and has become hurt or aloof.[4] In any case the loss is genuine—resolutions without external sanctions are self-enforcing contracts that are maintained by the value of your reputation with yourself, and you have injured that reputation. It does not matter whether you have retained—internalized—the rules you observed others using, or conceived new ones. You have a practical motivational basis for self-blame.

Your awareness that the loss of credibility your lapse caused was foreordained would not mitigate it. What would mitigate it would be an interpretation that removes your act from having been a test case for your self-control. A list of permissible excuses is intuitively clear: you did not know what you were doing; you did not realize your diet forbade it; you had an overriding justification; you could not have done otherwise; and so on. When you say you "could not have done otherwise" you do not mean that your act was predetermined but that it was constrained—not subject to motivation or, more controversially, subject to overwhelming motivation. The bottom line is whether or not your act tells you something about what you can expect from yourself in the future. Intertemporal bargaining is a practical tool for self-control, and an awareness of determinism would not make it cease to function. A Laplacean demon might know whether or not your self-control is about to suffer a setback, but you do not know it; getting an estimate about it was one of the expected outcomes of your current choice, and thus one of the incentives for this choice. Your choice was based upon your imperfect self-prediction; and this is true whether or not there was a demon that knew for sure and whether or not you believed that such a demon could exist.

People do not all wield this tool well. Some are too ready to accept excuses for themselves, and hence they suffer from a reduced expectation of actually doing what they intend. Some stretch the obvious criteria in the other direction and blame themselves for outcomes that were outside their control, such as failing a test that was beyond their abilities. Self-blame is not immune to wishful thinking, the rationale in the case of excessive blame being a hope that perhaps the unfortunate phenomenon really is subject to your intentions—"If failing this test is my fault, it means I can still believe I am smart enough to have passed it." However, there are intrinsic constraints on wishful thinking, and however much it distorts our ascription of responsibility, it does not change the nature of the process. Self-blame is a primitive, an intrinsic contingency of recursive self-prediction, and it operates without regard to the question of ultimate causality. If our choice gives us bad news about ourselves, we unavoidably "kick ourselves" for it, that is, pay a hedonic cost over and above the cost of the choice itself. This is the *cogito* of personal responsibility. In a theory that holds the person to be intrinsically unitary this extra cost would be puzzling and possibly superfluous, but it makes perfect sense for a population of successive selves in a limited warfare relationship with one another.

Social Blame

A crude case could be made for interpreting self-blame in a pure deterrence model: Long-range interests would threaten the current short-range interest with guilt and impose guilt as a sanction if the threat failed. However, guilt arising from intertemporal bargaining is not literally an action but the perception of a loss that has already happened. Certainly the notion of someone taking revenge on a past self would be odd. The threat that faces a person in bargaining with her future selves is not retaliation but a prediction of poorer reward in the future as those selves simply try to maximize it. She does not *choose* to blame herself but suffers from her awareness of blameworthiness. It might then make sense to ask whether our sense of social blameworthiness is modeled on our internal experience. Might social blame be vicarious self-blame rather than self-blame be internalized social blame?

My proposal is that people perceive social blame as an empathic extension of their personal processes of self-blame: "I blame her because in her shoes I would blame myself." If we understand social blame as our perception of another's conduct through the filter of our own intertemporal bargaining situation, it appears not mainly as a contingent incentive bearing on the control of that person's behavior but as an event in its own right, a loss that has already happened. It would be hard to say what the loss consists of—of trust, of some sort of credit, perhaps of the extent of possible empathy—but my point is that this kind of blame is not imposed but discerned, and discerned by analogy with our personal responsibility for our own lapses.

The foregoing analysis suggests that the characterization of self-blame as an internalization of social blame is backward. Admittedly blame has a major role as a social deterrent. The criminal justice system is only the procedural extreme of the informal accounts kept among small groups and families. But the view of blame simply as social manipulation is too Machiavellian. In practice the assignment of social blame appears to be quick and sure, a process more of "affective intuition than deliberative reasoning" (Greene & Haidt, 2002, 517). Despite academic theories about when a person is blameworthy, people tend to base judgments on a sense of deservingness. For instance, theoretical tests for legal insanity vary widely from state to state in the United States, from merely being impelled by a mental disease to not even knowing right from wrong, but the rate at which juries accept this defense varies little from state to state (Cirincione, Steadman, & McGreevy, 1995) or within a state when the charge to the jury is changed (McGreevy, Steadman, & Callahan, 1991). Furthermore, however much people may endorse a need to deter wrongdoers, punishing someone just "so as to make an example of him" is regarded as unfair.

The difference between this proposal and the deterrence model is best illustrated by comparing the intertemporal prisoner's dilemma with an interpersonal one. Given a recent history of cooperation, perception of your partner's defection in an interpersonal prisoner's dilemma causes a loss of trust in the partner, which gives you an incentive to punish her. Perception of your own defection in an intertemporal prisoner's dilemma causes a loss of expected trust among your future selves, and this loss of trust *is* the punishment. In the interpersonal case the punishment is an action, deliberate and tactical. In the intertemporal case the punishment is an inescapable perception of lowered prospects. The idea of a social loss as the root of interpersonal blame accords better with the intuition of deservingness or a "debt to society" than do pure deterrence theories. In both personal and social cases the loss of trust can be repaired by credible evidence, either subsequent cooperations or a side-transaction involving penance (in religion, "atonement"), in which you assure your partners, or your future selves, that there will be no defections without a commensurate cost. In many situations the empathic extension model and the pure deterrence model will make the same predictions, but empathic extension also describes the sense of deservingness. Neuroimaging reports of a basic tendency to put ourselves into others' situations (Iacoboni & Dapretto, 2006) accord with this hypothesis.

Given the truth of the empathic extension hypothesis, the legitimacy of social blame is not threatened by determinism. Why shrink from blaming someone else for transgressions when you would blame yourself for them? However, this legitimacy is limited by the extent to which another person's self-control functions resemble our own. Clearly we would not want to see justice administered by someone on the far end of the autistic spectrum, someone who cannot vicariously model another's motives,[5] or by a sociopath, who is not moved by them. Both, if intelligent, could follow a contingency plan for deterrence, but they could not assess the quality of deservingness that goes beyond deterrence. We are suspicious of even ordinary folks' empathic abilities and look for ways to correct for differences of experience and condition. The legal principle of trying the accused by a jury of peers is one example.

What to Do with the Drunken Sailor

Still, different juries intuit differently and have often appeared from the outside to have miscarried justice. Judgments by individuals are even more variable. Thus we search for objective criteria that could divide the blameworthy from the merely hapless, without our having to imagine ourselves in various different shoes. Unfortunately there seem to be no distinct lines in nature that match our personal tests for blame with any better than fair regularity. The most popular has been whether the behavior was caused (or, more weakly, influenced) by a disease. Alcoholism and other addictions have been shown to have a large hereditary component (Goodwin, 1986). To the extent that an inborn appetite for a substance varies among people, those at the high end of the scale might be said to have a disease. And yet addicts have often been observed to resist "irresist-ible" cravings (Heyman, 2009) and have changed their behavior when given even relatively small structured payments to do so (Stitzer & Petry, 2006). To have an itch is a disease. To scratch it is a choice. Almost everyone is especially tempted by one kind of impulse or another. But is an itch sometimes so intense or persistent that a person should not be held responsible for scratching it?

Cause by a disease has always been a gold-standard excuse. Subjects who are told of hypothetical misbehaviors report that they excuse the perpetra-tors much more often if the antecedents were physiological (e.g., low levels of a particular neurotransmitter) as opposed to experiential (e.g., severe parental abuse—Monterosso et al., 2005). Subjects also feel freer to misbehave after hearing arguments for determinism (Holton, 2009; Vohs & Schooler, 2008), suggesting that they irrationally interpret determinism, which they fail to differentiate from fatalism, as a sort of universal disease. In the addictions the identification of changes in addicts' brains pushes the argument toward a disease model. However, as science is increasingly able to identify physical proximate causes for behaviors, it is becoming apparent that such causes are universal. A physical change does not necessarily imply that the person is coerced by a motive that used to be considered resistible. Often it is the motive that induces the physical change; decisions themselves can be seen happening in the brain by functional magnetic resonance imaging (fMRI) (Daw, Niv, & Dayan, 2005; Glimcher, Kable, & Louie, 2007). Identification of a physical basis for motives has always been crude as a test for responsibility, but by chance the level of our ability to observe them used to apportion our sympathy to an extent that felt about right. The recent rise in our observational ability has spoiled this test, leading to what Dennett calls "creeping exculpation" (Dennett, 1984, 156–169). We can no longer pardon every behavior of which we can see physical roots. Nor does there seem to be any other independent indicator of blameworthiness.

What, then, should we make of the cases where our best understanding of an addict's state of mind leads to the conclusion that she is *unable* to resist temptation—that failing an epiphany she would not be able to recruit enough motivation for a sustained period of abstinence? The unusually great rewarding quality for a particular person of a particular modality—drinking, gambling, buying—might reasonably be called a disease, but the resourcelessness that follows her repeated defections in intertemporal bargaining is more like a budgetary crisis. When the addict cannot find enough credibility to stake against her temptations to consume, we might say that she was no longer responsible for her choices—but because of bankruptcy, not sickness. There is no natural test for whether such bankruptcy "exists" or not, nor even a test for when we should recognize it. Such a recognition would necessarily be culture-bound and would resist theoretical benchmarks just as attempts to define legal insanity have done. And whereas the financially bankrupt are not able to discover the funds they need by a radical restructuring of their books, sudden regenerations of will sometimes happen as addicts reframe their choices (Heyman, 2009,

44–64; and Premack's smoking example, above). The addict is not without motivation, after all; her long-range interests just cannot get adequate leverage. The determination of a motivational bankruptcy in place of a disease is not apt to make much practical difference, and it will not resolve the issue of blame any more than financial bankruptcies do. It will merely let us understand addiction's psychological damage within a marketplace model of decision making.

A Mechanism for Free Choice

Descartes was struck by how the developing laws of physics, particularly mechanics, applied to the human body, but the motivational process seemed to be a world apart. His solution was that physical activity is mechanistic but that mental activity is independent: "I have a clear and distinct idea of myself as a thinking, non-extended thing, and a clear and distinct idea of body as an extended and non-thinking thing" (quoted in Klein 1970, 346). Descartes may have had additional reasons for the distinction, but it looks on the surface as if he was responding to a simple difference in observational standpoint: He could see his body move in the world of things, but he could observe his "self" only introspectively. Thus he could conceive his arm as a system of levers but had no picture to which he could analogize his self. We still have not agreed upon a picture of the self, although I am suggesting one here, and thus we keep circling the intellectually forbidden dualism, as if hoping to find a permissible rationale for it.

Eccles's subatomic indeterminist model (Eccles, 1994) could be anchored easily in Descartes's pineal gland. Compatibilist models avoid specifying this kind of nexus, but still they shift awkwardly between the external viewpoint of objective science and the introspective description of moral responsibility (Haji, 2002). Incompatibilists scoff at these efforts, but they have accounted for the robust introspective experience of freedom only as an illusion (Smilansky, 2000), if perhaps an illusion anchored firmly in our evolved cognitive apparatus (Greene & Cohen, 2004). Strictly speaking, a self united by intertemporal bargaining is never an unmoved mover; and yet it is an emergent phenomenon. The experience of free will is not an empty perception, or illusion. If we are dominated by any illusion it is one that we also inherited from Descartes, that in contrast to the body, "the mind is entirely indivisible" (quoted in Klein, 1970, 346). A person who is a population of partially conflicting interests in a limited warfare relationship is continually engaged in negotiation. Her choice is based only on incentives, but these incentives include the effect she expects to have on her own future motivational states, an expectation that arises and shifts freshly as she tries out ways of framing her choice. Her assessment of these incentives, knowing that the resulting conclusions will be fed back as further incentives, or even knowing that they might be so fed back, should create both genuine surprise and an accurate sense of personal initiative. It will not create the sense of being an unmoved mover, whatever that would feel like.

In discussing moral responsibility most compatibilists shift the frame of reference from the chain of causality to the robustness of the concept in personal experience. This shift is necessary, but the resulting discussions arrive at either blame as social manipulation, consistent with strict determinism, or blame as something deserved, an intuition that goes beyond the manipulation hypothesis but is seemingly inconsistent with determinism. However, this intuition can be better grounded by a rationale for deservingness in self-blame, a phenomenon that has heretofore seemed secondary. An understanding of intertemporal bargaining reveals self-blame to be a loss of self-trust rather than a nonsensical retaliation against a former self. This loss is unaffected by the question of whether it is strictly determined by a chain of prior causes. Perceiving social blame as an empathic extension of self-blame likewise makes determinism cease to be relevant to its assessment. The intertemporal bargaining hypothesis provides a deterministic model that permits, to paraphrase Daniel Dennett, all the aspects of free will worth having.

Notes

1. Some have pushed this idea even further, perhaps unnecessarily far, by denying that "content neutral" mechanisms are enough to make the will free without an origin in the person's core values (e.g., Benson, 1994; Wolf, 1990).

2. Of course what literally governs the bidding in the internal marketplace is the *prospect* of reward, which does not itself occur until after the choice is made; but choosing according to prospects is also the process in literal markets.

3. Richard Holton gives a good example of two sequential stages of temptation in a passage from Ignatius Loyola: "One sins venially when the . . . thought of

committing a mortal sin comes and one gives ear to it, dwelling on it a little or taking some sensual enjoyment from it . . ." (Holton, 2009, 421). Presumably failing to avoid the thought is sinful because it raises the amount of willpower needed to avoid the deed.

4. It might seem that unwillingness to hurt the other was itself the motive for self-control, but we are talking about the case where the other's knowledge of your behavior—and possibly the very existence of the other—is fantasied. I have hypothesized that the factor promoting this hypothetical case above mere imagination is the verifiability of its effect on intertemporal bargaining (Ainslie, 1975): If you believe that Saint X will help you avoid a temptation, this will be a self-confirming prophesy, as will be the effect of lapsing and disappointing her. To the extent that the imagined other is a way of understanding a larger class of incentives at stake in individual choices, she becomes not just a fantasy or a memory but a substantive factor in choice making.

5. The actual deficit in autistic spectrum disorders is probably more complex, perhaps "a disconnection between a strong naive egocentric stance and a highly abstract allocentric stance" (Frith and deVignemont, 2005).

References

Ainslie, G. (1975). Specious reward: A behavioral theory of impulsiveness and impulse control. *Psychological Bulletin, 82,* 463–496.

Ainslie, G. (1992). *Picoeconomics: the strategic interaction of successive motivational states within the person.* Cambridge: Cambridge University Press.

Ainslie, G. (2001). *Breakdown of will.* New York: Cambridge University Press.

Ainslie, G. (2005). Précis of breakdown of will. *Behavioral and Brain Sciences, 28,* 635–673.

Ainslie, G. (2007). Can thought experiments prove anything about the will? In D. Spurrett, D. Ross, H. Kincaid, & L. Stephens (Eds.), Distributed cognition and the will: individual volition and social context (pp. 169–196). Cambridge, MA: MIT Press.

Ainslie, G., & Monterosso, J. (2003). Building blocks of self-control: Increased tolerance for delay with bundled rewards. *Journal of the Experimental Analysis of Behavior, 79,* 83–94.

Bain, A. (1859/1886). *The emotions and the will.* New York: Appleton.

Benson, P. (1994). Free agency and self-worth. *Journal of Philosophy, 91,* 650–658.

Bodner, R., & Prelec, D. (2001). The diagnostic value of actions in a self-signaling model. In I. Brocas & J. D. Carillo (Eds.), Collected essays in psychology and economics. New York: Oxford University Press.

Bratman, M. E. (1999). *Faces of intention: selected essays on intention and agency.* Cambridge, UK: Cambridge University Press.

Broad, C. D. (1966). Determinism, indeterminism and libertarianism. In B. Berofsky (Ed.), Free will and determinism (pp. 135–159). New York: Harper & Row:

Cirincione, C., Steadman, H. J., & McGreevy, M. A. (1995). Rates of insanity acquittals and the factors associated with successful insanity pleas. *Bulletin of the American Academy of Psychiatry and the Law, 23,* 399–409.

Darnton, R. (1995). *Forbidden best-sellers of pre-Revolutionary France.* New York: Norton.

Daw, N. D., Niv, Y., & Dayan, P. (2005). Uncertainty-based competition between prefrontal and dorsolateral striatal systems for behavioral control. *Nature Neuroscience, 8,* 1704–1711.

Dennett, D. C. (1984). *Elbow room: the varieties of free will worth wanting.* Cambridge, MA: MIT Press.

deWaal, F. (2007). *Chimpanzee politics.* Baltimore: Johns Hopkins University Press.

DuBreuil, B. (2009). Paleolithic public goods games: The evolution of brain and cooperation in mid-Pleistocene hominins. Available at: <http://african.cyberlogic.net/bdubreuil/pdf/PPGG.pdf>.

Dworkin, G. (1988). *The theory and practice of autonomy.* Cambridge: Cambridge University Press.

Eccles, J. (1994). *How the self controls its brain.* Berlin: Springer.

Frith, U., & de Vignemont, F. (2005). Egocentrism, allocentrism, and Asperger syndrome. *Consciousness and Cognition, 14,* 719–738.

Garson, J. W. (1995). Chaos and free will. *Philosophical Psychology, 8,* 365–374.

Gibbon, J. (1977). Scalar expectancy theory and Weber's law in animal timing. *Psychological Review, 84,* 279–325.

Glimcher, P. W., Kable, J., & Louie, K. (2007). Neuroeconomic studies of impulsivity: Now or just as soon as possible? *American Economic Review, 97,* 1–6.

Goodwin, D. W. (1986). Heredity and alcoholism. *Annals of Behavioral Medicine, 8,* 3–6.

Green, L., & Myerson, J. (2004). A discounting framework for choice with delayed and probabilistic rewards. *Psychological Bulletin, 130,* 769–792.

Green, L., Myerson, J., Holt, D. D., Slevin, J. R., & Estle, S. J. (2004). Discounting of delayed food rewards in pigeons and rats: Is there a magnitude effect? *Journal of the Experimental Analysis of Behavior, 81,* 39–50.

Greene, J., & Cohen, J. (2004). For the law, neuroscience changes nothing and everything. *Philosophical Transactions of the Royal Society of London. Series B, Biological Sciences, 359,* 1775–1785.

Greene, J., & Haidt, J. (2002). How (and where) does moral judgment work? *Trends in Cognitive Sciences, 6,* 517–523.

Haji, I. (2002). Compatibilist views of freedom and responsibility. In Kane, R., ed. The Oxford handbook of free will (pp. 202–228). Oxford: Oxford University Press.

Henderson, M. (2009). Chimpanzee's plan to attack zoo visitors shows evidence of premeditated thought. *Times (London, England),* March 10. Available at <http://www .timesonline.co.uk/tol/news/science/article5877764.ece>.

Heyman, G. M. (2009). *Addiction: a disorder of choice.* Cambridge, MA: Harvard University Press.

Hobbes, T. (1996). *Leviathan.* Cambridge: Cambridge University Press (Original work published 1651).

Hofmeyr, A., Ainslie, G., Charlton, R., & Ross, D. (in press). The relationship between smoking and reward bundling in a group of South African university students. *Addiction (Abingdon, England).*

Holton, R. (2009). Determinism, self-efficacy, and the phenomenology of free will. *Inquiry, 52,* 412–428.

Hume, D. 1962. An inquiry concerning human understanding. In A. Flew (Ed.), Hume on human nature and understanding (pp. 21–163). New York: Collier (Original work published 1748).

Humphrey, N., & Dennett, D. C. (2002). Speaking for our selves: an assessment of multiple personality disorder. In N. Humphrey (Ed.), The mind made flesh: essays from the frontiers of psychology and evolution (pp. 19–47). Oxford: Oxford University Press (Original work published 1989).

Iacoboni, M., & Dapretto, M. (2006). The mirror neuron system and the consequences of its dysfunction. *Nature Reviews. Neuroscience, 7,* 942–951.

James, W. (1890). *Principles of psychology.* New York: Holt.

James, W. (1896). The dilemma of determinism. In The will to believe and other essays in popular philosophy (pp. 145–183). New York: Longmans Green. (Original work published 1884).

Kane, R. (1989). Two kinds of incompatibilism. *Philosophy and Phenomenological Research, 50,* 220–254.

Kant, I. (1966). *Critique of pure reason.* (F. M. Muller, Trans.). New York: Doubleday Anchor (Original work published 1781).

Kapitan, T. (1986). Deliberation and the presumption of open alternatives. *Philosophical Quarterly, 36,* 230–251.

Kavka, G. (1983). The toxin puzzle. *Analysis, 43,* 33–36.

Kirby, K. N. (1997). Bidding on the future: evidence against normative discounting of delayed rewards. *Journal of Experimental Psychology. General, 126,* 54–70.

Kirby, K. N. (2006). The present values of delayed rewards are approximately additive. *Behavioural Processes, 72,* 273–282.

Kirby, K. N., & Guastello, B. (2001). Making choices in anticipation of similar future choices can increase self-control. *Journal of Experimental Psychology. Applied, 7,* 154–164.

Klein, D. B. (1970). *A history of scientific psychology.* New York: Basic Books.

Klein, B., & Leffler, K. B. (1981). The role of market forces in assuring contractual performance. *Journal of Political Economy, 89,* 615–640.

La Mettrie, J. (1999). *Man a machine.* Chicago: Open Court (Original work published 1748).

Landé, A. (1961). The case for indeterminism. In S. Hook (Ed.), Determinism and freedom in the age of modern science (pp. 83–89). New York: Collier.

Mazur, J. E. (1987). An adjusting procedure for studying delayed reinforcement. In M. L. Commons, J. E. Mazur, J. A. Nevin, & H. Rachlin (Eds.), Quantitative analyses of behavior V: The effect of delay and of intervening events on reinforcement value. Hillsdale, NJ: Lawrence Erlbaum.

Mazur, J. E. (2001). Hyperbolic value addition and general models of animal choice. *Psychological Review, 108,* 96–112.

McClennen, E. F. (1990). *Rationality and dynamic choice.* New York: Cambridge University Press.

McGreevy, M. A., Steadman, H. J., & Callahan, L. A. (1991). The negligible effects of California 1982 reform of the insanity defense test. *American Journal of Psychiatry, 148,* 744–750.

Mele, A. R. (1995). *Autonomous agents: from self-control to autonomy.* New York: Oxford University Press.

Merali, Z. (2007). Free will: is our understanding wrong? *New Scientist, 2615,* 10–11.

Miller, W. R. (2003). Comments on Ainslie and Monterosso. In R. Vuchinich and N. Heather (Eds.), Choice, behavioural economics, and addiction (pp. 62–66). New York: Pergamon Press.

Monterosso, J. R., Ainslie, G., Toppi-Mullen, P., & Gault, B. (2002). The fragility of cooperation: A false feedback study of a sequential iterated prisoner's dilemma. *Journal of Economic Psychology, 23*(4), 437–448.

Monterosso, J., Royzman, E. B., & Schwartz, B. (2005). Explaining away responsibility: effects of scientific explanation on perceived culpability. *Ethics & Behavior, 15,* 139–158.

Nadelhoffer, T., Morris, S. G., Nahmias, E. A., & Turner, J. (2005). Surveying freedom: Folk intuitions about free will and moral responsibility. *Philosophical Psychology, 18,* 561–584.

Nozick, R. (1981). *Philosophical explanations.* Cambridge, MA: Belknap Press.

Poundstone, W. (1992). *Prisoner's dilemma: John von Neumann, game theory, and the puzzle of the bomb.* New York: Doubleday.

Premack, D. (1970). Mechanisms of self-control. In W. A. Hunt (Ed.), Learning mechanisms in smoking (pp. 107–123). Chicago: Aldine.

Railton, P. (1984). Alienation, consequentialism, and the demands of morality. *Philosophy & Public Affairs, 13,* 134–171.

Rescorla, R. A. (1988). Pavlovian conditioning: Its not what you think it is. *American Psychologist, 43,* 151–160.

Russell, P. (1992). Strawson's way of naturalizing responsibility. *Ethics, 102,* 287–302.

Sappington, A. A. (1990). Recent psychological approaches to the free will versus determinism issue. *Psychological Bulletin, 108,* 19–29.

Smart, J. J. C. (1961). *Philosophy and scientific realism.* New York: Humanities Press.

Schelling, T. C. (1960). *The strategy of conflict.* Cambridge, MA: Harvard University Press.

Smilansky, S. (2000). *Free will and illusion.* Oxford: Clarendon Press.

Smilansky, S. (2002). Free will, fundamental dualism, and the centrality of illusion. In R. Kane (Ed.), The Oxford handbook of free will (pp. 489–505). Oxford: Oxford University Press.

Stapp, H. P. (1998). Pragmatic approach to consciousness. In K. H. Pribram (Ed.), Brain and values (pp. 237–248). Mahwah, NJ: Lawrence Erlbaum.

Stitzer, M., & Petry, N. (2006). Contingency management for treatment of substance abuse. *Annual Review of Clinical Psychology, 2,* 411–434.

Strawson, P. (2003). Freedom and resentment. In G. Watson (Ed.), Free will (2nd ed., pp. 72–93). Oxford (Original work published 1962).

Strawson, G. (1986). *Freedom and belief.* New York: Oxford University Press.

Vohs, K. D., & Schooler, J. W. (2008). The value of believing in free will: Encouraging a belief in determinism increases cheating. *Psychological Science, 19,* 49–54.

Watson, J. B. (1924). *Behaviorism.* New York: The Peoples Institute Publishing Co.

Wolf, S. (1990). *Freedom within reason.* New York: Oxford University Press.

4 Addiction, Responsibility, and Ego Depletion

Neil Levy

Are addicts responsible for their drug-related behavior, that is, for the range of activities in which they must engage in order to procure, prepare, and consume their drug? In this chapter, I argue that the answer is no, at least with regard to much of this behavior and including some of the actions that are least easily excused in rival models. In defending the view that addictive behavior is not responsible behavior, I defend a view that is very popular, especially with the scientific community. But the account of addiction I offer will differ markedly from the account offered by most proponents of this view.

Addiction as Compulsion: Reactivity and Responsiveness

There are two currently influential ways of understanding responsibility for addictive behavior. On the *moral* model, addictive behavior, whatever its differences from ordinary behavior, is sufficiently under the control of the agent for him or her to be held responsible for it. In this view, addictive behavior is normal (enough) behavior; only the goal of the behavior is abnormal. This view is often encountered in the mass media—where it is invariably advanced in the service of blaming addicts for their behavior—but there are instances of the view in scholarly writing where it is sometimes advanced in the service of the claim that addictive behavior reflects *different* choices, rather than *vicious* choices (Foddy & Savulescu, 2006).

The second model for understanding addictive behavior, the *medical* or *scientific* model, holds that the behavior is grossly abnormal and *therefore* not responsible behavior. In this view, addictive behavior is often characterized as *compulsive*, sometimes even as robotic. Because addictive behavior is compulsive behavior, the agent lacks control over its manifestation and therefore cannot be held responsible for it.

The claim that lack of control over a behavior excuses is surely very plausible. But what do proponents of the medical model mean when they say that addicts lack control over their behavior? The claim, at least typically, seems to be that agents *cannot prevent* the behavior. I think we can best capture the claim using the theoretical apparatus of a very influential account of moral responsibility, that offered by John Martin Fischer, alone and together with Mark Ravizza. In this view, agents are directly responsible for behavior over which they exercise *guidance control*, where guidance control is a kind of counterfactual sensitivity to reasons (Fischer & Ravizza, 1998). An agent exerts guidance control over a behavior if she acts on a moderately reasons-responsive mechanism, which is to say, roughly, that the mental mechanisms that issue in her behavior must be *responsive* to reasons (that is, were the agent to be presented with a sufficient reason to act in a different way, she would be capable of recognizing it as a sufficient reason) and *reactive* to reasons (the mechanism would actually cause her to act otherwise in response to at least some sufficient reasons to do otherwise, if it is allowed to act unhindered). Because guidance control combines responsiveness and reactivity, agents can fail to control their behavior in two different ways. Usually, however, the claim that addicts lose control of (some of) their drug-taking behavior is best understood as the claim that they are subject to failures of reactivity: They act on their urges to consume despite recognizing that they have better reason to refrain.

However, it is very difficult to make a convincing case that addictive behavior is compulsive, when compulsion is understood as a failure of reactivity. The difficulty is great enough with regard to what we might call *proximate* addictive behavior: the behavior required for immediate consumption of the drug. It is exponentially greater with regard to *distal* addictive behavior: the behavior instrumentally required to procure the drug and the opportunity to consume it. Let us briefly review the resources of the medical model to see how it tries to establish that addictive behavior is compulsive, in the sense at issue.

Addictive drugs bring about a variety of different changes in the brain, which make addicts multiply vulnerable to continued consumption. Some of these changes might plausibly be taken to affect the reactivity of mechanisms to reasons that the agent nevertheless recognizes. Addiction produces neuroadaptations that increase the "pull" of the drug while they decrease the ability of the agent to resist it. Neuroadaptations increase the reward value of drugs (Dackis & O'Brien, 2001; Robinson & Berridge, 2003) and thereby their motivational force. Some of these changes might make the pull of drugs far greater than the attraction of natural rewards, by bypassing mechanisms that have the role of adjusting expectations of the reward value of a behavior. Unlike natural rewards some addictive drugs might always produce a "better than expected" signal, thereby preventing satiation (Hyman, 2005).

Whereas these adaptations increase the attractiveness of the drug, others might reduce the ability of the agent to resist. There is evidence that decision making by addicts is impaired globally, not only with regard to their drug. Perhaps some of these deficits reflect preexisting vulnerabilities in decision-making mechanisms, rather than neuroadaptations caused by persistent substance abuse. Some of these vulnerabilities should be considered as much cognitive as motivational (and therefore to affect responsiveness rather than reactivity). For instance there is evidence that addicts have steeper discount curves than nonaddicts; that is, they devalue delayed rewards to a greater extent than matched controls (Ainslie, 2001). But other deficits in decision making are more clearly problems with translating desires into action. On tasks requiring subjects to inhibit prepotent responses, addicts perform poorly relative to controls (Garavan & Stout, 2005). This clearly reflects a failure of reactivity of the relevant mechanisms.

In principle it seems possible for the strength of cravings, or the aversiveness of withdrawal, to be sufficient to render addictive behavior compulsive. We can easily grasp how compulsiveness produced by either of these mechanisms could be excusing due to failures of reactivity. If a craving is of sufficient strength to move the agent all the way to action, regardless of her explicit beliefs and values, then she cannot react to incentives to do otherwise. Compulsiveness produced by the aversiveness of withdrawal might function to excuse in precisely the same way; the aversiveness might produce a desire to escape of sufficient strength to undermine reactivity. Alternatively, given the actual range of alternatives, the aversiveness of withdrawal might make consumption of the drug the best action available and, therefore, justified.

But are these mechanisms sufficient to render addictive behavior genuinely compulsive? Inability to inhibit a prepotent response (for instance) might translate into an excuse via a failure of reactivity under certain circumstances, but these are circumstances that will rarely be encountered. Actual addictive behavior, even proximate addictive behavior, will rarely consist of a series of actions in all of which the agent engages despite herself; that is, despite attempting to inhibit the behavior. Even when an action (if indeed "action" is the right descriptor) is genuinely such that it cannot be inhibited, it is almost always preceded and followed by stages at which the agent could, if she so desired, be able to stop, to leave the scene, or to undo the action; the inhibition failure data therefore cannot explain addictive behavior. Scientists sometimes defend the compulsiveness of drug consumption by reference to a "habit system." For Redish, Jensen, & Johnson, (2008, 424), the habit system renders addictive behavior "unintentional, robotic, perhaps even unconscious." Certainly habitual behaviors can be tic-like, and subjects can fail to be conscious of engaging in them. But very little addictive behavior, which is, after all, relatively complex, is like this. The planning system alone is capable of driving flexible behavior; to the extent to which the agent is likely to meet with unexpected contingencies along the route to consumption, the behavior will require the input of the planning system (Neal, Wood, & Quinn, 2006). On a standard dual process account of the mind, this will ensure that the agent is conscious of the behavior and that it is effortful and therefore voluntary. At most, only a fraction of addictive behavior (probably only the most proximate of addictive behavior, under the most routine circumstances) can be genuinely unconscious, rather than overseen by the agent.

It might be objected, however, that complex voluntary action is compatible with failures of reactivity—perhaps when the motivating desire upon which the agent acts is of sufficient strength. It is very difficult to judge whether a desire is sufficiently strong to undermine reactivity; indeed, some philosophers have been skeptical that the idea even makes sense (Feinberg, 1970). The difficulty lies in distinguishing between a desire that the agent *could* not resist and one that she *chose* not to resist. In the absence of any means (as yet) for measuring the strength of a desire and calculating its power to overwhelm the agent's resistance, the best we can do is to estimate the strength of a desire by reference to the ability of agents to react to incentives. If an agent is able to respond to relatively *normal* incentives, then the desires to which they are subject cannot be sufficiently strong to overwhelm reactivity. Reactivity only to extraordinary incentives—like the reactivity of an agoraphobic to a fire burning his house down around him—is not evidence for reactivity to more typical incentives (Mele, 1990) and therefore is not evidence that the agent retains the relevant capacities. The evidence available suggests that the strength of the craving for drugs is (at least typically) insufficient to undermine reactivity. Given (intuitively) quite ordinary incentives to refrain from drug taking, addicts seem regularly to succeed. One piece of evidence is the fact that many addicts eventually "mature out" of their habit, without outside aid. Successful abstinence often occurs in response to an incentive that is strong, although not extraordinary, such as the incentive to look after a new baby (Carlson, 2006). Moreover, much less powerful incentives can be shown to moderate addictive behavior. Price increases affect the amount of drugs consumed by addicts (Elster, 1999; Neale, 2002). Alcoholics are sensitive to the cost of alcohol even after a priming drink (Fingarette, 1988, 36–42). Moreover, addicts sometimes deliberately abstain for prolonged periods in order to lower their tolerance for the drug, and thereby decrease the dose they will need to achieve the high they want (Ainslie, 2000, 82). All of this evidence suggests that reactivity is preserved: given incentives in the normal range, addicts are capable of responding appropriately.

Much of the evidence against the hypothesis that the strength of addictive desires is sufficient to undermine reactivity is equally evidence against the hypothesis that the aversiveness of withdrawal undermines reactivity. In order for addicts to react to incentives by giving up their drug or by deliberately abstaining in order to cheapen their habit or simply to moderate intake, they must be able to tolerate the effects of withdrawal for greater or lesser periods of time. Many of these actions require them voluntarily to abstain for the entire withdrawal period. Moreover, some highly addictive drugs—for instance cocaine—produce little in the way of withdrawal symptoms. It therefore seems false that agent reactivity is undermined by addiction and therefore false that addictive behavior is compulsive as that term is normally understood.

Most glaringly it is not plausible that addicts fail in reactivity with regard to *distal* addictive behavior. Addictive behavior includes not only the actions involved in consuming the drug, which are relatively easily conceptualized as subject to desires of unusual strength and persistence. It also includes the prior acts that must be performed before consumption is possible: buying the drug, obtaining the money to buy the drug, and so on. It has been suggested that even these distal activities might themselves be performed compulsively; through the mechanisms of operant and classical conditioning, stimulus-response (S-R) behaviors might be prompted by cues associated with procuring and preparing the drug (Everitt & Robbins, 2005). Moreover, there is some evidence that drug addicts show a heightened reward response to money, perhaps because for the long-term addict it is itself closely associated with the opportunity to consume (Bechara, 2005), but it is implausible to think that all the activities instrumentally required to procure drugs are themselves either rewarding or triggered habitual behaviors. Addicts notoriously engage in degrading and often dangerous actions in order to earn the money for their drugs. No one can think that they are subject to a desire to do so. The flexibility of response required, in real life situations, to procure drugs rules out S-R explanations of distal behaviors.

When reactivity is undermined, agents are unable to conform their behavior to their beliefs as to how they ought to act. Now, many of the neuroadaptations produced by addiction affect addicts' evaluations rather than their reactivity. Indeed, some of the evidence cited above, in support of the hypothesis that neuroadaptations increase the pull of addictive desires, might instead be better understood in these terms. For instance neuroadaptations increasing the reward value of the drug are likely to influence addicts' evaluation of the choiceworthiness of consumption as well as (or sometimes instead of) increasing the desire for it independent of such evaluations. Some cognitive evaluations bias addicts' memories, making them more likely to recall positive outcomes of consumption than negative, or leading them to miscategorize alike situations as unlike (or vice-versa). For instance, a gambling addict might erroneously distinguish situations predictive of reward from situations predictive of losses (Redish et al., 2008). Adverse consequences may be less salient to addicts, perhaps due to impaired somatic marker systems, as a result of which they may fail to generate the anticipatory autonomic system responses seen in normals (Bechara, 2005). Other neuroadaptations have the effect not of directly affecting the evaluation of consumption but of biasing attention, such that drug-related cues are very salient to addicts (Lubman, Peters, Mogg, Bradley, & Deakin, 2000). Further, addicts may find it difficult to avoid ruminating obsessively on courses of action that would lead to drug consumption (Redish et al., 2008).

These cognitive alterations in the mental processes of addicts have sometimes been described as rendering their behavior compulsive (e.g., Everitt & Robbins, 2005). Clearly if they excuse, they do so not by affecting reactivity but responsiveness. Were the addict unable to perceive incentives to do otherwise, the addict would not be properly responsive to reasons and therefore would be excused. But even though these neuroadaptations decrease responsiveness, they are far from eliminating it. Reactivity is subsequent to responsiveness: an agent must first be capable of recognizing incentives to do otherwise before she can react to these incentives. Hence, the evidence cited above showing that addicts are moderately reactive to reasons is, ipso facto, evidence that they are responsive to reasons. The effects of addiction on cognition are real, but they are best thought of as producing decreased sensitivity to reasons to do otherwise; decreased, that is, relative to normal controls. But the incentives to do otherwise are often so great for addicts that their decreased sensitivity is more than enough for them to grasp that they have reason to do otherwise than consume.

Given these facts, ought we to return to the moral model of addiction, according to which addicts choose freely, and therefore responsibly, to consume their drugs? Even though I believe that addictive behavior is best thought of as very similar to normal behavior—indeed, as produced by the same mechanisms that drive much of the behavior in which normal agents engage—it would be hasty to conclude that it is responsible behavior. It might be, instead, that addictive behavior, *and many instances of entirely normal behavior*, are produced by mechanisms that render it non-responsible.

Beyond Responsiveness and Reactivity

Reactivity-based accounts understand loss of control to occur when the agent loses the ability to act as they believe they ought: control is control over our overt behavior. But there is no reason to limit the scope of control to overt behavior: mental life too is something over which agents can (fail to) exercise control. We cannot capture such failures by reference to reactivity, since the agent who loses control over his mental life does not judge that he ought to act otherwise than he does: his loss of control over his mental life leads him to judge that he ought to act as he does. But nor can we understand failures of control over our mental life as failures of responsiveness to reasons. Such responsiveness is a global capacity of agents and may be retained even while the agent loses control over an aspect of his mental life. Yet intuitively, such a loss of control should constitute an excuse.

To see how such failures excuse, it is worth comparing the loss of control over mental life with the analogous, and uncontroversially excusing, loss of control over overt action (that is, of reactivity). An agent can lose the ability to control a piece of behavior—say, the movements of his arm, which might become subject to an uncontrollable twitch—and therefore fail to be responsible for this piece of behavior, even while it remains true that he retains control over the rest of his behavior. Loss of control is local, not global. But by requiring moderate reasons responsiveness as their standard, Fischer and Ravizza rule out the possibility that a local failure of mental self-control can excuse. Indeed, they are explicit on the point, arguing that such local failures are not possible. As they put it, "reactivity is all of a piece" (Fischer & Ravizza, 1998, 73); that is, if a mechanism is reactive to *some* incentive to do otherwise, than the mechanism is reactive to *any* incentive to do otherwise. Thus, they do not make room for a local failure of control of an agent over some aspect of his mental life.

It is therefore a significant problem for the Fischer and Ravizza view if local failures of control over the agent's mental life can occur. Indeed, the trouble goes much further; so far as I can tell, no account of moral responsibility makes room for the possibility of such a loss of control. Of course it is an empirical question whether such losses occur: Fischer and Ravizza might be right in claiming that reactivity is global and not local.

How do ordinary failures of agents to conform their behavior to their prior judgments occur? Such failures are, notoriously, a common feature of everyday life. Indeed, they are a primary contributor to health problems and early death on a grand scale. The major causes of early death in Western countries are all lifestyle related: poor diet, lack of exercise, excessive drinking, and smoking all take a heavy toll; other lifestyle-related problems are also significant contributors to the burden of disease and unhappiness (consider, for instance, risky sexual behavior). Now all these behaviors occur, in significant part, as a product of failures of self-control: a large proportion of those people who eat excessively, for instance, do so despite judging that they ought to eat less or to eat different foods (the very existence of the billion-dollar diet industry testifies to this fact). All of us, I think, suffer failures of self-control at least sometimes, and many of us are subject to such failures on a regular basis.

How should we understand these self-control failures? Clearly, at least in typical cases, they are not permanent failures of responsiveness. Some agents certainly engage in the kinds of behavior mentioned above because they are not responsive to the reasons against such behavior, but they are almost certainly a minority. Very many agents engage in behavior that is bad for them even while they recognize the reasons they have for moderating their behavior. Once again, the existence of the diet industry is testament to this fact: the fact that people spend large sums of money and a great deal of mental effort, usually in vain, in attempting to manage their weight is evidence that they recognize that they have good reason to do so. If these agents are subject to failures of responsiveness, these failures are temporary. Moreover, unless we are very mistaken about these kinds of things, they are local failures: the agent who fails to be responsive to some incentive to, say, moderate his eating behavior (on some occasion) nevertheless remains responsive to other incentives.

Should these failures instead be understood as failures of reactivity? In other words, is the loss of control seen in overeating the product of the failure by agents to control their overt behavior, despite (wholeheartedly) judging that they ought to do so? There is a rich philosophical literature on this question. Writers on *akrasia* or weakness of the will can be divided into two camps (for our purposes; actually the classification is not exhaustive): those who hold that weakness of the will involves what Holton (1999) calls *judgment shift*, and those who hold that it involves the agent's being overcome by his desires—that is, a failure of reactivity. Writers in the first camp argue that weakness of the will involves the agent (temporarily) changing his mind as to how he ought to act, whereas writers in the second hold that weakness of the will involves a failure of reactivity.

How can we settle the debate between these two views? Some authors simply urge us to look within. Introspecting on his own mental states, FitzPatrick, for example, tells us that he has no doubt that he sometimes wholeheartedly judges that he ought not act in the way he nevertheless finds himself doing, at the very moment he acts (FitzPatrick, 2008). However, introspection is notoriously an unreliable methodology. For my part, when I look within I do not know how to interpret what I find. Of course when I act akratically there is *some* sense in which I know, at the same time, that I ought not to act in the way I do, but is this knowledge dispositional or occurrent? Is it wholehearted or (as it were) inverted commas knowledge? I cannot tell, and I suspect that FitzPatrick's confidence in his own introspective clarity outruns its content. If it is possible, we ought to answer questions like this empirically and not by consulting our intuitions. I turn, then, to the empirical evidence.

Ego Depletion

The evidence here comes from studies on the (unfortunately named) ego-depletion hypothesis. It is perhaps best to introduce the hypothesis simply by describing paradigm experiments that probe it. The classic research on ego depletion proceeds as follows: subjects are divided into two groups, an ego-depletion group and a control group. The depletion group is given a task that draws on its members' self-control reserves—say, watching a funny movie without smiling—while the control group is given a task matched for demandingness but that does not require much self-control—say, rating various options in terms of desirability. Then both groups are given a common task that requires self-control: for example holding one's hand in icy water (the cold-pressor task) or attempting to solve an anagram puzzle that is in fact insoluble. The finding is that subjects in the ego-depletion group persist a significantly shorter time at the self-control task than do subjects in the control group. The conclusions of researchers are that self-control resources are temporarily depleted when they are drawn upon and that when self-control reserves are low, engaging in tasks that require self-control becomes much more difficult.

Is ego depletion a good model for ordinary failures of self-control? Clearly, when subjects enter the laboratory they do not come with a pre-existing commitment to, say, persisting at anagrams or holding their arms in icy water. Perhaps ego depletion does not model ordinary failures of self-control at all; perhaps, that is, it is not ecologically valid. Worries like this one can be allayed: several ego depletion experiments have examined the behavior of subjects with preexisting commitments to self-control. Vohs and Heatherton (2000) measured the consumption of ice cream in subjects ostensibly engaged in a flavor-rating exercise. Ego-depleted chronic dieters ate significantly more than ego-depleted nondieters as well nonde-pleted dieters. Kahan et al. (2003) measured the consumption of cookies of depleted dieters in what was ostensibly a taste-perception test; once again, "restrained" eaters consumed significantly more. Restrained eaters come to the experimental situation with a preexisting resolution; the ego-depletion paradigm led them to act contrary to it. Thus ego depletion does not (for example) increase basic appetites or lower resistance to aversive experiences. Instead, it seems to lead to failures of self-control.

Intuitively, ego depletion can model at least many ordinary failures of self-control. On the ego-depletion hypothesis, self-control is a limited resource: an agent's ability to control himself is a function of the state of that resource, and the state of that resource is, in turn, a function of the number and demandingness of self-control tasks in which that agent has recently engaged. Obviously, ordinary agents often encounter multiple self-control tasks within the course of a single day; if these tasks deplete self-control resources, we ought to expect to be able to correlate the agents' difficulty in exercising self-control with the number and difficulty of these challenges.

On the assumption that ego depletion is a good model for ordinary failures of self-control, the debate between those who hold that weakness of the will involves a failure of reactivity and those who hold that it involves judgment shift is settled in favor of the latter. There are two lines of evidence supporting this conclusion. The first comes from experiments that ask ego-depleted subjects to choose options to be delivered at some specific time in the future—say, asking them on a Wednesday to select a film to be watched on the weekend. Depleted subjects select fewer high-brow films than nondepleted subjects (Wang et al., in press). Now, the desire-based explanation of weakness of the will predicts that agents will be overcome by the immediate attractiveness of available goods, but, given that the agents continue to believe that other goods are preferable all things considered, it seems to predict that they will make future choices in line with their judgments.

There are two reasons why this evidence supports the judgment-shift hypothesis. First, an agent's explicit statement about his judgment at a time is good (although certainly not infallible) evidence about his judg-ment at that time. Importantly, the kinds of processes and states that sometimes make such statements unreliable (self-deception and the like) are not at issue in this context. Thus, we are entitled to suppose that when subjects express a preference for lower-brow films at a future date, they express their all-things-considered judgment as what kind of films they have most reason to see at that date. The rival hypothesis, that the strength of their desires overcome *despite* their contrary judgment, commits us to supposing that although these agents *say* one thing, they *judge* another; with this view, not only does their desire cause an overt action that conflicts with their judgment, but it also takes over their voice box as well. This is implausible. It may be that desires work to change what we say, but if they do, they surely accomplish this by changing what we judge.

Second, the available evidence, from animal studies and human studies alike, suggests that immediately available rewards work far more power-fully on our desires than do distant rewards and that the choice of distant rewards that conflict with one's resolutions reflects a change in judgment. Thus, when subjects sincerely judge, at t, that they ought to perform some act at a future time t_1, they are capable of putting that judgment into effect at t: minimally by expressing it. Consider the evidence from hyperbolic discounting (Ainslie, 2001). Hyperbolic discounters, both human and animal, judge at t that they ought to act in one way, yet at t_1 they find themselves judging in a way that conflicts with that judgment. For instance, they might judge that they ought to refrain from consuming some desir-able good at t, but when the opportunity to consume the good is available, they act on it. This suggests that temporal distance significantly reduces the effects of the desirability of goods on our behavior: even pigeons who learn that they are subject to hyperbolic discounting, such that they are unable to resist consuming a small reward when it is available despite the fact that were they to wait they would receive a larger later reward, are able to learn to use commitment devices to maximize their rewards. By pecking a button before the smaller reward becomes available, they prevent themselves consuming the small reward, thus forcing themselves to wait for the larger later reward (Rachlin, 2000). Thus, the immediate availability of a reward acts powerfully on agents (whether by altering their preferences or compelling them to act against their preferences).

Now, this evidence is important for the following reason. Suppose that failures of reactivity, as a consequence of the power of a desire to move an agent against her own (concurrent) judgment, sometimes occur. Then we would expect them to occur when the opportunity for consumption is imminent, given the evidence that even a brief delay greatly reduces the power of the desire. Thus, if an agent expresses a judgment with regard to a temporally distant good, we have strong evidence that the expressed preference really reflects their judgment at the time they make it.[1]

A second line of evidence for the claim that ego depletion causes weakness of the will via a change in judgment, not via the influence of a desire over an agent who continues to make judgments in line with her own resolutions, comes from studies focusing directly on the attitudes of ego-depleted subjects. Wheeler, Briñol, and Hermann (2007) gave subjects counterattitudinal arguments. Some of these arguments were designed to be strong, some weak. Depleted and nondepleted subjects were equally convinced by strong arguments, but depleted subjects were significantly more convinced by weak arguments. The increase in persuasiveness for depleted subjects of weak arguments does not seem to be due to the effort they make in processing these arguments, at least if their self-report is reliable. Instead, ego depletion seems to lead to lower-quality processing of the message content. There is strong evidence that accepting truth claims is the cognitive default position. This is the result of the apparent fact that to understand a proposition is to take it to be true, if only momentarily (Gilbert, 1991). In the absence of the processing resources needed to retrieve or to generate contradictory information and apply it to the message content, the default tendency to acquiescence takes over, and we accept the message as true. This hypothesis is supported by the fact that depleted subjects in the study of Wheeler et al. (2007) reported significantly more positive thoughts while assessing weak counterattitudinal arguments than did nondepleted subjects.

Not only does this suggest that judgment shift is the proximate cause of weakness of the will; it also suggests a (judgment-based) mechanism whereby this shift occurs. In response to temptation the subjects spontaneously generate or retrieve from memory arguments in favor of weak-willed action. Since they lack the cognitive resources to reject these arguments, they experience judgment shift. They come to judge that the benefits of succumbing to temptation are higher than they previously had thought, or the costs of giving in are lower, or both, and they act accordingly. The suggestion that this mechanism explains weakness of the will is plausible only if it is true that generating or retrieving arguments in favor of acquiescence is less effortful than assessing these arguments. Why should that be the case? Temptations, I suggest, automatically generate arguments in their favor. They might even be said to *constitute* arguments in their favor: for typical temptations, the major argument in their favor is that consumption of the tempting good is pleasurable. Ego-depleted individuals exhibit a stronger preference for the affective properties of products than do nondepleted individuals (Baumeister, Sparks, Stillman, & Vohs, 2008), suggesting a greater susceptibility to such pleasures.

But there is another route whereby arguments in favor of succumbing might effortlessly be generated: simply by retrieval from memory. Typically, we experience weakness of the will with regard to goods whose attractions we know all too well; often they are goods we have resolved to resist. We are therefore likely to have considered arguments in favor of giving in to temptation and be able to retrieve them without effort. It is worth noting that rote memory is not affected by ego depletion (Schmeichel, Vohs, & Baumeister, 2003).[2]

Ego Depletion and Addiction

The ego-depletion hypothesis coheres well with a range of (otherwise puzzling) phenomena characteristic of addictive behavior. It explains, first, the apparent discrepancy between the phenomenological intensity of a craving and its motivational power. At first sight, it might seem that we can explain this phenomenon by reference to the dissociation between the "incentive salience" of a goal and its hedonic value; between, that is, its being "wanted" and its being "liked" (Robinson & Berridge, 2003). But the dissociation between intensity and motivational force is not the dissociation between liking and wanting; it is a dissociation between motivation and *any* phenomenal state at all. As Loewenstein (2000) suggests, however, we can explain the dissociation by reference to what he calls the expenditure of willpower. If self-control is a depletable resource, it can be drawn down by a temptation of any strength, so long as it persists for a sufficient period of time.

On a closely related note, the ego-depletion hypothesis coheres with the temporal pattern characteristic of addiction. Addicts find it relatively easy to resist temptation in the short term. The problem of abstinence is not solved by getting through withdrawal (as we saw above). Abstaining is relatively easy for addicts, in the short term, *despite* withdrawal. It is longer-term abstinence that is truly difficult. Because short-term abstinence is not especially difficult, some "high functioning" addicts choose to engage in an abstain/binge cycle. They abstain from the drug for relatively long periods, allowing them to engage productively in work and family activities, and then withdraw entirely from such activities for a shorter or longer period, during which they binge (Loewenstein, 2000). A similar cycle, over a much shorter time span, is seen in disorders on the obsessive-compulsive spectrum (Leckman, King, & Cohen, 1999). If self-control is a depletable resource, the temporal pattern is easily explicable: while reserves are high (in the aftermath of a binge, for instance) abstinence is not especially difficult, but its maintenance draws down the reserves, making succumbing increasingly likely.

Third, the effects of cue dependence upon addiction cohere with the ego-depletion hypothesis. Addicts are known to have relatively little trouble giving up their drugs if the cues that trigger cravings are absent; hence the fact that few of the many American GIs who returned from Vietnam addicted to heroin remained addicted for long (Loewenstein, 2000). Why should cues be so significant? Cues trigger the desire for consumption, requiring the subject to draw on self-control resources to resist: if the temptation is persistent—if, for instance, the cue, or similar cues, remains salient to the agent—self-control reserves will fall until judgment shift occurs, and with it consumption.

Most importantly, the picture presented here helps explain the major mystery with regard to addiction: distal addictive behavior. Unless we postulate that addicts prefer to consume their drug to abstaining from it, not only when the opportunity for consumption is imminent but also when they are engaged in distal addictive behavior, we cannot explain this behavior. On the medical model this behavior is entirely mysterious, insofar as the medical model tries to explain addictive behavior as consequent on a failure of reactivity. The moral model does a little better here, but its success comes at the cost of failing to explain the ways in which addicts are impaired in their self-control. Unless addiction genuinely causes some kind of impairment in self-control, we cannot explain two of its central effects: the lengths addicts will go to attempt to be free of their addiction and the costs they will pay as a consequence of failing (West, 2006).

The ego-depletion hypothesis, understood as I have urged, not only explains distal addictive behavior, it also explains how such behavior is explicable in the very same subject who (sincerely) avows that she wants above all to be free of her addiction. Failures of self-control caused by ego depletion will lead to a characteristic oscillation of preferences: when the agent's self-control resources are plentiful, she will truthfully claim that she prefers abstinence to consumption and may resolve never to consume again; but when her self-control reserves are sufficiently depleted by cues triggering cravings, she will experience judgment shift. At that point, she may consume the drug or engage in distal addictive behavior. The oscillation of preferences described by the hyperbolic discounting literature is an expected consequence of the ego-depletion hypothesis.

Many of the multiple vulnerabilities documented in the literature on addiction can best be understood as vulnerabilities to ego depletion. Neuroadaptations that increase the reward value of drugs are likely to increase the degree to which drugs deplete self-control resources. Similarly, adaptations that make drug-related cues salient to addicts make these cues themselves ego depleting by reducing the ability of addicts to distract themselves from them. Other neuroadaptations, for instance those that make it difficult for addicts to inhibit prepotent responses, may reflect a direct effect of addiction on the state of the self-control system itself. Thus not only will addicts have their self-control resources depleted by cues associated with drug taking; these resources may themselves be pathologically low.

Finally, there is direct evidence suggestive that ego depletion is at least part of the explanation for the failures of self-control seen in addiction. Muraven and Shmueli (2006) have shown that resisting the temptation to drink depletes self-control reserves. Muraven et al. (2002) have also shown that ego depletion leads to higher alcohol consumption. A limitation of this work is that it was carried out with social drinkers and not addicts. Nevertheless, it is supportive of the view advanced here.

Of course, not all distal addictive behavior occurs subsequent to ego depletion. Some addicts may be ambivalent, or even wholehearted about their drug consumption: for them such behavior is not the consequence of a failure of self-control. Moreover, some addicts may engage in such behavior not because they have experienced a failure of self-control but because they *expect* to fail at control: they may therefore be moderating the negative consequences of such a predictable failure.

Ego Depletion and Responsibility

As we have seen, standard accounts of moral responsibility cannot satisfactorily explain failures of control over mental life like those we see in ego depletion. When a subject experiences judgment shift, she is experiencing neither a failure of reactivity nor of reasons responsiveness, as these are standardly understood. Ought we to conclude that she is responsible for her subsequent behavior? I suggest not. If failures of reactivity excuse, then so ought failures of control over one's mental life.

Failures of reactivity excuse, roughly, because such failures entail that we cannot infer ill will on the part of the agent. The agent's (wrongful) overt action, for instance, does not reflect contempt toward its victim or even an indifference toward the victim's welfare. Things are more complicated when the failure is of control over one's mental life. Whereas failures of reactivity need tell us *nothing* about the agent or the quality of her will, beyond the bare fact that she has lost control over her ability to bring her actions into line with her judgments, failures of control over one's mental life, at least as produced by ego depletion, are informative about the agent. The judgment formed is genuinely representative of some aspects of the self forming it. Thus, for instance, the addict would not form the judgment that consumption is better *now* than abstaining unless it were the case that the drug was genuinely tempting for her. Nevertheless, I suggest, this fact is insufficient for us to hold her responsible for her failure.

For many failures of self-control, the failure does not reflect badly on the agents because the facts their failure reveals about them—their desires, preferences, and so on—do not distinguish them from other people. They are, instead, just the kind of desires that ordinary people typically have (indeed, many of the typical desires that are the proximate causes of self-control failures are—plausibly at least—innate). Addictive desires are different, of course: most of us will not experience self-control failures as a result of the temptation to consume cocaine or heroin, because most of us are not at all tempted to use cocaine or heroin. So the failure of control over her mental life experienced by the addict is, in this case, due to a fact about her that distinguishes her from others. But this fact is true of her not because of anything she does *at the time of her failure*; it is true of her due to her past actions. These past actions have altered her preferences and her brain in such a manner that the drug does constitute a challenge to her self-control. We may wish to blame the addict for her early drug taking; nothing in the ego-depletion hypothesis bears directly on this question. But we cannot blame her for her later failure, taken by itself. *Given how she is*, when she experiences her failure of mental control, there is nothing she can reasonably be expected to do to prevent her failure.

Objections, Caveats, and Conclusions

It might be held that the empirical evidence supports the view that continued resistance is possible for the ego-depleted agent. When subjects are reminded of their values, or offered cash incentives, they are able to hold out against the urge to succumb longer than otherwise (Baumeister et al., 2008). Accordingly, if we apply a Fischer and Ravizza style counterfactual test to the addict—asking whether she can respond and react to incentives—we get the result that she possesses the capacity to do otherwise (in the conditional sense favored by compatibilists). But whereas the suggested test tells us something about the agent that is relevant to whether she could have done otherwise—it tells us what capacities and skills she possesses—it does not tell us whether, *in the circumstances that actually prevailed*, exercising those capacities and skills could reasonably have been expected of her. Since ego depletion induces judgment shift, the agent cannot reasonably be expected to take action of a kind that would prevent her acting in accordance with her new judgment: After experiencing judgment shift, agents do not remind themselves of their values, or take other steps to test whether their (new) all-things-considered judgment coheres with their values, precisely because they *have* experienced judgment-shift and are satisfied with their decision. Of course, they might be able to prevent judgment-shift prior to its occurrence, by such means. But these antidotes are short-term ones, leaving the agent even more depleted than before (Baumeister et al., 2008). They do not prevent self-control failure; they merely delay it.

There is, however, a means whereby agents can avoid self-control failure. The ego-depletion hypothesis predicts that we inevitably give in to *continuously persisting* desires. If all desires were continuously persisting, then resistance would be impossible. Fortunately, we can take steps to make it less likely that our desires persist. In the normal case most of us can distract ourselves reasonably successfully most of the time. Addicts find this technique difficult to employ because the cues that trigger their cravings tend to capture their attention. However, they can take steps to avoid encountering the cues in the first place. The situations, places, and people associated with drug use trigger cravings, and avoiding these cues helps to keep the desires under control. If the desires persist, then addicts will consume, since their self-control resources are depleted. But if they can take steps to ensure that their cravings are only intermittent, addicts can significantly raise the probability that they will always have enough self-control to successfully resist on each occasion.

Addicts find it so hard to remain drug-free, then, because they are not able—or do not realize the need—to remove themselves sufficiently from the cues that trigger their cravings. If drug taking is a habitual response to stress, or if the addict usually uses with his partner, then removing himself from the relevant cues may be impossible or very costly. It is therefore not at all surprising that giving up an addiction is extremely difficult in a wide range of circumstances. Since many addicts find themselves unable to structure their lives in such a manner as to avoid drug taking—despite the fact that many of them genuinely desire to abstain permanently—and since many of them fail even to recognize the need to do so (the myth of "willpower" mitigates against them acquiring this knowledge), they are typically not responsible for their failures of self-control. To the extent, however, that they know what they ought to do, and are able to act accordingly, they may be indirectly responsible for their failures: responsible by virtue of failing to take steps to avoid the circumstances that would trigger the failures.

Mention of indirect responsibility brings us back to the question of whether addicts might be responsible for token acts of consumption by virtue of responsibility for becoming addicted. I assume that few will be tempted to hold addicts fully responsible for later failures on these kinds of grounds. The very existence of the debate whether addiction excuses, I take it, commits those who engage in it to holding that the question cannot be answered in this way, because these grounds are obviously available to all participants in the debate. It is worth adding that even these initial failures might sometimes be excused on precisely the kinds of grounds sketched above: initial uses might also be the product of an excusable failure of control over one's mental life. Here the proximate cause will not be the temptation of the drug—not, at least, the temptation as experienced by the addict—but perhaps the temptation of a new experience, or the temptation of engaging in "cool" behavior, and so on. It will be objected that excusing behavior on these grounds cannot be allowed because excuses will proliferate. So be it: we cannot allow the fact that we do not like its conclusion to prevent us following an argument where it leads.

I conclude, therefore, that despite the fact that addicts are moderately reasons-responsive, their failures of self-control are (often) excused. Because they cannot reasonably be expected to exercise greater control over their mental life than they do, they are not to blame for their failure. If this argument is correct, accounts of moral responsibility need supplementing: to failures of responsiveness and reactivity we must add failures to control our mental life. More importantly, the argument indicates that our responses to addicts must change.

Acknowledgment

I would like to thank Jeff Poland for very helpful comments on an earlier draft of this chapter.

Notes

1. It should be noted that Ainslie does not interpret the scope of judgment shift seen in hyperbolic discounting in the way I have suggested. He claims, rather, that hyperbolic discounters exhibit an indexical preference shift: when the time for consumption is imminent, they shift from judging they ought to refrain to judging that they ought to refrain *on every occasion except the present*. The evidence from Wang et al. seems to count against this claim: under the influence of temptation, the subjects shifted from preferring that they watch worthy movies now and in the future to preferring to watch trashy movies now and in the future. This issue requires further exploration, given that the kind of reasoning that Ainslie describes, in which a subject does not alter his view about how he ought to act in general but decides to make an exception of the current occasion, *seems* common.

2. Obviously, this suggestion is plausible only if we can explain an asymmetry in memory retrieval: why should the subject be able effortlessly to retrieve arguments in favor of consumption but not arguments in favor of maintaining the resolution? Elsewhere (Levy, forthcoming) I have argued that ego depletion tends to switch the subject to what psychologists call system 1: the fast, effortless, intuitive, and encap-

sulated mode of thinking. As a consequence, he or she will engage in a biased memory search, of the kind we see exemplified in the confirmation bias (Nickerson, 1998), a paradigmatically system 1 process.

References

Ainslie, G. (2000). A research-based theory of addictive motivation. *Law and Philosophy, 19*(1), 77–115.

Ainslie, G. (2001). *Breakdown of will*. Cambridge: Cambridge University Press.

Baumeister, R. F., Sparks, E. A., Stillman, T. F., & Vohs, K. D. (2008). Free will in consumer behavior: Self-control, ego depletion, and choice. *Journal of Consumer Psychology, 18*(1), 4–13.

Bechara, A. (2005). Decision making, impulse control and loss of willpower to resist drugs: a neurocognitive perspective. *Nature Neuroscience, 8*(1), 1458–1463.

Carlson, B. E. (2006). Best practices in the treatment of substance-abusing women in the child welfare system. *Journal of Social Work Practice in the Addictions, 6*(3), 91–115.

Dackis, C. A., & O'Brien, C. P. (2001). Cocaine dependence: a disease of the brain's reward centers. *Journal of Substance Abuse Treatment, 21*(3), 111–117.

Elster, J. (1999). *Strong feelings: emotion, addiction and human behavior*. Cambridge, MA: MIT Press.

Everitt, B. J., & Robbins, T. W. (2005). Neural systems of reinforcement for drug addiction: from actions to habits to compulsion. *Nature Neuroscience, 8*(11), 1481–1489.

Feinberg, J. (1970). What is so special about mental illness? In *Doing and deserving* (pp. 272–292). Princeton, NJ: Princeton University Press.

Fischer, J. M., & Ravizza, M. (1998). *Responsibility and control: an essay on moral responsibility*. Cambridge: Cambridge University Press.

Fingarette, H. (1988). *Heavy drinking: the myth of alcoholism as a disease*. Berkeley: University of California Press.

FitzPatrick, W. J. (2008). Moral responsibility and normative ignorance: answering a new skeptical challenge. *Ethics, 118*(July), 518–613.

Foddy, B., & Savulescu, J. (2006). Can addicted heroin users consent to the prescription of their drug? *Bioethics, 20*(1), 1–15.

Garavan, H., & Stout, J. C. (2005). Neurocognitive insights into substance abuse. *Trends in Cognitive Sciences, 9*(4), 195–201.

Gilbert, D. (1991). How mental systems believe. *American Psychologist, 46*(2), 107–119.

Holton, R. (1999). Intention and weakness of will. *Journal of Philosophy, 96*(5), 241–262.

Hyman, S. E. (2005). Addiction: a disease of learning and memory. *American Journal of Psychiatry, 162*(8), 1414–1422.

Kahan, D. Polivy, J., & Herman, C. P. (2003). Conformity and dietary disinhibition: a test of the ego strength model of self-regulation. *International Journal of Eating Disorders, 33*(2), 165–171.

Leckman, J. F., King, R. A., & Cohen, D. J. (1999). Tics and tic disorders. In J. F. Leckman & D. J. Cohen (Eds.), *Tourette's syndrome—tics, obsessions, compulsions* (pp. 23–41). New York: John Wiley & Sons.

Levy, N. (Forthcoming). Resisting weakness of the will. *Philosophy and Phenomenological Research.*

Loewenstein, G. (2000). Willpower: a decision theorist's perspective. *Law and Philosophy, 19*(1), 51–76.

Lubman, D. I., Peters, L. A., Mogg, K., Bradley, B. P., & Deakin, J. F. W. (2000). Attentional bias for drug cues in opiate dependence. *Psychological Medicine, 30*(1), 169–175.

Mele, A. R. (1990). Irresistible Desires. *Nous (Detroit, MI), 24*(3), 455–472.

Muraven, M., Collins, R. L., & Nienhaus, K. (2002). Self-control and alcohol restraint: a test of the self-control strength model. *Psychology of Addictive Behaviors, 16*(2), 113–120.

Muraven, M., & Shmueli, D. (2006). The self-control costs of fighting the temptation to drink. *Psychology of Addictive Behaviors, 20*(2), 154–160.

Neal, D. T., Wood, W., & Quinn, J. M. (2006). Habits—a repeat performance. *Current Directions in Psychological Science, 15*(4), 198–202.

Neale, J. (2002). *Drug users in society.* New York: Palgrave.

Nickerson, R. S. (1998). Confirmation bias: a ubiquitous phenomenon in many guises. *Review of General Psychology, 2*(2), 175–220.

Rachlin, H. (2000). *The science of self-control.* Cambridge, MA: Harvard University Press.

Redish, A. D., Jensen, S., & Johnson, A. (2008). A unified framework for addiction: Vulnerabilities in the decision process. *Behavioral and Brain Sciences, 31*(4), 415–437.

Robinson, T. E., & Berridge, K. C. (2003). Addiction. *Annual Review of Psychology*, *54*(1), 25–53.

Schmeichel, B. J., Vohs, K. D., and Baumeister, R. F. (2003). Intellectual performance and ego depletion: Role of the self in logical reasoning and other information processing. *Journal of Personality and Social Psychology*, *85*(1), 33–46.

Vohs, K. D., & Heatherton, T. F. (2000). Self-regulatory failure: a resource-depletion approach. *Psychological Science*, *11*(3), 249–254.

Wang, J., Novemsky, N., Dhar, R., & Baumeister, R. F. (in press). Tradeoffs and depletion in choice. *Journal of Marketing Research*.

West, R. (2006). *Theory of addiction*. Oxford: Blackwell Publishing.

Wheeler, S. C., Briñol, P., & Hermann, A. D. (2007). Resistance to persuasion as self-regulation: ego depletion and its effects on attitude change processes. *Journal of Experimental Social Psychology*, *43*(1), 150–156.

5 Lowering the Bar for Addicts

Gideon Yaffe

In public discussions of addiction and responsibility, it is common to find both those who are sympathetic to addicts who act badly and those who are not, holding, often merely tacitly, that addict responsibility is all or nothing. "It's a disease!" one side says, suggesting that we can hold the addict no more responsible for wrongdoing than we can the person with laryngitis who keeps quiet when speech is called for. "No, it's a matter of personal responsibility!" claims the other side, suggesting that wrongdoing by addicts is only cosmetically different, if even that, from wrongdoing by nonaddicts. What both sides overlook is the possibility that addicts should be given some kind of "break" but not be excused entirely. In fact, as this chapter argues, in overlooking this possibility, both sides overlook the truth.

Part of the reason that the all-or-nothing position tempts is that the alternative position raises vexing questions. The two central questions, in fact, seem to the pessimistic to be intractable: If addicts are not to be excused entirely, what should they be held responsible for? And, if addicts are to be given a "break," what should they *not* be held responsible for? What we seem to lack is a principled way of drawing the line, and this nudges us toward thinking that we must take a stand either for or against addict responsibility, period, or else give up on even trying to answer the question. But, as will be argued here, we ought not to let pessimism get the best of us. Both questions are answered here, albeit at a level of abstraction that makes it difficult to know what to say about borderline cases. Still, even an answer of this sort marks progress.

What will be argued here, in short, is that an addict is not responsible for violating a norm if he could comply with it only by giving up control of his behavior to someone or something that is independent of his own decision-making capacities. We cannot expect people, that is, to give up their autonomy in order to comply with norms. However, it is also argued that in virtually every case, if not all, of a norm violation by an addict, there is a less stringent norm that the addict can be held responsible for violating, precisely because he would not have to give up his autonomy in order to comply with it.

The structure of the argument for this view is as follows. The first three sections argue that, with some important qualifications, people cannot be expected to comply with norms when compliance would require them to guide their behavior without recourse to their own conception of the reasons for and against action. Toward this end, the first section, through a discussion of the analogy sometimes suggested between addiction and duress, distinguishes excusing someone on the grounds that he *cannot* comply with the norm he violated, on the one hand, with excusing him on the grounds that he *cannot be expected* to take on the burdens that compliance would require, on the other.

The second section identifies a very special sort of burden that compliance sometimes requires one to take on, namely the burden to compensate for defects that one has that make it more difficult for one to comply than for normal people to do so. The third section identifies a condition that, when a burden of this kind meets it, the agent cannot be expected to bear in order to comply with the norm. The section also specifies what norms those who face such burdens *can* be expected to comply with.

The fourth section argues briefly that a mounting pile of evidence from the neuroscience of decision making generally, and from the neuroscience of addict decision making in particular, suggests that compliance with norms would often require the addict to bear a burden that meets the condition of Burdens People Cannot be Expected to Bear identified in the third section. The result is that we ought to lower the bar for addicts: there is much that we cannot hold them responsible for doing wrong, but there is also much that we can and should. Exactly where the line should be placed in borderline cases turns out to be, in part, an empirical matter and one that, hopefully, further scientific work, especially in neuroscience, will help us to specify in a way that does justice to the facts about addicts.

Addiction and Duress

The view of addict responsibility defended in this chapter rests crucially on the idea that addicts are to be excused, when they are, not because addiction disables, but because, instead, it is too much to demand that addicts exercise their ability to comply with the norms that apply to non-addicts. In this way, there is some analogy in responsibility between action performed as a result of addiction and action performed under duress—action performed in response, that is, to powerful threats.

Theorists have often suggested that duress undermines responsibility by showing the agent to have had diminished opportunity to comply with the law or with what morality requires. Consider the person who robs a bank at the bidding of those who threaten to kill his child if he does not. Such a person does not have the same opportunity as the rest of us to refrain from robbing the bank; the reason is that, unlike him, we can refrain from robbing the bank *without thereby sacrificing our children's lives.* This explanation of the responsibility-undermining force of duress, however, is easily misconstrued. If a person who robs a bank lacks the opportunity *to refrain* from robbing the bank, then that shows that he *cannot* refrain, and that might be enough to excuse him for the robbery.[1] But someone who admits that he *could* refrain, but notes that he would have had to bear a very great burden to do so (namely the loss of his child's life), offers a different kind of argument in his defense. Such a person notes that there was a road to compliance that he could have traveled; he claims, however, that he should not have been expected to travel such a rocky road. There is a gap, that is, between "cannot" and "cannot be expected to." When they assert truths, both of these pleas excuse. But they excuse for different reasons, and this is obscured by the claim that duress undermines responsibility by showing opportunity to have been lacking. The opportunity lacked—namely the opportunity to refrain from the robbery and at the same time preserve the child's life—is not needed for it to be the case that the agent *could* have complied with the norm he is charged with violating, namely the norm against robbing banks. Rather, the fact that the agent lacked the opportunity he lacked shows that compliance would have required him to take on a substantial burden of the sort that we do not demand people to take on when complying with the norm. This is why the person who robs the bank when he is threatened with exclusion from a gang if he does not—imagine that this is part of a gang initiation ceremony—cannot excuse himself on the grounds of duress. He also lacks an opportunity—namely an opportunity to both refrain and join the gang—that he would like to have (and, perhaps, others enjoy), but the burden that he would have to bear in order to comply with the norm, namely exclusion from the gang, is not of the sort that supports the claim that he cannot be expected to comply.

A number of theorists have explored the possibility that addiction undermines responsibility for the reasons that duress does (see, for instance, Husak, 1999; Morse, 2000; Watson, 1999). The idea is that addicts lack opportunities that the rest of us enjoy in something like the way in which those under duress do. It is attractive to elaborate this point by noting that nonaddicts have the opportunity to refrain from drug use without suffering withdrawal, whereas addicts lack such opportunities. Assuming that withdrawal is the sort of burden that we cannot expect people to suffer in order to comply with the norms that addicts routinely violate, it would follow that addicts lack responsibility for reasons parallel to those involved in duress. It is not that they cannot comply; it is, rather, that they cannot be expected to bear the burdens of withdrawal that compliance would lead them to suffer.

Three problems plague this line of thought. First, the variation in the nature of withdrawal is far greater than the variation in the responsibility-diminishing force of addiction. To explain, compare one of the common and leading symptoms of methamphetamine withdrawal, namely sleeplessness, to one of the common and leading symptoms of cocaine withdrawal, namely craving. What one cannot be expected to do when doing it would involve sleeplessness is likely to be very different from what one cannot be expected to do when doing it would involve unsatisfied craving. Both sleeplessness and unsatisfied craving are bad things. But they are different bad things and so will have differential impact on the responsibility of the agent who fails to comply in order to avoid them. Yet methamphetamine addicts and cocaine addicts appear to be alike in the respect crucial to the question of responsibility; namely, they are both addicts. Addiction's relevance to responsibility, that is, does not seem to vary with the nature of the withdrawal involved, as would be expected if addiction were appropriately analogized to duress in which the threatened consequence of compliance with the norm at issue is withdrawal.

Second, addiction seems to be relevant to responsibility, in *some* elusive way, even when the addict violates a norm that has nothing to do, per se, with drug use. Consider, for instance, a heroin addict with a $30 per day habit, whose family calls in favors to get him a dull job that will pay him $130 per day. He has no other means for earning anything close to this amount of money. If he were to turn down the job, he would find himself feeding his habit through a mixture of pressuring family members for handouts, panhandling, and petty crime, all of which would add up to much less than $130 per day. When the addict fails to do the job competently and is fired, it seems that his failure is due in some way to his addiction. This isn't to say that we necessarily provide him with a full excuse for such behavior in light of his addiction. We might fully recognize that he deserves to be fired. But his addiction is surely *relevant* to the question of the degree to which he is responsible for his bad behavior at work. He might be responsible enough to warrant being fired, while nonetheless not being *as* responsible as a nonaddict who did the same objectionable things. But if this is right, then it cannot be the prospect of suffering withdrawal that is of relevance to the addict's responsibility. In fact, in this case, his chances of suffering withdrawal would be *lower* were he to behave well at work since he would then have enough money to feed his habit and pay his rent. The point is that addiction's relevance to responsibility seems to extend beyond the limited context in which drugs are involved. The addict's condition seems to infect a great deal of his behavior beyond his use of drugs or even his pursuit of use.

Third, even addicts who will suffer withdrawal if they comply with the norms they violate rarely pursue drugs *in order* to avoid withdrawal. Although it is not limited to this case, the most obvious support for this contention comes from cases of relapse. By the time relapse occurs, the addict is past the point at which refraining from use would result in withdrawal, so avoiding it cannot be his reason for use. But even addicts who would suffer withdrawal often use for other reasons than in order to avoid it. Now, imagine that while it is shown that the child of the man in our earlier example will be murdered if he does not comply with the threat and rob the bank, it is also shown that he robs the bank for independent reasons—merely for the money, for instance. Perhaps it is clear that he would have robbed the bank even if he had not been under duress. Perhaps there is evidence that he was making plans to do so prior to the issuance of the threat. This undermines his duress excuse, a fact that is reflected in many criminal codes. The relevant section of the *Model Penal Code*, for instance, which has been imitated in many jurisdictions, reads,

It is an affirmative defense that the actor engaged in the conduct charged to constitute an offense because he was coerced to do so by the use of, or a threat to use, unlawful force against his person or another . . . (*Model Penal Code*, §2.09(1), v. 1, p. 37)

The crucial word here is "because." While the man in our example is coerced, he does not comply *because* he is coerced, and so he would not have an affirmative defense under this section of the *Model Penal Code*. Similarly, the addict who would suffer withdrawal, but uses for some other reason, would not have diminished responsibility thanks to the fact that not using imposed the burden of withdrawal. And yet such an addict seems to have as much a claim to diminished responsibility as the addict who uses *because* he would otherwise suffer withdrawal. Something has gone wrong in the analogy between addiction and duress when the burdens of withdrawal are thought to do the excusing work for the addict.

Burdens of Compensation

In rejecting the most natural analogy between addiction and duress, there is a danger that the baby will be thrown out with the bathwater. Perhaps there is some other burden that the addict would bear, were he to comply with the norms he violates, that we cannot expect him to bear, and which is distinct from the suffering of withdrawal. In fact, as will be argued, this is the case, although in some important ways that will become clear, the analogy between addiction and duress breaks down once we appreciate the nature of the burdens that the addict would have to suffer to comply. The burdens of relevance are called here "the burdens of compensation": burdensome steps that one needs to take in order to compensate for obstacles to one's compliance with norms. In order to comply with certain norms, addicts must take steps to compensate for defects that they suffer from thanks to their addiction.

In fact all of us suffer from burdens of compensation thanks to our weaknesses. Consider people who find it difficult to wake up in the morning. Imagine someone who invariably falls back to sleep for 30 minutes after turning off his blaring alarm clock. It is harder for this man to make it to work on time than it is for the person who jumps from the bed to the shower immediately when the alarm goes off. In order to be at work on time, the late sleeper has to take steps to manage his weakness, and these steps involve burdens. For instance, he might have to buy himself an alarm clock with a "snooze" button. Or he might need to buy more than one alarm clock. Or he might need to set his first alarm 30 minutes earlier than those who do not have this problem and so go to sleep earlier the night before. These are the burdens of compensation. A sentry with a small bladder may need to endure a certain degree of thirst because he must drink less than those with larger bladders if he is to remain at his post for the full length of his watch. An epileptic may need to suffer the sometimes substantial side effects of anticonvulsant drugs if he is to meet his obligations as a father. A construction worker may need to spend money on an electric tool if he lacks the arm strength to use the manual tool supplied by his employer. The list goes on and on. Norms apply, in the first instance, to the normal. Those of us who are less than normal in some way or another—as all of us are—find that compliance with norms often requires that we compensate for our weaknesses, and such compensation almost always involves undertaking a burden of some sort.

The burdens of compensation differ in an important way from the burdens involved in standard duress cases. In duress, a threatener attaches some abnormal consequence to compliance with the norm that is in some way bad for the agent he is aiming to manipulate, or he attaches some abnormal consequence to noncompliance that is in some way good for the agent, or both.[2] In all such cases the burdens in question become consequences of compliance with the norm. If the man in our example complies with the norm against robbing banks—if he does not rob the bank—then the result is that his child dies. The burdens of compensation, by contrast, are suffered *prior* to compliance with the norm and so are not causal consequences of it. The money must be spent to buy a second alarm clock *in order* to be on time to work; this contrasts with a case in which a fine is issued for being late. The burdens of compensation are undertaken in order to enable compliance; not so with the burdens involved in duress.[3]

The very idea of the burdens of compensation shows there to be unexpected room for error in classifying an excusing condition as showing that the agent *cannot* comply, or, instead, as showing that he *cannot be expected* to comply. Does the late sleeper lack the ability to get up on time without the aid of a second alarm clock? It is because of something intrinsic to him that he cannot do this, and so his problem is one of ability. This is the conclusion we reach when we phrase the question with respect to the ability to get up on time *without the aid of a second alarm clock*. But notice that his inability to get up on time without the aid of a second alarm clock does not amount to an inability to get up on time, *period*. If he has the ability to get a second alarm clock, he has the ability to get up on time. So if he says, when he is late, "But I couldn't be on time!" what he says is not literally true, and this is why his irate boss would be justified in replying, "Yes, you could have; you could have gotten a second alarm clock."

Now it is true that a failure to exercise one's ability to bear the burdens of compensation can result in a change in what one can do later. And this is the case here. The late sleeper cannot get up on time *given that he failed to buy a second alarm clock*. Given this complexity, it is easy to get mixed up about what fact is, in fact, ameliorating an agent's responsibility when burdens of compensation are involved. When the burdens of compensation are so great that we cannot expect someone to undertake them in order to comply with a certain norm, and so we excuse his noncompliance on those grounds, we are likely to get confused as to whether we are excusing on the grounds of absence of ability or on the grounds that his opportunities are different from those who do not face such burdens. Such a person faces the burdens because of something intrinsic to him, and so it seems that it is something about his limited abilities that excuses him. But, in fact, it is not. His limited abilities are nonetheless great enough to make compliance possible for him, since he has the ability to bear the burdens of compensation, and so his excuse is not one of ability. Rather, his limited abilities have resulted in a limitation in his opportunities: he lacks the opportunity to comply without suffering the burdens of compensation. And, if, unlike the late sleeper, those burdens are very great, it is this fact about his opportunities that makes it inappropriate to hold him accountable for noncompliance.

Burdens of Compensation People Cannot Be Expected to Bear

What kinds of burdens associated with compliance with a norm are sufficient to excuse, or at least ameliorate, responsibility for violation of the norm? This is an extraordinarily difficult question that requires an answer in particular cases whether the burdens in question are burdens of compensation, or not. For instance: Does a person who anticipates injury to himself from a threatener if he does not inflict injury on a victim deserve reduced responsibility for inflicting that injury on the victim? Surely, the answer turns, in part at least, on both the nature of the injury that was anticipated and the nature of the injury inflicted. The fact that your pinkie would otherwise be scratched, or your feelings would otherwise be hurt, is of little or no relevance to your responsibility for maiming another. But darkness descends when the burdens anticipated are closer in value to those imposed. How close do they need to be to support reduction of responsibility? And close on what scale and in what way? These are hard questions to answer even in this kind of case, and the issue is that much harder when loss of apples is anticipated if a loss of oranges is not inflicted. It is not clear that we can even hope for a complete theory in this domain. It may be simply impossible to identify necessary and sufficient conditions of the needed sort, namely conditions that a burden B associated with compliance with a norm N meets just in case the fact that B is associated with compliance excuses or mitigates responsibility for violation of N.

But even though we may not be able to hope for a full theory in this domain, we can, as argued here, make this much progress: we can identify a sufficient, although not necessary, condition. That is, we can identify a condition that, when a burden associated with compliance with a norm meets it, an agent cannot be expected to comply with the norm. As we shall see, the sufficient condition to be identified is such that only burdens of compensation ever meet it. Hence, what is to be proposed here does not help us to understand the circumstances under which duress excuses. But it does help us to understand the circumstances under which addiction does. As we shall see, however, frequently when this condition is met, and so the agent in question is excused on the grounds that he could not be expected to comply with the norm he violated, there is another, distinct norm that the agent can be expected to comply with and with which he may not have complied. Addicts cannot be expected to comply with all of the norms that nonaddicts are held to; but they can be expected to comply with closely related norms and so are often responsible for their failures to comply with those. The bar is lower for addicts. But there is still a bar over which they can be expected to go and can be held responsible for failing to go over. This position will become clearer in what follows.

Consider an agent with the following problem: he cannot comply with a particular norm, at a particular time, so long as he makes the decision about how to act himself. However, if he simply defers to some other trustworthy person, or commits himself to slavishly following a rule without consideration of the reasons for and against following it, or relies without rational reflection on the position of the spots on the sun (which happen, inexplicably, to be an accurate guide), then he can comply with the norm. What he cannot do is to comply through appreciation of the reasons that actually favor compliance. Such a person faces a very peculiar and particular burden of compensation: to compensate for his problem, and so to comply with the norm, he must give up autonomous control of his behavior; instead of making decisions himself, he needs to decide to let someone or something make them for him. Since he has the ability to give up autonomous control of his behavior, he has the ability to comply. His problem is not one of inability. But can he be expected to comply? For reasons to be explained in a moment, and with some important qualifications, the answer is no. In general people cannot be rightly held responsible for norm violations when compliance involves this kind of burden of compensation. If this is right, then we have identified a condition such that, when a burden meets it, a person cannot be expected to suffer that burden in order to comply with a norm. This is true when the burden is to have one's behavior guided by a mechanism (such as another's decision, or the position of the sunspots) that does not involve an appreciation of the reasons for the behavior.

By way of example, consider those with mental disabilities that make them much slower than the rest of us to appreciate what they do and do not have reason to do. Such disabilities interfere radically with one's capacity to recognize what it is best for one to do when the time to act is now, even in situations in which one is clear about the facts. There is every reason to believe that people with such problems will face situations in which their only chance to do what they ought—their only chance to comply with moral and legal norms—is to allow their decisions to be made by others. Compliance requires giving up autonomy. This is the burden of compensation of people with such mental disabilities. When such a person fails to comply with a norm because he does not give up autonomous control to another, is he responsible for his failure? It seems that his responsibility is at least diminished. Or, put another way, he has the right to risk noncompliance in order to maintain autonomous control over his behavior. To bring out the intuition here expressed, compare such a person to someone who also does not comply but was fully able to appreciate the reasons for and against the act he performed. Surely the mentally disabled person is not responsible in the same way, or to the same degree, if at all, in comparison, even though he, too, had the ability to comply? How can we ask the intellectually slow to give up their autonomy in order to act quickly?

It is important to note that the decision to give up one's autonomy can be, itself, an *exercise* of one's autonomy. The mentally disabled person may be given all the time he needs to decide whether to give up control of his later decisions to a caretaker. There is, therefore, a derivative sense in which he is autonomous when deferring, later, to his caretaker: he has autonomously decided, earlier, to defer, and the autonomy of this earlier decision may color our judgment about whether his conduct later is or is not autonomous. This is true, but it is compatible with recognizing that there remains an important sense in which his later conduct is *not* autonomous: it does not spring from an exercise, on his part, of his capacities for recognizing the reasons for and against *that* behavior. There is, therefore, a kind of autonomy that he gives up in order to comply with certain norms, even if there is another kind that he maintains, and it is the giving up of this kind of autonomy that is the burden of compensation for compliance.

Consider a somewhat different example. Imagine a soldier heading into battle who tends to panic quite easily. Enough loud noises and flying shrapnel, and he is simply unable to think clearly and finds himself with a powerful desire to flee, even when he would be fleeing into the arms of the enemy. Let us stipulate what he lacks the ability to do in such circumstances: weigh the reasons for and against fleeing versus staying the course and guide his conduct in accordance with the outcome of such a process of weighing. In particular, in such circumstances, he has the ability and the opportunity to flee, and he has the ability and the opportunity to stay the course. (If there are intuitions to the effect that he cannot stay the course, these derive from the fact that what he can do is determined by more than ability and opportunity; perhaps he can stay the course only if he can try to do so, and perhaps he lacks the ability to do that.) If it turns out that, in the heat of battle, the right thing to do is to stay the course, then our soldier has a problem, for so long as he makes the decision himself, in the heat of battle he will flee, since he will not be able to recognize the good reasons for staying the course. To solve this problem he needs to take steps before he goes into battle to see to it that, during the battle, his conduct is not guided by his judgment at the time about what he has most reason to do. Depending on what he is like, various strategies might be open to him. He cannot just decide to stay the course no matter what, since, for all he knows, there will be better reason to flee. Rather, he needs to depend on something that will have a differential response depending on what he actually has good reason to do, and he must guide his behavior by its response. For instance, he might commit himself to slavishly following a friend, or a superior, who he knows will not panic, someone he can count on to see what the right thing to do is. If he does that, then, when the time comes, and his panic sets in, everything in him will be telling him that he should flee, while what he will do is whatever it is that the person whom he is relying on is doing.

Let us imagine that our soldier does not give over control of himself to something else but, instead, heads into battle, and, at a moment when he should stay the course, he flees. He has violated a norm—he should have stayed the course—but is he as responsible for doing so as someone who kept a clear head in battle but who also fled? Or, to put the question in the language developed here, could the soldier be expected to take on the burden of compensation in this case, the burden of giving up his own autonomy for a time, or is that too great a burden to demand that he take on in order to comply with the norm he has violated? It matters to the answer whether the soldier has made a prior decision to be a soldier, recognizing that in so deciding he commits himself to giving up autonomous control of his behavior in various ways, including the one at issue here. If he has made that decision—if he is not an involuntary conscript and was properly informed about his role when recruited—then he is under an independent obligation to give up his autonomy by committing himself to blindly follow his sergeant. He therefore has no reduced responsibility for his failure to comply with the norm and stay the course. However, such cases are importantly different from those of greatest concern to us here. To see this, imagine a conversation with the soldier who fled when he should have stayed the course:

Judge: You should have stayed the course.

Soldier: But to do so I would have had to give up my autonomy.

Judge: But you agreed to give up your autonomy in this respect when you agreed to be a soldier.

Notice that the judge's rejoinder does not involve citing the obligation to obey the norm requiring the soldier to stay the course; rather, the judge identifies an independent source of normative pressure to do that. Imagine that the judge were to respond to the soldier's remark in this dialogue differently:

Judge: Well, then in order to stay the course you should have given up your autonomy.

In this case, the judge takes the very norm the soldier violated, the norm requiring him to stay the course, to require him to give up his autonomy. That is, the judge, asserts that people can be expected to take on the burden of compensation at issue in order to comply with the norm independently of any other norms to which they are subject. At this point, the judge makes an error. The soldier who has agreed to be a soldier can be expected to give up his autonomy as he would need to in order to comply with the norm, but he cannot be expected to do so *merely because* he is expected to comply with the norm he violated. This kind of case, then, is similar to a duress case in which the victim has previously agreed, without coercion, to suffer the burden that the threatener threatens. In such cases the fact that compliance would require taking on the burden does not ameliorate responsibility for noncompliance.

It is important to see that it is not the case, across the board and without exception, that people who voluntarily take on roles are thereby required to give up their autonomy in order to meet the obligations associated with those roles. This is true often enough, but it is not always true. Consider, for instance, the obligation to give a gift to one's spouse on an anniversary. This is the sort of obligation that it only makes sense to meet if one does so autonomously. A person who cannot meet this obligation without giving up his autonomy cannot meet it at all. This is part of the reason that spouses (barring special arrangements) have the right to complain when it turns out that some third party picked out the anniversary gift. Further, not all role obligations are as stringent as the soldier's even if it is possible to meet them while relinquishing one's autonomy. Professors are obligated to meet with the students whom they are advising; but they are not required to do so when doing so would require giving up their autonomy. The role obligation in such a case is substantially less demanding than the soldier's. It follows, therefore, that alternative sources of obligation only sometimes place one under pressure to bear the burden of compensation of loss of autonomy in order to comply.

What the example of the soldier helps us to see is a qualification to the claim that people cannot be expected to give up their autonomy when that is what is required to comply with a norm: this is true *if* there is no independent normative pressure to give up their autonomy, as there is in the soldier case. But we still have a sufficient condition of the sort we seek:

If S, in order to A in circumstances C, would have to give up his power to decide whether or not to A in C on the basis of appreciation of the reasons for and against A-ing in C, and if S is not under independent normative pressure to give up his autonomy in this way, then S is not responsible for failing to A in violation of a norm requiring agents to A in C.

This *seems* true, but is there any reason other than its seeming so for thinking it is? One possibility is that the burden of giving up one's autonomy has particular importance to responsibility—greater importance than other sorts of burdens—because of the nature of blame and punishment, because, that is, of the kinds of acts that blaming and punishing are. Blaming and punishing for a norm violation are both examples of what Stephen Darwall has called "the second personal address of second personal reasons" (Darwall, 2006; for discussion see Yaffe, 2008). That is, to blame or to punish is to generate, through the act of blaming or punishing, an additional reason for a person not to have acted as he did. Blaming and punishing, then, are special forms of communication that are to be addressed to those who are capable of uptake. To blame or to punish is not merely to assess or grade a person's conduct; it is also to thereby alter the landscape of reasons. The act itself generates reasons for the agent to act otherwise than he did. Further, and importantly, to take place, the act of blaming S for what he did at time *t*, requires that, *at time t,* S was equipped to guide his behavior in accordance with the reason for action generated, later, by the act of blaming. Put more intuitively, blaming makes sense only when the agent blamed was in a position, at the time of the act for which he is blamed, to comply with the norm from a recognition that a later act of blame would generate a reason for him to comply. Given this, to say to someone, in blaming him, "You should have given up your autonomy in order to A" is the equivalent of saying to him, "You should have taken steps to make yourself an inappropriate object of this very act of communication." The person who insists that another should have given up his autonomy in order to comply with a norm expresses the desire that the other person appreciate, at the time of noncompliance, the reason that is generated, through the act of address. But, at the same time, such a person expresses the desire that the other have complied without exercising the capacity to appreciate reasons of the very sort that are generated by the assertion. Such a person is involved in a kind of incoherence that undermines the success of his act of blaming or punishing. If we were to say to the involuntarily conscripted soldier in the earlier example, "You should have just blindly followed your sergeant," then we are saying to him that among other things he would not have been subject to this very act of blame had he blindly followed the sergeant, and that itself is a reason to have done so. But the soldier has an apt reply: "Had I blindly followed the sergeant, I wouldn't have been in a position to appreciate that your blaming me was a reason not to flee. So how could you have expected me to guide myself in accordance with that reason?" The very purpose of the act of blaming, in such a case, is undermined by what the agent is told he should have done.

It is important to see how different this explanation is from the sort that might be issued to explain why a person cannot be expected to bear the threatened burden in duress. In the usual duress case, such as the case of robbing the bank to prevent the threatener from killing the child, assessing whether the agent can be expected to comply with the norm he violated requires weighing the *values* of the threatened consequence and the harmful, or otherwise objectionable, act performed by the agent. You can be expected to suffer a scratch to your finger in order to avoid maiming another because a scratch to the finger is *so much less bad* than the maiming you inflicted. But the burden of giving up one's autonomy in order to comply with a norm makes it inappropriate to expect compliance with the norm independently of any comparison between the value of the autonomy to be given up and the (dis)value of the act performed in violation of the norm. People cannot be expected to give up such autonomy (when they are not under independent normative pressure to do so) *even if* it would be much less bad all told for them to do so than for them to fail to comply with the norm. The reason is that to demand that someone give up such autonomy is to demand that he do something that would make demanding it of him pointless or inappropriate. The act of demanding (which is what blaming and punishing *are*), in such a case, is self-undermining. Not so in most cases of responsibility-diminishing duress in which the demand can be coherently made, but what would be demanded oughtn't to be.

Why We Should Lower the Bar

What does all of this have to do with addiction? We will be in a position to answer that question after one more step is taken. Consider someone who suffers from the following defect: he just cannot learn correctly from his mistakes about what value to assign to particular alternative actions and outcomes. An animal in the wild that had this problem would be very lucky to survive long enough to reproduce. A butterfly with this defect, for instance, might initially judge that the red flowers are better sources of nectar than the yellow. But when it discovers that, in fact, the red flowers have no nectar at all, it does not update its judgment in a way that will guide it next time when faced with the choice between red and yellow flowers. If it cannot learn from its disappointment, it will spend its energy flying to and attempting to harvest nectar from a red flower next time, and the time after, and so on and thereby give up the opportunity to expend those energies in at least exploring the possibility that the yellow flowers are a better choice. Such a butterfly might have no defect at all, relative to other butterflies, when it comes to learning the facts. It might learn from its experience, for instance, that red flowers do not have nectar in them, just as any other butterfly would. What it has trouble doing is recognizing that fact as a reason not to expend energy to fly to red flowers. Animals must update their algorithms for determining what reasons they have to perform various acts, or pursue various outcomes, in light of the factual information they have about those acts and outcomes. An animal that has a defect in this regard has a serious defect indeed.

People, of course, vary rather radically in their capacity to learn from their errors about what reasons they have. And they vary radically in this capacity across different domains of action. Someone capable of making excellent assessments about what stocks to buy and sell—someone who can recognize subtle differences in the facts about companies as reasons for and against betting on their success—might find himself, over and over, getting involved with women with characteristics that provide him with powerful reasons to run the other way, reasons that, for some reason or other, he just cannot learn to recognize in a way that will guide his behavior. But imagine that someone fails to comply with a norm in a domain of action in which he is much less good than most people at learning from his errors about reasons and values. Consider the extreme case first: he is not just less good at learning from his errors about what characteristics of mates are worth pursuing and avoiding; he is incapable of such learning; he will always, and invariably, take himself to have a powerful reason to pursue a woman like his mother, say, no matter what other toxic qualities she happens to possess. When such a person should not pursue the woman he pursues—when he is in violation of a norm in doing so—is it true that he is *unable* to avoid violation? No, for he could allow someone else to make his decisions for him. He could, for instance, sign on to a service that arranges marriages; or he could just slavishly follow the advice of his level-headed friends. What he cannot do is to comply with the norm *through a recognition of the reasons for compliance*. He thus faces a burden of compensation of the sort identified in the previous section. To compensate for his learning problem he would need to give up guidance of his conduct in this domain by his own decision-making capacity. Can we hold him responsible for doing what he should not when the burden of compensation in such a case is as described? If the sufficient condition identified earlier is correct, we cannot. His learning problem saddles him with a burden of compensation that we cannot ask him to take on in order to comply with the norms he violates (assuming that he is not under independent normative pressure to give up his autonomy in this way). Imagine the following conversation with such a man:

Friend: You shouldn't be chasing her.

Defective Man: But I can't help it.

Friend: Not true. You could pursue whoever I tell you to pursue, independently of your predilections.

Defective Man: That's too much to ask.

Defective Man's claim that he lacks the ability to comply, as Friend notes, is simply false. But Defective Man is right in responding to Friend's rejoinder when he says that the burden of compensation in this case is more than he can be expected to take on. People simply cannot be asked to give up their autonomy in order to compensate for defects in their capacity to learn from mistakes about what reasons they have for action.

Now consider the case in which Defective Man's learning problem is a deficit, not an inability. His problem is that he learns much more slowly than the rest of us and requires more radical disappointment to come to recognize and guide his conduct in accordance with the reasons he has for avoiding relationships with women with certain characteristics. Where one bad date would be enough for normal people, he requires three bad divorces and years of misery in order to get the message. But he does get it eventually. When he has not yet had as much experience as he needs and is, once again, pursuing a woman he ought not to pursue—he is in violation of a norm—what should be said about his responsibility?

In moving toward an answer, imagine, as is often the case, that there are different degrees of noncompliance. In this case, imagine that Defective Man can pursue the woman he ought not to pursue either zealously or weakly. If we consider this modeled in its simplest form, we might imagine that if he were to spend 2 hours each week pursuing her, he would be pursuing her weakly, whereas if he were to spend 30, he would be pursuing her zealously. Perhaps there is a sharp line between the two categories of pursuit—perhaps it is weak pursuit below 10 hours and zealous above—or perhaps there is a gray area with paradigm cases only above and below it. Either way, under even this very simple way of distinguishing between weak and zealous pursuit, both reflect the agent's conception of his reasons, and those conceptions stand in a hierarchical relation. If he pursues her weakly but not zealously, he takes himself to have a reason to be romantically involved with her but does not grant much weight to that reason. If he pursues her zealously, then he grants that reason a great deal of weight. The difference in the conduct, then, reflects a difference in the agent's conception of his reasons: zealous pursuers see greater reason to pursue than do weak pursuers.

In fact, the respective acts serve to express the same kind of thing about the agent's conception of his reasons even if we model the weak-zealous distinction in a way that gets closer to tracking the morally relevant facts. Imagine, for instance, that we appeal not merely to the time the agent is willing to invest in the task but instead to the full range of losses he is willing to bear in order to engage in it. In such a case it is harder to decide if a particular agent's pursuit is zealous or weak—if he is willing to give up his trip to the beach with his nephew but not willing to give up the dog to whom the woman he pursues is allergic, is his pursuit weak or zealous? But, still, the question turns on the nature of the attitude toward his reasons evidenced by the agent's conduct. So, for our purposes, imagine that weak and zealous pursuits are distinguished in this way: the zealous pursuer evidences through his conduct recognition of more or greater reason to pursue than is evidenced by the conduct of the weak pursuer.

Since, in our example, Defective Man should not pursue the woman at all, we have two norms: he ought not to pursue her weakly, and he ought not to pursue her zealously. After all, he has reasons to *avoid* becoming attached to her at all, and both weak and zealous pursuit involve a failure to recognize and respond to such reasons. Now, since both zealous and weak pursuit would be in violation of the first norm, but only zealous would be in violation of the second, the second norm is less stringent, or less demanding, than the first. "If you must pursue her," Friend might say, "at least don't pursue her *zealously*." Let us assume that given his defects, in order to avoid violation of the norm against weak pursuit, Defective Man would have to give up his autonomy; if he is going to make his decisions himself, he is going to pursue her either zealously or weakly. But in order to avoid violation of the norm against zealous pursuit, he does not need to give up his autonomy. He has learned enough, let us assume, to see that there is reason not to pursue her zealously. What he cannot yet see is that there is reason not to pursue her at all. Giving up his autonomy is not one of the burdens of compensation for compliance with the norm against zealous pursuit; but it is one of the burdens of compensation for compliance with the norm against weak pursuit. We now have two cases to consider—he pursues her weakly or he pursues her zealously—and two norms—the norm against zealous pursuit and the norm against weak. Consider table 5.1.

What we learn from table 5.1 is that a person with Defective Man's problem can be held responsible for *zealously* pursuing the person he ought not pursue, but he cannot be held responsible for pursuing her *weakly*. He ought not pursue her at all, but his defect diminishes his responsibility only for weak pursuit. If he goes ahead and pursues her zealously, he cannot shield himself from blame or punishment on the grounds that he

Table 5.1

	Norm against Zealous Pursuit	Norm against Weak Pursuit
Pursues Zealously	I. Violates; can be expected to comply	II. Violates; cannot be expected to comply
Pursues Weakly	III. Complies	IV. Violates; cannot be expected to comply

could avoid such conduct only by taking on a burden that he cannot be expected to take on. He could have pursued her only weakly and thus complied with the norm against zealous pursuit without taking on any such burden.

The lesson of this example can be generalized. When a person has a learning defect of the sort under consideration—a defect in learning what value to attach to actions and outcomes in light of his experience—that makes it harder for him to learn, but it does not undermine the possibility entirely. We can often identify a less stringent norm from the one that we hold everyone to and with which he can be expected to comply. The relevant norm is the most stringent norm that he could comply with without giving up his autonomy. In the example above there are just two kinds of pursuit, zealous and weak, and it is stipulated that the man in the example can comply with the former without taking on the burden of giving up his autonomy, whereas he cannot comply with the latter without doing so. In real cases, things will be much messier. There are often many different ways of failing to comply, differing both in degree and in kind from one another. And the burdens of compensation associated with compliance with each can vary only by degree from one another, or can vary in kind in some respects and not in others. What such messiness shows is that it is not as though the approach that the analysis of the example recommends takes moral reasoning out of our hands. But, still, it helps us to see how the issue needs to be framed when a person suffers from this kind of learning deficit.

Now consider addiction. A growing body of work in neuroscience, particularly in the subfield of neuroeconomics, is providing support for the claim that those addicted to various drugs suffer from a learning deficit of just the sort under consideration here: they are much less good than the nonaddicted at learning from their mistakes about the values of actions and outcomes in a way that guides their behavior (for an overview, see Montague, Hyman, & Cohen, 2004). Much, although not all, of this work concerns the functioning of the midbrain dopamine system, which is known to be affected by drugs of abuse (see, for instance, Di Chiara & Imperato, 1988). A large amount of evidence, provided primarily by studies in monkeys, indicates that the dopamine signal represents not the value that a subject attaches to a particular action or outcome but the difference between that value and the value the subject expected the action or outcome to have (see, for instance, Schultz, Apicella, & Ljungberg, 1993; Hollerman & Schultz, 1998; Schultz, 1998). When a monkey is shown a signal and then, a few seconds later, given a reward, the dopamine signal goes up initially when the reward is received. But after the monkey has learned that the signal precedes reward, dopamine goes up when the signal is received, and it remains flat when the reward is obtained. Further, when the signal is issued and no reward is given, the monkey's dopamine signal goes up initially on seeing the signal, but it goes down when the monkey realizes that it will not receive a reward. A plausible explanation for these observations is that the initially unexpected reward shows the monkey's condition to be better than it expected it to be, and so the dopamine signal goes up. Later, when the monkey has learned to associate the signal and the reward, it finds on seeing the signal that its condition is better than expected, and so, again, the dopamine signal goes up on seeing the signal. But, since the appearance of the signal resets the monkey's expectations—having seen the signal, the monkey now expects the reward—the dopamine signal remains flat when the monkey receives the reward, and its expectations are met. And the signal goes down when the monkey does not receive the reward, and things turn out to be worse than expected.

What function could be served by a representation in the brain of the difference between the value one expects an act or outcome to have and the value it turns out to actually have? It is plausible to think that the information carried by such a representation is of particular use *for learning what value to attach to particular acts and outcomes in light of experience.* It helps the organism to update its algorithm for determining what reasons it has to act in light of the facts as it sees them. In fact many of the most predictively powerful computational algorithms of evaluative learning use this piece of information (among others, see Sutton & Barto, 1998). What this strongly suggests, then, is that dopamine signals play a crucial role in learning from one's mistakes what values to attach in prospect to actions one is considering performing and to outcomes one is considering pursuing (see, for instance, Waelti, Dickinson, & Schultz, 2001; Bayer & Glimcher, 2002; Berridge & Robinson, 1998). Further, there is a growing body of evidence to suggest that the dopamine signal in addicts is defective in comparison to nonaddicts. In the first instance this is because many drugs of abuse directly drive up the dopamine signal independently of the experienced and expected value of the action of using (see Redish, 2004). The experienced cocaine user may have a perfectly accurate expectation about the value of his next experience of use. So, when he uses and finds that it is just as good as he expects, a correctly functioning dopamine signal would remain flat; things are no better or worse than expected. But since cocaine drives up the dopamine signal, the cocaine user's dopamine signal goes up on use, thereby representing use as better than expected. Thus, an error is registered of just the form that would be found were use to have been found through experience to be worth much more than the cocaine user expected it to be at the time he decided to use. If it is this signal that informs the cocaine user's evaluations of alternatives next time, then next time he is considering using he will represent that act as that much better than he represented it as being last time; he will correct his "error." Among other things this means that he will be moved to act as though he thought use was worth that much more money than he was willing to pay for it last time. Or, more generally, there is now more that he would be ready to sacrifice for use, including things of tremendous nonmonetary value.

Importantly, there is evidence to suggest that the dopamine signal in addicts is disrupted not just when they are using drugs but even when they are not. Their defects in evaluative learning extend, that is, to times at which they are not intoxicated. In addition these defects appear to extend to at least some domains of action in which drugs are not at stake. In experimental settings, for instance, addicts do not appear to learn from evaluative errors in investment games and other games in which they are not being asked to make choices about using or refraining from use (see Chiu, Lohrenz, & Montague, 2008). As more work in neuroscience is completed—especially in conjunction with psychological and computational work on decision making—more and more will be learned about the exact nature and extent of the addict's learning deficits.

What do these results from the neuroscience of addiction show about addict responsibility? When combined with the sufficient condition identified above under which a burden of compensation ameliorates responsibility for a norm violation, we find that addicts face just the same kind of burden of compensation as the man in our earlier example who needs much deeper and more troubling disappointment than the rest of us before he can learn whom he has reason not to pursue romantically. In the domains with respect to which the addict has trouble learning from his mistakes about what reasons he has—most notably, but not confined to those cases in which he is considering using or pursuing use of drugs—the addict cannot be expected to conform to the most stringent norms that are appropriate for nonaddicts. To conform to such norms, the addict would have to give up reliance on his own decision-making capacities and so sacrifice his autonomy in a significant respect. But, still, we can ordinarily identify a less stringent norm that he could comply with without undertaking any such burdens. Imagine, analogously to before, that the addict can pursue drugs zealously or pursue them weakly; he can, for instance, kill people for them, or he can merely deceive and manipulate his relatives in order to get them. He should not do either. But imagine, further, that to avoid even weakly pursuing drugs he would need to give up control of his behavior; he would need to rely entirely on someone or something else to make his decisions for him. But he knows enough to see the reasons against zealous pursuit and is capable of guiding his behavior in accordance with such reasons; he thus need not give up his autonomy in order to comply with the norm against zealous pursuit.

If what has been said here is correct, it follows, as in the earlier example, that the addict cannot be expected to comply with the norm against weak pursuit, but he can be expected to comply with the norm against zealous pursuit. There are thus some things that we can hold the addict responsible for doing in service of his addiction and others we cannot. The line between these two is determined by the burdens of compensation involved in performance. Where the addict would have to compensate for his learning deficit by giving up his autonomy, we cannot expect compliance, and so we cannot hold the addict responsible for failure; but where he would not, we have no reason to believe that we cannot, and so we should.

Conclusion

Even if the view of addict responsibility presented here is correct, darkness surrounds the details. When an addict deceives and manipulates his family members in order to get them to give him money to buy drugs, is he responsible? And if so, what, exactly, is he responsible for? The answer is that he is responsible for whatever he did that he could have avoided doing without giving up his autonomy to do so. But this is not the answer that his family or police, prosecutors, and judges seek. They want a more specific answer. They will find this answer all but useless until they know whether the addict was, in fact, in a position to recognize and guide his conduct in accordance with reasons not to push quite as hard as he did, or not to tell lies of such great significance as he did, or something else of that nature. They want to know the precise content of the norms that the addict is and is not responsible for violating. All that can be said in response to this concern is that we have to wait and see. All we can do is to make the best guesses that we can on the basis of the best empirical research available. But we can also have hope that more empirical research will give us more guidance. How much more experience does the addict need in order to learn what reasons he has and how weighty they are? It is an empirical question. But if what has been said here is correct, at least now we know what to look for.[4]

Notes

1. In fact, I don't think it does all by itself since I follow Harry Frankfurt and many others in rejecting the so-called Principle of Alternate Possibilities, according to which the ability to do otherwise is a necessary condition of responsibility for wrongdoing. There is a large literature on this topic. For a start, see Frankfurt (1969) and the essays collected in Widerker and McKenna (2006).

2. It is famously difficult to adequately distinguish between threats and offers. As a start, see Nozick (1969).

3. It is possible to construct duress cases in which the burden is suffered prior to compliance with the norm because it becomes clear to the threatener prior to the moment of compliance that the agent will, in the future, comply with the norm. In such cases, the burden is still a consequence of compliance, but it is not a *causal* consequence.

4. Thanks to Doug Husak and to the editors of this volume for thoughtful comments on an earlier draft, and thanks to Jacob Ross for helpful conversation.

References

Bayer, H. M., & Glimcher, P. W. (2002). Subjective estimates of objective rewards: using economic discounting to link behavior and brain. *Society of Neuroscience Abstracts*, 28, 358–360.

Berridge, K. C., & Robinson, T. E. (1998). What is the role of dopamine in reward: hedonic impact, reward learning, or incentive salience? *Brain Research. Brain Research Reviews*, 28, 309–369.

Chiu, P., Lohrenz, T., & Montague, P. R. (2008). Smokers' brains compute, but ignore, a fictive error signal in a sequential investment task. *Nature Neuroscience*, 11, 514–520.

Darwall, S. (2006). *The second-person standpoint: morality, respect, and accountability.* Cambridge, MA: Harvard University Press.

Di Chiara, G., & Imperato, A. (1988). Drugs abused by humans preferentially increase synaptic dopamine concentrations in the mesolimbic system of freely moving rats. *Proceedings of the National Academy of Sciences of the United States of America*, 85, 5274–5278.

Frankfurt, H. (1969). Alternate possibilities and moral responsibility. *Journal of Philosophy*, 66, 829–839.

Hollerman, J. R., & Schultz, W. (1998). Dopamine neurons report an error in the temporal prediction of reward during learning. *Nature Neuroscience*, 1, 304–309.

Husak, D. (1999). Addiction and criminal liability. *Law and Philosophy*, 18, 655–684.

Montague, P. R., Hyman, S. E., & Cohen, J. D. (2004). Computational roles for dopamine in behavioural control. *Nature*, 431, 760–767.

Morse, S. (2000). Hooked on hype: addiction and responsibility. *Law and Philosophy*, 19, 3–49.

Nozick, R. (1969). Coercion. In S. Morgenbesser, P. Suppes, & M. White (Eds.), Philosophy, science, method: essays in honor of Ernest Nagel (pp. 440–472). New York: St. Martin's Press.

Redish, A. D. (2004). Addiction as a computational process gone awry. *Science*, 306, 1944–1947.

Schultz, W. (1998). Predictive reward signal of dopamine neurons. *Journal of Neurophysiology*, 80, 1–27.

Schultz, W., Apicella, P., & Ljungberg, T. (1993). Responses of monkey dopamine neurons to reward and conditioned stimuli during successive steps of learning a delayed response task. *Journal of Neuroscience*, 13, 900–913.

Sutton, R., & Barto, A. (1998). *Reinforcement learning: an introduction.* Cambridge, MA: MIT Press.

Waelti, P., Dickinson, A., & Schultz, W. (2001). Dopamine responses comply with basic assumptions of formal learning theory. *Nature*, 412, 43–48.

Watson, G. (1999). Excusing addiction. *Law and Philosophy*, 18, 589–619.

Widerker, D., & McKenna, M. (Eds.), (2006). Moral responsibility and alternative possibilities: essays on the importance of alternative possibilities. Burlington, VT: Ashgate Publishing.

Yaffe, G. (2008). Reasonableness in the law and second-personal address. *Loyola Law Review*, 40, 939–976.

6 Decision-Making Capacity and Responsibility in Addiction

Louis C. Charland

A Change in Tactics

It is perilous to generalize about the scope and nature of responsibility in addiction. Personal and social circumstances of addiction vary widely, as do the effects of various addictive substances and the manner in which they are metabolized in the individual. The nature, duration, and severity of addiction are also relevant variables that are often ignored. Admittedly, most addictive drugs have reasonably well-demarcated profiles of action, which permits some degree of extrapolation on the level of prognosis, pathology, and treatment. Nonetheless, despite these and other advances in our understanding of addiction, it is still impossible to reliably predict who will be successful in treatment and who will relapse. The standard of care appears to be to treat substance abusers as if they are all equally responsible for their recovery, even though it is not clear to what degree they can in fact exercise responsibility and control over their substance use.

Philosophers often approach the question of responsibility for addiction from the vantage point of "free will" or some other philosophically related conception of "choice." The analysis is typically purely conceptual in nature (e.g., Davidson, 1980; Mele, 2004). It is the opinion of the present writer that there are probably no such philosophical "varieties of free will worth wanting" (Dennett, 1984). Although the amount of philosophical skill and acumen that is deployed in such discussions is undoubtedly impressive, the clinical benefits are difficult to assess. The problem is that there is no clear way to move from the proverbial philosophical armchair to clinical testing and intervention.

One solution to this conundrum is to try and do away with unfettered philosophical conceptual speculation. It is the solution proposed here. However, adopting this solution does not mean discarding the problem that interests us. We are still concerned with elucidating the problem of responsibility in addiction. The difference is a change in tactics. Instead of addressing the problem of responsibility in addiction philosophically, we address it empirically. This shall be done by formulating the problem of responsibility in terms of the clinical concept of decision-making capacity. The proposed change in tactics still leaves a lot of room for philosophical analysis and discussion. What has changed is the locus of accountability, which is now the tribunal of experience rather than the proverbial armchair.

According to the proposed new strategy anything that cannot be clinically formulated and tested must be rejected as mere anecdote and speculation. All relevant terms and notions must be operationally defined and amenable to clinical formulation and testing according to measurable parameters. Progress on a practical level is imperative, even if the first steps that need to be taken are primarily theoretical. This last point is important to emphasize. This is because there are presently no specific studies and results on the nature of decision–making capacity in addiction to build on. There are, however, many studies that investigate how decision-making capacity figures in other mental disorders and a large body of supporting theoretical discussion that can serve as inspiration. What follows then is really a tentative sketch of a research program on the relationship between decision-making capacity and addiction and its theoretical rationale, along with a special focus on the problem of responsibility. An important part of the new strategy will be to try and avoid overgeneralization by attempting to build on specific individual types and cases of addiction. In the present discussion our focus will be severe, chronic, treatment-refractory, heroin addiction.

One immediate and important consequence of adopting a decision-making capacity approach to the problem of responsibility in addiction is that generalizations in the area are automatically subject to severe limitations. The reason is that decision-making capacity is not a global concept but, rather, a decision-specific one. A person is never decisionally capable in general. Only a specific decision, at a particular time, for a particular individual, can be assessed for decision-making capacity. Thus generalizations are automatically curtailed by theoretical fiat when responsibility is approached from the vantage point of decision-making capacity. In this alternate framework, it is meaningless to speak of responsibility in general. There is no single general answer to the question whether addicts— in some general sense—can be said to be responsible for their addiction or their recovery. This is not to say that generalization is impossible or unimportant. It simply means that concrete particular determinations of capacity are the ultimate foundation for any account of responsibility in addiction.

In conformity with the requirement that discussions of responsibility in addiction always address specific addictions in specific circumstances, the present discussion focuses on a particular case that has recently been at the forefront of controversy. This is the prescription of heroin, usually in injectable form, to chronic, treatment-refractory, heroin-dependent individuals (Perneger, Giner, & Mino, 1998). The question that will concern us is whether such individuals can be considered decisionally capable ("mentally competent") to give informed consent to their drug of choice, namely heroin (Charland, 2002). It is important that in this study the individuals in question are living in dire social circumstances, with some involved in drug-related criminal activity. Not surprisingly, many of the study subjects suffer from physical and mental health problems other than addiction, for example, anxiety, depression, HIV infection, and suicidal behavior (Perneger et al., 1998).

Paradox and Politics

Unfortunately, we are forced to begin with an ostensibly counterintuitive paradox. On the one hand, there is the hypothesis that decision-making capacity, a clinical concept, can help elucidate the problem of responsibility in addiction. Yet, on the other hand, there is the frustrating fact that the requisite clinical studies on decision-making capacity have not yet been carried out (Anderson & DuBois, 2007; Jeste & Saks, 2006). If decision-making capacity in addition is so important, then why has it not been extensively studied?

Of course, for legal reasons, decision-making capacity is normally considered in both addiction treatment and research. However, with few exceptions, the standard of care in the field is to presume that addicted individuals are capable of making their own decisions regarding substance use. This, in turn, is normally held to imply that addicted individuals are also *prima facie* "responsible" for making those decisions and assuming their consequences. In general, the rule is to presume capacity except in moments of acute intoxication or withdrawal (College on Problems of Drug Dependence, 1995, 171; National Bioethics Advisory Commission, 1998).

Even in exceptionally controversial cases, such as research on the administration of heroin to severely heroin-dependent individuals, the assessment of capacity is apparently a routine informal affair that requires no specialized capacity testing. For example, in the study we are concerned with, we are simply told that, " . . . the psychiatrist, confirmed the patient's eligibility, explained program procedures, obtained informed consent" (Perneger et al., 1998). In sharp contrast, extensive specialized capacity testing has been conducted for most other major mental disorders (Appelbaum, 2006; Appelbaum & Grisso, 1995; Appelbaum, Grisso, Frank, O'Donnell, & Kupfer, 1999; Dunn, 2006; Tan, Stewart, Fitzpatrick, & Hope, 2006). Why then the absence of capacity testing in the case of addiction? In particular, how can we *unilaterally* presume that severely addicted individuals are capable of freely and voluntarily consenting to their drug of choice, when by *definition* their diagnosis implies that they have "lost control" over their use of that drug (Charland, 2002; Elliott 2002)? It is easy to dismiss this formulation of the issues as overly simplistic, as a naive literal-minded reading of current diagnostic terms and categories (Hall, Carter, & Morley, 2003a, 2003b). However, taking scientific terms and theories at face value is a perfectly reasonable way to generate missing caveats and refinements. In this case it even leads to quite interesting results.

Paradoxically, it would appear that the field of addictions considers itself off limits when it comes to research on decision-making capacity and specialized capacity testing. There even appears to be active resistance to the idea. For example, the suggestion that such capacity research be carried out for controversial cases such as heroin prescription has sometimes been dismissed with more than a hint of ridicule (Ling, 2002; O'Brien, 2002). At the same time, the debate has reached the top journals in the field (Charland, 2003; Hall, 2006; Hall et al., 2003a, 2003b; Hall, Carter, & Morley, 2004). The issue is now openly acknowledged in many policy-oriented discussions on the ethics of addiction research (Ashcroft, Dawson, Draper, & McMillan , 2007; Foddy & Savulescu, 2006; Geppert & Bogenschutz, 2009; Harwood & Myers, 2004; Levy, 2006; Roberts, 2002). And yet, despite all this attention, the requisite testing has apparently still not been done. In such a paradoxical situation, one can hopefully be excused for speculating on possible "political" motives behind the absence of the relevant testing.

One possible "political" reason why the relevant testing has not been carried out may be the fear that, if capacity were carefully assessed using specialized accepted measures, many addicts would be found incapable of consenting to treatment or participation in research. The worry is that there would be costly and timely practical consequences if decision-making capacity in addiction were *routinely* assessed rather than *unilaterally* presumed. Important research that needs to be done would be greatly constrained (Hall et al., 2003a). In this impasse it is natural to look to the intermediate stages of the addictive cycle—periods in between intoxication and withdrawal—as the opportune time to assess capacity (Carter & Hall, 2008; Cohen, 2002; Walker, 2008). So-called "loss of control" is less evident and pronounced there, or so it may seem. It is therefore easy to consider addicts as if they were capable of normal decision making during these intermediate periods. However, this is an illusion.

Let us instead ask why "loss of control" in addiction should not extend to all phases of the addictive cycle? In the case of the heroin prescription referred to above, careful reflection on the chronic, cyclical, and relapsing nature of addiction suggests that this may in fact be the case. Succinctly, decision-making capacity may be impaired in a significant sense at less obvious moments of the addiction cycle, even though "loss of control" is not always explicitly manifest in directly observable behavior. This is a point on which it is important to be nuanced. Note also that just as "loss of control" is usually a gradual worsening process that cannot be restricted to single momentary occurrent states or episodes, recovery is equally—but not always—a gradual process of improvement, where control is reclaimed and reinforced. In sum the manner to approach the issue of "loss of control" in addiction is not through a description of directly observable isolated behavioral *states* but, rather, by focusing on the values that under-lie the entire behavioral *process* in addiction. Once we look at the role of values in this process, the manner in which decision-making capacity can help contribute to our understanding of the problem of responsibility in addiction will be easier to state and understand.

Pathological Values in Addiction

Many theoretical models of addiction focus on the cognitive determinants of addictive behavior. They investigate how addicts think and reason and attempt to model the apparent irrationality of addictive behavior using theoretical models derived from decision theory and cognitive neuroscience (e.g., Ainslie, 1999; Becker & Murphy, 1988; Campbell, 2003; Hyman, 2007; Ole-Jorgen, 1999). The focus in this kind of investigation is addictive thinking. Without a doubt it must be conceded that this general approach has yielded valuable and interesting results. But its explanatory scope is limited, a shortcoming that is usually insufficiently recognized. The reason is that "cognitive" theoretical models of addictive behavior fail to get to the real causal roots of addiction.

The roots of addiction do not lie in the cognitive domain of thinking, which may even be largely epiphenomenal, but rather are in the affective domain of feeling. These roots lie in very strong visceral feelings (Elster, 1999; Lowenstein, 1999). Note however that the adjective "strong" here is sometimes apt to mislead. For there are also subtle and elusive feelings in addiction that are just as effective in precipitating relapse. This however does not affect the point at hand. Addiction is not primarily a function or manifestation of faulty reasoning or irrational thinking, and "loss of control" in addiction is not really "cognitive" loss of control, properly speaking (see, e.g., Hyman, 2007). Neither is addictive behavior primarily a matter of disordered volition or impaired will (Appelbaum, Lidz, & Klitzman, 2009; Campbell, 2003; Roberts, 2002). Undoubtedly, both impairments in thinking and volition are evident in addiction. But the roots of addiction lie *primarily* in the area of affectivity. It is feelings and the mechanisms that govern them that are fundamentally disordered in addiction. The problem lies primarily in the so-called "pleasure" centers of the brain (Panksepp, 1998, 164–186).

Investigating addiction from the vantage point of cognition and disordered thinking is tempting in many ways. Decision theory and cognitive neuroscience provide reasonably well-developed experimental methods that yield ostensibly clear and interesting results. But the real truth about addiction lies elsewhere. It lies in the affective and not the cognitive domain. The relevant branch of neuroscience is not cognitive neuroscience but instead affective neuroscience (Charland, 2007b). Likewise, the elements of decision theory and psychology that need to be emphasized are not cognitive posits such as beliefs and probability functions but, rather, feelings and their underlying values. The problem of course is that affective posits such as feelings and emotions are notoriously elusive and are much harder to investigate empirically than their cognitive counterparts (Berrios, 1985). However, that is no reason to ignore them, and progress in the area is certainly possible, as recent developments in the affective sciences amply testify (see especially Panksepp, 1998, for details, and Sander & Scherer, 2009, for a general survey of recent developments).

Therefore, according to the proposed alternative, addiction is primarily a matter of strong and at the same time subtle and elusive feelings. It involves an affective reorientation driven by deep-seated pathological values, which gradually emerge as the main motivational elements and determinants of addictive behavior. The feeling dimension of addiction is often reflected and manifest in cognitive activities such as thinking and reasoning. But this is largely an intellectualization of another, deeper, and far more elusive reality that lies in the domain of affectivity. Admittedly, sometimes changing faulty thinking and reasoning patterns and assumptions can help to alter some of the feelings implicated in addiction (Beck, 1976; Ellis, 1962). However, as long as the strong feelings emanating from values derived from physiological and psychological dependence continue to exercise their grip on the addicted individual's mental economy, addictive behavior remains stubbornly recalcitrant and resistant to long-term change through cognitive means. This is because the addict's self-destructive thinking and faulty reasoning is only a symptom of a much larger, deeper, problem whose causes lie in the affective domain, where change is often slow and laborious.

An interesting way to frame these observations is in terms of values. This is an approach that has proven helpful in understanding the pathology of other mental disorders, especially anorexia (Tan et al., 2006; Vollman, 2007). Framed in such terms, addictive behavior is based on core pathological values that arise from affective reorientations in the pleasure and reward circuits of the brain. Those values are expressed through feelings. The result is an overall affective reorientation of the brain, which is then manifested in addictive behavior. Note that none of these affective processes requires cognition or verbal behavior, although of course they may be accompanied by these. Examples of core pathological values are not easy to state. But they can be inferred from the relevant behavior, or even sometimes directly elicited by direct stimulation of the brain through surgical or pharmacological means. Examples of such values might be the feeling that one must have a particular drug, or the feeling that one must have the feeling that comes from using a drug. Such feelings can of course vary in duration and intensity and may enter into competition with other feelings. They also have a dispositional nature, meaning that they can remain latent at times, although they also resurface regularly at periodic intervals. What makes those motivational addictive feelings and their underlying values "pathological" is the fact that the values in question are initially caused and reinforced by long-term use of addictive drugs themselves. The values in question are not freely—or authentically—chosen by the individual but rather are a toxic by-product of the drug (Charland, 2007a). Further social reinforcement and elaboration occur as addiction progresses, and change becomes increasingly difficult to initiate and sustain.

According to this alternative sketch, it is not the addicted individual's thinking that is fundamentally disordered but his feelings that are. Addiction is fundamentally and primarily a disorder of affectivity rather than cognition. Obviously, this is only a sketch. Innumerable details and qualifications still need to be spelled out in response to questions and objections. Nonetheless the sketch arguably has at least one commanding virtue. It is deliberately limited in scope. The specific addiction we are investigating is severe treatment-refractory heroin dependence, usually accompanied by additional co-morbid mental disorders such as anxiety and depression, in individuals who are in great social distress (Perneger et al., 1998). Visceral factors and subcortical mechanisms associated with affectivity play a determining role in addictions of this sort (e.g., Gardner & David, 1999; Lowenstein, 1999; Panksepp, 1998). Many of the feelings involved are bodily feelings or stem from such feelings. But the range of affective states involved also extends to short- and longer-term emotional states and processes.

No automatic generalization to other kinds of addictions is presumed or intended by the vague use of the term "addiction" in the present sketch, nor indeed in this chapter as a whole. Hopefully readers will appreciate how difficult it is to argue that our philosophical craving for generalizations ought to be curtailed in addiction research, while the relevant issues are often stated in such general terms. There is a tension in this juggling act, since at the same time as generalizations are supposed to be curtailed, we also hope to arrive at a general methodological prescription of reasonably wide scope, namely, that decision-making capacity ought to be assessed separately, for each different kind of addiction and its respective token instances across individuals. This very disciplined, laborious, clinical method is what the concept of decision-making capacity is supposed to bring to the question of responsibility in addiction.

Decision-Making Capacity

Having momentarily settled what we mean by "addiction," we can now look at the concept of decision-making capacity to see what it can bring to our understanding of the problem of responsibility in addiction. Because this is a complex field, we will have to settle on a particular conception of how decision-making capacity ought to be understood (Charland, 2008). To start we must distinguish decision-making *capacity* from common-sense *agency*. Addicts obviously make choices (Freckelton, 2002). They also appear to think and reason as they make those choices. In this simple sense, addicts display agency. However, agency of this sort is not the same as capacity. For our purposes "capacity" will be understood to mean decision-making capacity. This is a much narrower and restricted concept than simple agency and its associated concept of "choice."

Decision-making capacity is a fundamental concept of Western medical law and ethics. It derives from the doctrine of informed consent, which requires that consent be informed, free, and "capable" in order to be deemed valid. There are several leading theoretical visions of how the relevant concept of capacity should be theoretically formulated and clinically operationalized (Sturman, 2005). Probably the most influential formulation of the concept in North American jurisdictions is the "MacArthur" model developed by Paul Appelbaum, Thomas Grisso, and colleagues (Appelbaum & Grisso, 1995; Grisso & Appelbaum, 1995; Grisso et al., 1995). Its main operationalized clinical measure is referred to as the MacCAT-T (Grisso & Appelbaum, 1998). The MacCAT-T is a semistructured questionnaire with a simple scoring system that takes about 15–20 min to administer. According to the MacCAT-T, decisional capacity is divided into four subcapacities. These are (1) understanding, (2) appreciation, (3) reasoning, and (4) choice. In other models, capacity is sometimes said to include an additional feature that is not explicitly mentioned in the Mac-CAT-T but that its authors say is largely implicit (Grisso & Appelbaum, 2006). This is (5) values. The basic elements of capacity and their rationale are briefly reviewed below.

1. *Understanding*   Perhaps the most basic element of capacity is understanding (Buchanan & Brock, 1989, 23). Obviously, in order to be capable of consenting to or refusing a given treatment, a subject must have some basic understanding of the facts involved in that decision. Yet this apparently simple requirement can turn out to be rather complex depending on how "understanding" is defined (Drane, 1984). Basic comprehension and knowledge or cognition of facts is one minimal interpretation (Grisso & Appelbaum, 1998, 37–42). However, most commentators recognize that this mental ability alone is not enough for generating the sort of health care decisions we are concerned with (Berghmans, Dickenson, & Ter Meulen, 2004; Breden & Vollman, 2004; Moberg & Kniele, 2006).

2. *Appreciation*   In addition to understanding, most writers on capacity agree that subjects must also have some appreciation of the nature and significance of the decision that they are faced with (Grisso & Appelbaum, 1998, 42–52). Thus, in addition to understanding, subjects must be able "to appreciate the nature and meaning of potential alternatives—what it would be like and 'feel' like to be in possible future states and to undergo various experiences—and to integrate this appreciation into one's decision making" (Buchanan & Brock, 1989, 24). The appreciation requirement has clout. A subject can understand what addiction is and what a commitment to recovery entails but fail to appreciate that it is *they* who are addicted and that this is really *their* decision to make—further, that it is *they* who will experience the consequences of making, or not making, that decision. Denial in alcoholism thus represents a failure in appreciation. Pathological values of the sort we have discussed might compromise appreciation in this sense because they artificially alter what counts as meaningful and worth pursuing for an individual.

3. *Reasoning* Without the mental ability to engage in reasoning and manipulate information rationally, it is impossible for understanding and appreciation to issue in a decision (Buchanan & Brock, 1989, 24–25; Grisso & Appelbaum, 1998, 52–58). The concept of reasoning is often left vague in discussions of decisional capacity. Probably this is because insisting on too high or specific a normative standard of reasoning might risk making a majority of health care subjects decisionally incapable; a reductio ad absurdum of any theory of decisional capacity that implied such a result. Yet normative standards of reasoning sometimes do get mentioned: for example, consistency and the ability to derive conclusions from premises (Freedman, 1981). Reasoning is also usually said to include the ability to weigh risks and benefits and evaluate putative consequences.

4. *Choice* Unless subjects can express their choice in some outward way, it is impossible to know their intended decision. The condition is not trivial, since some patients—for example, stroke victims—can have an active mental life and satisfy our first three conditions for capacity but are unable to express anything verbally or otherwise. This has led some commentators to add the ability to express a choice to the list of elements that comprise capacity (Grisso & Appelbaum, 1998, 34–37).

5. *Values* In addition to the above four elements of capacity, some theorists explicitly state that capacity requires a set of values (Buchanan & Brock, 1989, 24–25). Because a subject's values can be expected to change over time, what is required is not an immutable, fixed set of values but a minimally consistent and stable set of values (Buchanan & Brock, 1989, 24). Another way of expressing this point is to say that capacity requires "a conception of what is good" (Buchanan & Brock, 1989). The reason for this last requirement should be obvious. Weighing the risks and benefits of various alternative choices requires values, also called "utilities" or "preferences." So does selecting one option over others. This can be argued to imply that capacity requires affective capacities such as feelings and emotions (Charland, 1998a, 1998b; see also Appelbaum, 1998, 2007).

Recall that capacity as defined above is always specific to a particular person at a particular time in a particular context. It therefore makes no sense to declare someone decisionally capable *tout court*—or in general. Admittedly, the law in most Western jurisdictions makes a general presumption of capacity: persons are assumed to be decisionally capable of making their own decisions unless there is reason to suspect otherwise. Nonetheless, the foundation of the concept of capacity is a decision-specific determination for a particular person at a particular place and time. We have already seen that this condition has important consequences for understanding how responsibility figures in addiction. Basically, it means that responsibility is not a fixed or uniform construct that can be unilaterally applied or denied across different cases and situations. It needs to be assessed for individual cases based on their particular circumstances.

There is one last feature of capacity assessments that needs to be mentioned. It is that assessments for decision-making capacity are typically all-or-nothing. Thus, even though it is evident that many of the subcapacities that underlie capacity come in degrees, capacity itself is invariably treated as a threshold concept. This requirement derives from the practical fact that the law normally requires an all-or-nothing determination in adjudicating matters of informed consent. Practically, there is a need to distinguish individuals who are capable of making their own decisions, and therefore do not need assistance to aid them in this task, from individuals who lack the requisite capacity to make their own decisions and therefore need the assistance of surrogate decision makers.

Evidently, applying the notion of decision-making capacity to addiction immediately restricts the manner in which questions of responsibility can be framed and answered. First, there is the focus on situations of consent, whether it be consent to treatment or consent to participate in clinical research. Second, there is the decision-specific nature of decision-making capacity. This severely narrows the scope of any proposed related concept of responsibility. Third, there is the threshold nature of the concept of decision-making capacity. This all-or-nothing—yes or no—nature of the concept of capacity also extends to any related concept of responsibility. Finally, fourth, understood from the point of view of decision-making capacity, the concept of "responsibility" acquires an empirical basis that it does not have otherwise. This is because capacity is an operationalized empirical measure.

Accountability and Responsibility

It should now be clear that the concept of decision-making capacity suggests a distinct but quite restricted notion of "responsibility." The key here is accountability: whether a person's decisions, and the values those decisions are based on, are truly theirs (Elliott, 1991, 1999, 91–103; 2002). Recall the fact that in the example we have chosen, the addicted individuals are treatment refractory. That is, they have repeatedly failed at all existing treatment options. This indeed is a common qualifying condition for participation in heroin prescription trials of the sort we are discussing. Cases like this constitute a good example of what is meant by saying that addiction is a chronic relapsing condition. The example also highlights another important feature of addiction, namely, ambivalence (Elster, 1999, 10, 74). Addicted individuals routinely commit to recovery and often achieve some degree of abstinence or control over their drug use. However, sadly, these periods of remission are often short-lived, and relapse occurs.

The central place of ambivalence in addiction is reflected in the fact that many addicted individuals routinely say that they desperately want to quit, yet soon afterward they relapse and apparently contradict their earlier commitment. There are interesting theoretical models that purport to describe these patterns of commitment and relapse in addictive thinking (Elster & Skog, 1999). However, as noted above, many of them fall short on the explanatory side. This is because the real causal roots of addictive behavior lie in the domain of feeling rather than thinking, affectivity rather than cognition. It is the peculiar periodic dispositional nature of the underlying pathological values in addiction that explains ambivalence. At one point in time, the addicted person really feels as if she wants to quit, and says so, usually with remarkable sincerity. However, as the addictive cycle progresses and enters its periods of craving and seeking, these earlier feelings are apparently overwhelmed or annulled, and other, more powerful, feelings take over. The feeling that one must seek and use drugs wins out.

Although the above explanation may be simplistic, it appears reasonably robust. It nicely captures and combines widely accepted facts about addiction, from the neurobiology of craving and withdrawal, to the baffling chronic nature of relapse. It also explains the common sense observation that once an addicted individual starts using, she "become like another person." The ambivalence that addicted individuals manifest in their behavior is sometimes so periodic that it can lead family members to believe that they cannot be trusted to keep their promises of abstinence. This is a profoundly self-defeating attitude to adopt when confronted with addiction; however, it does reflect the chronic relapsing character of addiction and related ambivalence.

It is simply a clinical fact that, much of the time, for many addicted individuals, the commitment to recovery and related momentary consent to treatment cannot usually be sustained: "most addicts who try and quit their habit will typically experience numerous relapses before they succeed" (Ole-Jorgen, 1999, 192). That relapse will repeatedly occur on the road to recovery is indeed one of the most pervasive and robust truths about addictions of the sort we are describing. Relapse will usually occur. In this sense, much of the time, for many addicted individuals, the decision to enter treatment is not strictly speaking accountable. Because the evaluative capacities and dispositions that underlie, motivate, and orient their decision making are mostly governed by pathological values instilled by the drug, those decisions are not truly theirs. Such decisions should of course be encouraged, but as a matter of fact that stems from the cyclical nature of their condition, addicted individuals cannot actually be counted on to predictably realize their stated aims. The reason is that as long as the pathological values that underlie addictive behavior remain operative—something that can continue long after detoxification—addicted individuals often can and will vacillate between promises to control their addiction and relapse. This often leads to profound shame and disillusionment and a lack of self-confidence that pose added obstacles to recovery.

Lack of accountability in the above sense would amount to a serious failure in decision-making capacity. Most importantly, it indicates a failure in appreciation. Decisions are based on values. There is a periodic fluctuation in the dispositional activation of pathological values that occurs in addiction. At one period of the cycle, the addicted individual does not feel like using her drug of choice, but at other times she apparently does feel like using her drug of choice. How and to what extent the drug of choice is valued thus changes over the periodic cycles of addiction. As a matter of principle, such systematic and pathological changes in value are incompatible with the kind of stability in values that is required for acceptable decision-making capacity. The situation is not unlike some cases of dementia, where momentary changes and fluctuations in personality severely compromise the accountability, and therefore the decision-making capacity, of patients to comply with treatment decisions. Sometimes these changes are the manifestation of cognitive deficits, but they can also emanate from altered values underlying feelings and emotions, hence the analogy with addiction.

Conclusion

Addiction of the variety discussed in this chapter is a condition that, by its very nature, compromises decision-making capacity across the decisional spectrum. The impairment is present not only in moments of withdrawal and intoxication but at all stages of the addictive cycle, as long as the pathological dispositions to overvalue addictive drugs remain entrenched and operative.

In light of this pervasive and entrenched reorientation in pathological values, it seems reasonable to question the unilateral presumption of capacity for cases of this sort. The reason is that there is an important, but restricted, sense in which the addicted individuals in question *are* not "responsible" for their decisions regarding drug use. The high likelihood of repeated relapse means that, as a clinical matter of fact, they are usually not accountable. At the same time, clinical experience also suggests that we should treat addicted individuals *as if* they are responsible because that empowerment is often crucial to their recovery (Di Clemente, 2006). In the end, there is probably only one safe course of action to take when faced with such a difficult situation. This is to suspend the unilateral global presumption of capacity and instead assess decision-making capacity on a case-by-case basis, with careful monitoring and encouragement.

References

Ainslie, G. (1999). The dangers of will power. In J. Elster & S. Ole-Jorgen (Eds.), Getting hooked: rationality and addiction (pp. 65–92). Cambridge: Cambridge University Press.

Anderson, E. E., & DuBois, J. M. (2007). The need for evidence-based research ethics: a review of the substance abuse literature. *Alcohol and Drug Dependence, 86* (2–3), 95–105.

Appelbaum, P. S. (1998). Ought we to require emotional capacity as part of decisional competence? *Kennedy Institute of Ethics Journal, 8*(4), 377–387.

Appelbaum, P. S. (2006). Decisional capacity of patients with schizophrenia to consent to research: taking stock. *Schizophrenia Bulletin, 32,* 22–25.

Appelbaum, P. S. (2007). Assessment of patient's competence to consent to treatment. *New England Journal of Medicine, 357,* 1834–1840.

Appelbaum, P. S., & Grisso, T. (1995). The MacArthur Treatment Competency Study. I. Mental illness and competence to consent to treatment. *Law and Human Behavior, 19,* 105–126.

Appelbaum, P. S., Grisso, T., Frank, E., O'Donnell, S., & Kupfer, D. J. (1999). Competence of depressed patients for consent to research. *American Journal of Psychiatry, 156* (9), 1380–1384.

Appelbaum, P. S., Lidz, C. W., & Klitzman, R. (2009). Voluntariness of consent to research: a conceptual model. *Hastings Center Report, 39* (1), 30–39.

Ashcroft, R. E., Dawson, A., Draper, H., & McMillan, J. R. (2007). *Principles of health care ethics.* New York, London: John Wiley & Sons.

Beck, A. (1976). *Cognitive therapy and the emotional disorders.* New York: International Universities Press.

Becker, G., & Murphy, K. (1988). A theory of rational addiction. *Journal of Political Economy, 96,* 675–700.

Berghmans, R., Dickenson, D., & Ter Meulen, R. (2004). Mental capacity: in search of alternative perspectives. *Health Care Analysis, 12* (4), 251–263.

Berrios, G. E. (1985). The psychopathology of affectivity: conceptual and historical aspects. *Psychological Medicine, 15,* 745–758.

Breden, T. M., & Vollmann, J. (2004). The cognitive based approach of capacity assessment in psychiatry: a philosophical critique of the MacCAT-T. *Health Care Analysis, 12* (4), 273–283.

Buchanan, A. E., & Brock, D. W. (1989). *Deciding for others: the ethics of surrogate decision making.* Cambridge: Cambridge University Press.

Campbell, W. G. (2003). Addiction: a disease of volition caused by a cognitive impairment. *Canadian Journal of Psychiatry, 48* (10), 669–674.

Carter, A., & Hall, W. (2008). Informed consent to opioid agonist maintenance treatment: recommended ethical guidelines. *International Journal on Drug Policy, 19* (1), 79–89.

Charland, L. C. (1998a). Appreciation and emotion: theoretical reflections on the macarthur treatment competence study. *Kennedy Institute Journal of Ethics*, *8*(4), 359–377.

Charland, L. C. (1998b). Is Mr. Spock mentally competent: competence to consent and emotion. *Philosophy, Psychiatry, & Psychology*, *5* (1), 67–95.

Charland, L. C. (2002). Cynthia's dilemma: consenting to heroin prescription. *American Journal of Bioethics*, *2*(2), 37–57.

Charland, L. C. (2003). Heroin addicts and consent to heroin therapy: a comment on Hall et al. (2003). *Addiction (Abingdon, England)*, *98* (11), 1634–1635.

Charland, L. C. (2007a). Anorexia and the MacCAT-T test for mental competence: validity, value, emotion. Commentary on Jacinta Tan's "Competence to make treatment decisions in anorexia nervosa: thinking processes and values." *Philosophy, Psychiatry, & Psychology*, *13* (4), 283–287.

Charland, L. C. (2007b). Affective neuroscience and addiction. *American Journal of Bioethics*, *7* (1), 20–21.

Charland, L. C. (2008). Decision-making capacity. In E. N. Zalta (Ed.), *The Stanford encyclopedia of philosophy* (Fall 2008 edition). Available at <http://plato.stanford.edu/archives/fall2008/entries/decision-capacity/>.

Cohen, P. (2002). Untreated addiction imposes an ethical bar to recruiting addicts for non-therapeutic studies of addictive drugs. *Journal of Law, Medicine & Ethics*, *30*, 73–81.

College on Problems of Drug Dependence. (1995). Special report: human subjects issues in drug abuse research. *Drug and Alcohol Dependence*, *37*, 167–175.

Davidson, D. (1980). How is weakness of the will possible? In D. Davidson (Ed.), Essays on actions and events (pp. 21–42). Oxford: Clarendon Press.

Dennett, D. C. (1984). *Elbow room: the varieties of free will worth wanting*. Cambridge, MA: MIT Press.

Di Clemente, C. C. (2006). *Addiction and change*. New York, London: Guilford Press.

Drane, J. F. (1984). Competency to give an informed consent. *Journal of the American Medical Association*, *252* (7), 925–927.

Dunn, L. B. (2006). Capacity to consent to research in schizophrenia: the expanding evidence base. *Behavioral Sciences & the Law*, *24* (4), 431–445.

Elliott, C. (1991). Competence as accountability. *Journal of Clinical Ethics*, *2* (3), 167–171.

Elliott, C. (1999). *A philosophical disease: bioethics, culture, and identity*. London, New York: Routledge.

Elliott, C. (2002). Who holds the leash? *American Journal of Bioethics, 2* (2), 48.

Ellis, A. (1962). *Reason and emotion in psychotherapy.* New York: Lyle Stuart.

Elster, J. (1999). *Strong feelings: emotion, addiction, and human behavior.* Cambridge, MA: MIT Press.

Elster, J., & Skog, O.-J. (Eds.), (1999). Getting hooked: rationality and addiction. Cambridge: Cambridge University Press.

Foddy, B., & Savulescu, J. (2006). Addiction and autonomy: can addicted people consent to the prescription of their drug of addiction? *Bioethics, 20* (1), 1–15.

Freckelton, I. (2002). Choice, rationality, and substance dependence. *American Journal of Bioethics, 2* (2), 60–61.

Freedman, B. (1981). Competence, marginal and otherwise. *International Journal of Law and Psychiatry, 4,* 53–72.

Gardner, E., & David, J. (1999). The neurobiology of chemical addiction. In J. Elster & S. Ole-Jorgen (Eds.), Getting hooked: rationality and addiction (pp. 93–137). Cambridge: Cambridge University Press.

Geppert, C., & Bogenschutz, M. (2009). Pharmacological research on addictions: a framework for ethical and policy. *Journal of Psychoactive Drugs, 41* (1), 49–60.

Grisso, T., & Appelbaum, P. S. (1995). The MacArthur Treatment Competence Study. III. Abilities of patient's to consent to psychiatric and medical treatment. *Law and Human Behavior, 19,* 149–174.

Grisso, T., & Appelbaum, P. S. (1998). *The assessment of decision-making capacity: a guide for physicians and other health professionals.* Oxford: Oxford University Press.

Grisso, T., & Appelbaum, P. S. (2006). Appreciating anorexia: decisional capacity and the role of values. *Philosophy, Psychiatry, & Psychology, 13* (4), 293–297.

Grisso, T., Appelbaum, P. S., Mulvey, E. P., & Fletcher, K. (1995). The MacArthur Treatment Competence Study. II. Measures and abilities related to competence to consent to treatment. *Law and Human Behavior, 19,* 126–148.

Hall, W. (2006). Avoiding potential misuses of addiction brain science. *Addiction (Abingdon, England), 101* (11), 1529–1532.

Hall, W., Carter, L., & Morley, K. I. (2003a). Addiction, neuroscience and ethics. *Addiction (Abingdon, England), 98* (7), 867–870.

Hall, W., Carter, L., & Morley, K. I. (2003b). Heroin addiction and the capacity for consent: a reply to Charland. *Addiction (Abingdon, England), 98* (12), 1775–1776.

Hall, W., Carter, L., & Morley, K. I. (2004). Neuroscience research on the addictions: a prospectus for future ethical and policy analysis. *Addictive Behaviors, 29* (7), 1481–1495.

Harwood, H. J., & Myers, T. G. (2004). *New treatments for addiction: behavioral, ethical, legal, and social questions.* Washington, DC: National Academies Press.

Hyman, S. E. (2007). The neurobiology of addiction: implications for voluntary control of behavior. *American Journal of Bioethics, 7* (1), 8–11.

Jeste, D. V., & Saks, E. (2006). Decisional capacity in mental illness and substance use disorders: empirical database and policy implications. *Behavioral Sciences & the Law, 24* (4), 607–628.

Levy, N. (2006). Autonomy and addiction. *Canadian Journal of Philosophy, 36* (3), 427–447.

Ling, W. (2002). Cynthia's dilemma. *American Journal of Bioethics, 2* (2), 55–56.

Lowenstein, G. (1999). A visceral account of addiction. In J. Elster & S. Ole-Jorgen (Eds.), Getting hooked: rationality and addiction (pp. 235–264). Cambridge: Cambridge University Press.

Mele, A. R. (2004). Volitional disorder and addiction. In J. Radden (Ed.), The philosophy of psychiatry: a companion (pp. 78–88). Oxford: Oxford University Press.

Moberg, P. J., & Kniele, K. (2006). Evaluation of competency: ethical considerations for neuropsychologists. *Applied Neurology, 13* (2), 101–114.

National Bioethics Advisory Commission. (1998). *Report and recommendations of the National Bioethics Advisory Commission. Rockville, MD: National Institutes of Health* (Vol. 1). Research involving persons with mental disorders that may affect decision-making capacity Washington, DC: Academic Press.

O'Brien, C. P. (2002). Commentary: Cynthia's dilemma. *American Journal of Bioethics, 2* (2), 54–55.

Ole-Jorgen, S. 1999. Rationality, irrationality, and addiction—notes on Becker and Murphy's theory of addiction. In J. Elster & S. Ole-Jorgen (Eds.), Getting hooked: rationality and addiction (pp. 173–207). Cambridge: Cambridge University Press.

Panksepp, J. (1998). *Affective neuroscience: the foundations of human and animal emotions.* Oxford: Oxford University Press.

Perneger, T. V., Giner, F., & Mino, A. (1998). Randomised trial of heroin maintenance programme for addicts who fail in conventional drug treatments. *British Medical Journal, 317* (7150), 13–18.

Roberts, L. W. (2002). Addiction and consent. *American Journal of Bioethics, 2* (2), 58–60.

Sander, D., & Scherer, K. (2009). *Oxford companion to emotion and the affective sciences.* Oxford, New York: Oxford University Press.

Sturman, E. D. (2005). The capacity to consent to treatment and research: a review of standardized assessment tools. *Clinical Psychology Review, 25* (7), 954–974.

Tan, J. O. A., Stewart, A., Fitzpatrick, R., & Hope, R. A. (2006). Competence to make treatment decisions in anorexia nervosa: thinking processes and values. *Philosophy, Psychiatry, & Psychology, 13* (4), 267–282.

Vollman, J. (2007). But I don't feel it: values and emotions in the assessment of competence in patients with anorexia nervosa. *Philosophy, Psychiatry, & Psychology, 13* (4), 289–291.

Walker, T. (2008). Giving addicts their drug of choice: the problem of consent. *Bioethics, 22*(6), 314–320.

7   Addiction and Criminal Responsibility

Stephen J. Morse

A Moral Fable from Real Life

Let us begin with a tale of a genuine addict, Mr. Leroy Powell, whose criminal responsibility was addressed in a famous Supreme Court case, *Powell v. Texas* (1968) (all citations are from the case). Although some of the language used is outdated, the description of Powell's condition is consistent with how an alcohol addict's clinical problem would be described today.

In December of 1966 in Austin, Texas, Powell was arrested, charged, and convicted of public intoxication. His defense counsel had argued that because Mr. Powell was afflicted with "the disease of chronic alcoholism . . . his appearance in public [while drunk] was not of his own volition" (517), and thus, to punish Mr. Powell for this symptomatic behavior would be a violation of the Eighth Amendment prohibition of cruel and unusual punishment. The Supreme Court ultimately refused to hold that the Constitution was violated by convicting and punishing Mr. Powell and that there was no constitutional requirement of a compulsion defense to crime. For our purposes, however, the evidence in the case will set the stage for the argument of this chapter.

Mr. Powell's defense was supported by the testimony of an expert psychiatrist, Dr. David Wade, who testified that a "chronic alcoholic" is an "involuntary drinker" who is "powerless not to drink," and who "loses his self-control over his drinking" (518). Based on his examination of Mr. Powell, Dr. Wade concluded that Powell was a "chronic alcoholic" who, "by the time he has reached [the state of intoxication] . . . is not able to control his behavior, and . . . has reached this point because he has an uncontrollable compulsion to drink" (518).

Dr. Wade also opined that Powell lacked "the willpower to resist the constant excessive consumption of alcohol." The good doctor admitted that Powell's first drink when he was sober was a "voluntary exercise of will" but qualified this answer by claiming that alcoholics have a compulsion that is a "very strong influence, an exceedingly strong influence," that clouds their judgment. Finally, Dr. Wade suggested that jailing Powell without treatment would fail to discourage Powell's consumption of alcohol and related problems. One could not find a more clear expression of the medicalized, disease concept of addiction to ethanol.

Powell himself testified about his alcoholism. Indeed, there was no dispute about whether he was a chronic alcoholic. He also testified that he could not stop drinking. Powell's cross-examination concerning the events of the day of his trial is worth quoting in full.

Q: You took that one [drink] at eight o'clock [a.m.] because you wanted to drink?
A: Yes, sir.
Q: And you knew that if you drank it, you could keep on drinking and get drunk?
A: Well, I was supposed to be here on trial, and I didn't take but that one drink.
Q: You knew you had to be here this afternoon, but this morning you took one drink and then you knew that you couldn't afford to drink any more and come to court; is that right?
A: Yes, sir, that's right.
Q: Because you knew what you would do if you kept drinking, that you would finally pass out or be picked up?
A: Yes, sir.
Q: And you didn't want that to happen to you today?
A: No, sir.
Q: Not today?
A: No, sir.
Q: So you only had one drink today?
A: Yes, sir (519–520).

On redirect examination, Powell's attorney elicited further explanation.

Q: Leroy, isn't the real reason why you just had one drink today because you just had enough money to buy one drink?
A: Well, that was just give to me.
Q: In other words, you didn't have any money with which you could buy drinks yourself?
A: No, sir, that was give to me.
Q: And that's really what controlled the amount you drank this morning, isn't it?
A: Yes, sir.

Q: Leroy, when you start drinking, do you have any control over how many drinks you can take?
A: No, sir (520).

Powell wanted to drink and had that first drink, but despite that last answer, his compulsion did *not* cause him to engage in the myriad lawful and unlawful means he might easily have used to obtain more alcohol if his craving was desperately compulsive. And no one, I hope, wishes to suggest that poverty is a useful treatment for chronic alcoholism.

Addicts are not automatons. Even if they suffer from a chronic and relapsing brain disease, as one dominant model of addiction claims, if addicts have good enough reason not to seek and use, they do not. The questions are whether those reasons are available to them when they seek and use drugs or whether they are compelled to seek and use drugs even if they recognize and endorse the reasons not to.

Powell's case illustrates the issues this chapter will consider. What is addiction? What are the criteria for criminal responsibility, including the criteria for compulsion? Must the law adopt a medicalized view of addiction? Only after answering those questions can we finally turn to the ultimate question of how and in what cases addiction affects criminal responsibility.

The analysis begins by contrasting medical and moral views of addiction and how such views influence responsibility and policy analysis. It suggests that because addiction always involves action and action can always be morally evaluated, we must independently decide whether addicts do not meet responsibility criteria rather than begging the question and deciding by the label of "disease" or "moral weakness." To pursue this independent analysis, the chapter then turns to the criteria for criminal responsibility. This section shows that the criteria for criminal responsibility, like the criteria for addiction, are all behavioral, and therefore any scientific information about addiction must be "translated" into the law's folk psychological criteria. Before turning to the relation between addiction and criminal responsibility, the chapter then turns to an analysis of dangerous distractions in legal responsibility analysis. Among these distractions are the views that free will is a component of criminal responsibility and that causation of behavior is per se an excusing condition.

With the criteria for responsibility in place and dangerous distractions removed, the chapter then turns to the direct relation between addiction and criminal responsibility. It argues that most addicts retain sufficient rational and control capacities at the relevant times to be held responsible, especially for crimes that are not part of the definition of addiction itself. The chapter concludes by considering the social policy considerations addiction raises and suggests that there is good reason to excuse or mitigate addicts for the crimes of purchase and possession for personal use.

What Is Addiction?

As honest experts will admit, there is no consensual definition of "addiction" within any of the specialty disciplines that study the condition, and there is no definitive biological marker for it. There is broad agreement, however, that persistent and apparently compulsive seeking and using of drugs are the core phenomena to be explained. Some would include the presence of extremely deleterious consequences, but as we shall see, that appears to be a criterion for the requirement that the seeking and using is compulsive. To this core, many experts would add the subjective experience of "craving," but this is more controversial. Thus, the definition most people use is behavioral, including actions and mental states (Nestler, 2000).

Two ways of thinking about this condition dominate legal policy thinking. The medical model treats addiction as a chronic and relapsing brain disease. The definitional criteria are just signs and symptoms, akin to the signs and symptoms of other medical or psychiatric disorders. The legal model, in contrast, does not deny that addiction may be a disorder, but it nonetheless notes that the behavioral criteria indisputably include human action, such as seeking and using drugs. The implications for criminal responsibility of the two ways of looking at addiction are of utmost importance, but understanding the moral and legal responsibility of people for becoming addicted and for criminal conduct associated with their addictions has unfortunately been hindered by inadequate or superficial understanding of how explanatory models of addiction relate to responsibility. Even sophisticated people tend to think that the "man with the golden arm" is somehow an automaton, a puppet pulled by the narcotic strings of a biological disease, and that therefore the addict is not responsible for actions associated with his addiction. Evidence linking a genetic predisposition or neurological abnormality for this condition contributes powerfully, often confusingly, to this type of thinking (Keller, 2005). Conversely, many people think that addiction is purely a result of moral weakness. The various characterizations of addiction may be striking, heuristically rich, and contain much truth. For the law's purposes, however, the metaphors and models often obscure rather than clarify issues of criminal responsibility and of social policy generally in response to the deviant behavior many addicts exhibit. Therefore, let us first delve a bit more deeply into the medical and legal views.

The concepts of illness and disease have powerful associations in our culture, most of which are inconsistent with the sufferer's responsibility for the features of the illness. People can, of course, be responsible for initially contracting or risking contracting diseases. A person who is overweight, does not exercise, and smokes surely is responsible for risking hypertension; the person who in inappropriate circumstances engages in unprotected sexual activity surely risks contracting sexually transmitted diseases. And a person who suffers from many diseases can ameliorate the consequences by intentionally adhering to a prescribed medical regimen. But hypertension and infections are themselves mechanisms. The sufferer cannot terminate all the signs and symptoms of the disease simply by intentionally choosing to cease being hypertensive or infected.

Despite the potential contribution of human agency to the cause and maintenance of some diseases, no one denies that these are fundamentally diseases. Moreover, with many and perhaps most diseases, the sufferer is not responsible for contracting the disease, and for many diseases there is little or nothing the sufferer can do to help, other than to seek and cooperate with professional help and to wait for the disease to run its course. Although people sometimes can be complicit in their own diseases, the disease model is so powerful that people who are ill are not in general considered responsible for the signs, symptoms, and consequences. The dominant image of people with diseases is that they are the victims of pathological mechanisms who deserve sympathy and help and do not deserve condemnation.

The brain disease model of addiction borrows heavily from the powerful moral and social associations of the general concepts of illness and disease. It claims that addiction is a chronic and relapsing brain disease. Supported by highly technical anatomical, physiological, and genetic research demonstrating that addictions appear to have a biological basis, the brain disease model inevitably suggests that the addict is sick. The signs and symptoms of the disease—primarily compulsive drug seeking and use—are seemingly the mechanistic consequence of genetically driven pathological brain anatomy and physiology over which the addict has no control once prolonged use has caused the pathology. The following are recent excellent examples of this mode of thought that have appeared in prestigious journals. The first is by an eminent neuroscientist:

Dramatic advances over the past two decades in both the neurosciences and the behavioral sciences have revolutionized our understanding of drug abuse and addiction. Scientists have identified neural circuits that subsume the actions of every known drug of abuse, and they have specified common pathways that are affected by almost all such drugs. Researchers have also identified and cloned the major receptors for virtually every abusable drug, as well as the natural ligands for most of those receptors. In addition, they have elaborated many of the biochemical cascades within the cell that follow receptor activation by drugs. Research has also begun to reveal major differences between the brains of addicted and nonaddicted individuals and to indicate some common elements of addiction, regardless of the substance. (Leshner, 1997, 45)

The second is by an addiction researcher.

Addiction is a disorder of the brain's reward system. Functional imaging shows the vulnerable circuitry for addiction originating in the paleocortex. Paradoxically, humankind's greatest adaptive advantage, the neocortex, responsible for the phenomenon of consciousness, is at best only minimally protective from addictive disease and may pose a hurdle for recovery. Unlike most medical disorders, in addiction a net effect of supraphysiologic reward, impaired inhibition, or both paradoxically leads the limbic drive system to reinforce exposure to the disease vector. This is in direct violation of the principle of survival of the species. In individuals with underlying vulnerabilities, limbic drive progressively recruits neocortical function to protect continued access to abused substances, the polar opposite of self-preservation. (Gastfriend, 2005, 1514)

The first example, despite the concession to the behavioral sciences in its first sentence, describes solely biological advances, and the remainder of the article fails to note one "dramatic advance" in the behavioral understanding of addiction. The second example treats the intentional conduct of the addict solely as the product of brain mechanisms. There is no person present, no agent acting when the "organism" seeks and uses.

For those whose thinking is driven by the brain disease model, this image is applauded and promoted. For example, an editorial in the *American Journal of Psychiatry* opens as follows:

American psychiatry has made remarkable progress in recategorizing the addictive disorders from moral failures to brain diseases, but the need for community education continues. The concept of moral failure is by no means gone from the discussion of addictive disorders, as evidenced by our country's investment in criminal justice rather than treatment (Kosten, 1998, 11).

Such thinking can reflect in part battles over turf, funding, and the like, but it is undoubtedly sincerely motivated.

Virtually all mechanistic models of problems that bedevil society, including the medical model, are alluring because they imply that there are technical, "clean" solutions. Fix the "pathological mechanism," fix the social problem it produces; do not worry about refractory human behavior and messy moral accountability. The medical model is used here for rhetorical purposes because it is so dominant and because there is heartening progress in the biological understanding of addiction. But any black-box mechanical model of the phenomenon of addiction would have done as well.

The concept of compulsion or something like it is crucial to the medical model because without it addiction is just a habit like any other. Despite the current biologizing within the medical approach and scientific advances (e.g., Kasanetz et al., 2010), however, there is still no clear understanding of the biology of compulsively and persistently seeking and using substances. Once again, seeking and using are actions, not mechanisms. An adequate definition of compulsion that applies to action rather than to mechanism is needed to explore compelled action's biological basis, but such a definition does not exist.

The conclusion that the addict's behavior is compulsive is usually based on two types of evidence. The first is the person's objectively unverifiable self-report that he felt compelled, could not control himself, could not help himself, desperately craved, and the like. The second is an inference from all the negative and often horrendous social, occupational, health, and legal consequences that flow from persistent seeking and using, especially if the person claims that he wishes to stop. The inference is that the person would not continue to set back his own interests so disastrously by seeking and using unless those activities were in some sense compulsive. The current favored biological theory for addiction—a complex genetic vulnerability to have the neural systems of reward that are usually used for survival usurped by drugs—is certainly consistent with the view that some persistent drug users find it very rewarding to continue use, but it does not prove that the behavior is compulsive. Biological causation, even abnormal biological causation is not the equivalent of compulsion. If it were, all behavior would be compelled, but this is clearly false. An adequate independent definition of compelled action is crucial. We will return to the meaning of compelled action in the section below that relates addiction to criminal responsibility.

Criminal law's concept of the person, including the addict, is the antithesis of the medical model's mechanistic concept. Although all honest people will admit that biological and environmental variables beyond the person's rational control can cause an agent to be the type of person who is vulnerable to addiction and predisposed to commit crimes or can put the agent in the kind of environment that predisposes people to addiction and criminal activity, the law ultimately views the criminal wrongdoer as an agent and not simply as a passive victim who manifests pathological mechanisms. In *Powell*, for example, the Supreme Court held that a defense of "compulsion symptomatic of a disease" was not constitutionally required. The Court wrote that public drunkenness was behavior and thus unlike the simple status of being addicted; and it refused to hold that criminal blame and punishment were constitutionally impermissible under the circumstances. Indeed, Justice Marshall's plurality opinion observed that it was not irrational to respond to public drunkenness with the criminal sanction. The plurality also pointed out that Powell's own cross-examination at trial suggested that he was not powerless to stop drinking after he had taken his first drink.

As will be explained further below, unless either the person does not act or an excusing condition is present, agency entails moral and legal responsibility that warrants blame and punishment. Suffering from a disease *simpliciter*, such as addiction or schizophrenia, does not itself mean that the defendant did not act or that an excusing condition obtained, although diseases and other causes may negate action or produce an excusing condition, such as gross irrationality.

Action can always be evaluated morally, even if it is symptomatic of a disease state (Morse, 2007a). Most mental and physical diseases—even severe disorders—suffered by people who violate the criminal law do not have these exculpating effects because they do not sufficiently affect rational agency (Morse, 1999). Even if addiction is properly characterized as an illness, addicts may nonetheless be capable of being guided by good reasons, including the incentives law can provide (Satel & Goodwin, 1998). Whether they do have this capacity is a question that must be answered rather than begged by use of the disease model without further explanation. Indeed, it is an inconvenient fact for the disease concept that so many addicted people cease being addicts by intentionally quitting seeking and using without the aid of treatment (Heyman, 2009). Even if they relapse, they stopped being addicts during the period when they intentionally were not using. Few other diseases can be put in remission or cured in this manner.

In short, here is what we undeniably know about addictions. Some people who ingest drugs begin after some time persistently to seek and use drugs in a manner that they describe and observers infer is compelled and that the seeking and using then almost always creates further, often horrendous consequences for the user. Furthermore, some addicts intentionally stop being addicted. There is an enormous amount of other research about the biological, psychological, and environmental variables that influence the development, persistence, and termination of addiction. There is also a large body of often-conflicting research on how addiction affects executive function and other cognitive capacities. Such evidence might prove important in deciding an individual case. There is great behavioral heterogeneity among addicts, however, and our question is broader: Should addiction per se excuse an addict from immoral and illegal behavior? For these purposes, the statements at the beginning of the paragraph are the bedrock, uncontroversial observations. Why does it matter if we conceptualize drug-related problems medically as a brain disease, as the product of genetic predisposition and usurped or "hijacked" neural mechanisms of reward? Drugs undoubtedly cause vast and often catastrophic personal and social misery, and perhaps the program of research and intervention the biological disease model implies can ameliorate the misery. Why should internecine disputes among philosophers of biology and medicine about the boundaries of the disease concept, or the law's model of the person, or the pure moralizing of many stand in the way? They should not, of course; nothing should stand in the way of useful research and interventions. Unfortunately, however, otherwise useful images or models can have negative consequences if they exceed their rightful boundaries. Wrong or misleading images in an inapt domain can produce misguided policies.

Addiction always includes actions. Consequently, how those actions should be morally, socially, and legally evaluated is always an open question. The question should not be begged by any model's pre-suppositions. Legal policy is a matter of practical reason, of how we want to live together. It is not a matter of theoretical reason, a truth about the world. As long as the concept of action retains moral and legal significance, biological or other scientific understandings of the underlying mechanisms are not likely to have self-evidently necessitated legal consequences, although such understanding may provide guides to better policy.

The Legal Criteria for Criminal Responsibility

The criteria for criminal responsibility, like the criteria for addiction, are entirely behavioral, including actions and mental states. An agent is criminally responsible if the following six criteria are met. First, the agent must perform a prohibited intentional act in a state of reasonably integrated consciousness. Second, virtually all serious crimes require that the person had a further mental state regarding the prohibited harm. One definition of murder, for example, is the intentional killing of another human being. Thus, to be prima facie guilty of murder, the person must have intentionally performed some act that kills, such as shooting or knifing, and it must have been his intent to kill when he shot or knifed. If the agent does not act at all because his bodily movement is not intentional—for example, a reflex or spasmodic movement—then there is no violation of the prohibition. There is also no violation in cases in which the further mental state required by the definition is lacking. For example, if the defendant's intentional killing action kills only carelessly, then the defendant may be guilty of some homicide crime but not of intentional murder.

Criminal responsibility is not complete if the defendant's behavior satisfies the definition of the crime. Third, at the time of the crime the defendant must have had the reasonable capacity for rationality. Fourth, the defendant must have had the reasonable capacity for self-control (although the fourth is more controversial than the third). Fifth, the defendant must not have been acting under duress, coercion, or compulsion, which for our purposes can be treated the same. And sixth, the defendant must act unjustifiably. A justification exists if otherwise wrongful action would be right or permissible under the circumstances. For example, intentionally killing someone in self-defense who is wrongfully trying to kill you is certainly legally permissible, and many think it is right.

The last four criteria are always raised negatively as defenses to crime, such as legal insanity (arising from a rationality or self-control deficit), duress (arising from compulsion), and self-defense. In the cases of criteria three, four, and five, which are termed "excuses," the defendant has acted wrongly, but there is reason to believe he is nonetheless not a responsible agent. In cases of justification, there is nothing wrong with the agent. He is responsible but has acted properly under the circumstances. Addiction is always considered a potential excusing or mitigating condition, so this chapter will not address justification again. Note that the third and fourth criteria are expressed as capacities. If an agent possessed a legally relevant capacity but simply did not exercise it at the time of committing the crime or was responsible for undermining his capacity, no defense will be allowed. The degree of incapacity or coercion required for an excuse is a normative question that can have different legal responses depending on a culture's moral conceptions and material circumstances.

Some may think that the third and fourth criteria—the capacity for self-control and the absence of coercion—are the same, but for purposes of addressing the relation between addiction and responsibility, it is helpful to distinguish them. The capacity for self-control, some would say "will power," is conceived of as a trait possessed by the individual that can of course be influenced by external events, but that is nonetheless an aspect of the person (Holton, 2009). In some cases the capacity for control is poor characterologically; in other cases it may be undermined by variables that are not the defendant's fault, such as mental disorder. As we shall see in the section on the relation of addiction to responsibility, the meaning of this capacity is fraught. In contrast, compulsion exists if the defendant were metaphorically compelled to act by being placed in a "do-it-or-else," hard-choice situation. For example, suppose that a miscreant gunslinger threatens to kill me unless I kill another entirely innocent agent. I have no right to kill the third person, but if I do it to save my own life, I may be granted the excuse of duress. Note that in cases of metaphorical compulsion, unlike cases of no action, the agent does act intentionally.

This account of criminal responsibility is most tightly linked to retributive justifications of punishment, which hold that punishment is not justified unless the offender morally deserves punishment because the offender was at fault and responsible and that the offender never should be punished more than he deserves. It is generally conceded that, with exceptions that need not detain us and prove the point, desert is at least a necessary precondition for punishment in Anglo-American law. The account is also consistent with consequential justifications for punishment, such as general deterrence. No offender, however, including an addict, should be punished unless he at least deserves such punishment. Even if good consequences might be achieved by punishing nonresponsible addicts or by punishing responsible addicts more than they deserve, such punishment would require very weighty justification in a system that takes desert seriously.

Any potential relation of addiction to criminal responsibility will have to be addressed to the first five criteria, the first two of which define crimes and the next three of which deal with potential excusing conditions even if a crime's definition is met by the defendant's behavior. Note that all the criteria are essentially folk psychological and address acts and mental states. This means that the law's model of the person is an acting, conscious, potentially intentional, and potentially rational and well-controlled agent who can be responsive to reason. Responsibility concepts involve acting agents and not social structures, underlying psychological variables, brains, or nervous systems. The latter types of variables may shed light on whether the folk-psychological responsibility criteria are met or not, but they must always be translated into the law's five folk-psychological criteria. For example, demonstrating that an addict has a genetic vulnerability or a neurotransmitter defect tells the law nothing per se about whether an addict is responsible. Such scientific evidence must be probative of the law's criteria, and demonstrating this requires an argument about how it is probative.

Before we move to the relation between addiction and criminal responsibility, it is important to clarify some false starts and distractions that bedevil analysis of criminal responsibility of addicts or any other offenders. With that gnarled underbrush cleared, we will be ready finally to consider directly the relation of addiction to criminal responsibility.

False Starts and Dangerous Distractions

This section considers four false and distracting claims that are sometimes made about the responsibility of addicts (and others): (1) the truth of determinism undermines genuine responsibility; (2) causation, and especially abnormal causation, of behavior entails that the behavior must be excused; (3) causation is the equivalent of compulsion; and (4) addicts are automatons.

The alleged incompatibility of determinism and responsibility is foundational. Determinism is not a continuum concept that applies to various individuals in various degrees. There is no partial or selective determinism. Responsibility is possible or it is not, *tout court,* if the universe is deterministic. If human beings are fully subject to the causal laws of the universe, as a thoroughly physicalist, naturalist worldview holds, then many philosophers claim that "ultimate" responsibility is impossible from the start (e.g., Pereboom, 2001; Strawson, 1989). On the other hand, plausible "compatibilist" theories suggest that responsibility is possible in a deterministic universe (Wallace, 1994). There seems no resolution to this debate in sight, but our moral and legal practices do not treat everyone or no one as responsible. Determinism cannot be guiding our practices. If one wants to excuse addicts because they are genetically and neurally determined or determined for any other reason to be addicts or to commit crimes related to their addictions, one is committed to negating the possibility of responsibility for anything.

Our criminal responsibility criteria and practices have nothing to do with determinism or with the necessity of having so-called "free will" (Morse, 2007b). The capacity for libertarian freedom, the capacity to cause one's own behavior uncaused by anything other than oneself, is neither a criterion for any criminal law doctrine nor foundational for criminal responsibility. Criminal responsibility involves evaluation of intentional, conscious, and potentially rational human action. And almost no one in the debate about determinism and free will or responsibility argues that we are not conscious, intentional, potentially rational creatures when we act. Some neuroscientists and other scientists claim that "conscious will" is an illusion, but these arguments are at present conceptually and empirically unpersuasive, and they certainly have gained no acceptance in the law (Morse, 2007c). We may be deterministically caused to be the type of creature that acts intentionally, but determinism is not inconsistent conceptually or logically with the possibility of mind-brain causation of behavior. The truth of determinism does not entail that actions and nonactions are indistinguishable and that there is no distinction between rational and nonrational actions or compelled and uncompelled actions. Children are less rational than adults; most people most of the time do not act under severe threats. Our current responsibility concepts and practices use criteria consistent with and independent of the truth of determinism.

A related confusion is that once a nonintentional causal explanation has been identified for action, the person must be excused. In other words, the claim is that causation and responsibility are inconsistent and that causation per se is an excusing condition. This is sometimes called the "causal theory of excuse." Thus, if one identifies genetic, neurophysiological, or other causes for behavior, then allegedly the person is not responsible. In a thoroughly physical world, however, this claim either is identical to the determinist critique of responsibility and furnishes a foundational critique of all responsibility or is simply an error. I term this the "fundamental psycholegal error" because it is erroneous and incoherent as a description of our actual doctrines and practices (Morse, 1994). Noncausation of behavior is not and could not be a criterion for responsibility because all behaviors, like all other phenomena, are caused. Causation, even by abnormal physical variables, is not per se an excusing condition. Abnormal physical variables, such as neurotransmitter deficiencies, may cause a genuine excusing condition, such as the lack of rational capacity, but then the lack of rational capacity, not causation, is doing the excusing work. If causation were an excuse, no one would be responsible for any action. Unless proponents of the causal theory of excuse can furnish a convincing reason why causation per se excuses, we have no reason to jettison the criminal law's responsibility doctrines and practices that use other criteria for responsibility and excuse.

Third, causation is not the equivalent of lack of self-control capacity or compulsion. All behavior is caused, but only some defendants lack control capacity or acted under compulsion. Moreover, causation is not the equivalent of compulsion because lack of self-control and compulsion are normative standards. They apply only to some defendants. If causation were the equivalent of compulsion, all defendants would be compelled, and no one would be responsible for any criminal behavior. This is clearly not the criminal law's view.

A last confusion is that addicts are automatons whose behavioral signs are not human actions. We have addressed this issue before, but it is worth reemphasizing that even if compulsive seeking and using substances are the signs of a disease, they are nonetheless human actions and thus distinguishable from purely mechanical signs and symptoms, such as spasms.

Now, with a description of addiction and responsibility criteria in place and with an understanding of false starts, let us turn to the direct relation of addiction to criminal responsibility.

Addiction and Responsibility

I begin by making some basic distinctions among the types of phenomena for which addicts might conceivably be held responsible and among the types of crimes for which addiction might play some type of causal role. Then I turn to the responsibility of addicts for becoming addicted and for the foreseeable consequences of becoming addicted. Next I consider whether addiction bears on the act or mental state requirements for responsibility. Then, I consider whether addiction should be a full or partial excuse for criminal behavior. Finally, in this section I explore whether society or socioeconomic conditions should be held responsible for addiction. The ultimate conclusion is that most addicts should be held responsible for most crimes other than simple purchase and possession, for purely personal use and for use itself. In general addiction does not sufficiently undermine either cognitive or control capacities to excuse the addict for other crimes, and virtually all addicts can be held responsible for not taking the steps to prevent them from engaging in addiction-related crime.

Introductory Distinctions

Roughly speaking, addiction has four associated aspects or phenomena that might be objects of responsibility ascription: anatomical states, physiological states, psychological states, and actions (Fingarette & Hasse, 1979). Among these only action is a potentially appropriate object of moral and legal responsibility ascription and a justification for criminal punishment; status is neither an object of ascription nor a justification for blame and punishment (Robinson v. California, 1962). For the most part, people are held morally and legally responsible only for actions that are capable of being guided by reason. Although anatomical and physiological states, including one's genetic makeup, may be evaluated as desirable or undesirable, they are entirely or largely the product of mechanistic processes that are not under the agent's rational control. Those anatomical and physiological states that are signs of addiction are simply statuses of the agent's physical body, whether or not they are directly controllable through the person's rational agency. Similarly, a psychological state that is symptomatic of addiction, such as craving (or, according to many, ambivalence), is likewise just a status that is mechanistically produced by the underlying anatomical or physiological states associated with addiction and, in many cases, by environmental cues. Anatomical, physiological, and psychological states are not intentional human actions (albeit some mental states or processes can be produced intentionally). People may be responsible for the anatomical, physiological, and psychological states associated with addiction if they are responsible for becoming addicted, but the criminal law still would not punish those states because they are solely statuses.

The primary behavioral signs of addiction—seeking and using substances (Camí & Farré, 2003)—and other criminal behaviors related to the addiction are intentional human actions, even if the former are also signs of a disease that has genetic, anatomical, physiological, and psychological causes. Indeed, all intentional action has genetic, anatomical, and physiological causes, whether or not the action is the sign of a disease. The addict has an exceptionally powerful desire to consume the addictive substance, often described as craving, believes that consuming it will satisfy that craving by avoiding pain, causing pleasure, or some combination of the two, and therefore forms and acts on the intention to seek and to use the substance. Such explanatory practical syllogisms are the mark of all intentional actions.

Intentional action is the primary object of responsibility ascriptions. Seeking and using and other associated actions may therefore be morally and legally assessed. To assume that the addict is not responsible for addiction-related behavior just because it has biological causes or because the action is the sign of a disease generally commits the fundamental psycholegal error and therefore begs the question of responsibility. It is natural to think people are not responsible for signs and symptoms because mostly they are statuses mechanistically caused. But human action is distinguishable. It is not simply a status. The addict must be evaluated as an acting agent, a person who acts for reasons and not simply as a biophysical mechanism.

Crimes addicts commit may be divided into three classes. The first are those that involve behaviors that are criterial for addiction itself, such as buying, possessing, and using substances. The relation between the addiction and the criminal conduct is analytic in such cases. The second class comprises crimes committed in support of the addiction or as a noncriterial consequence of addiction, such as theft, burglary, or robbery to obtain the money to buy drugs, or Powell's public disorderly conduct. Crimes committed for dealers who will provide drugs as payment also fall into this category. Crimes in the second category may of course be overdetermined, driven not only by the desire for drugs but also for the pleasures that criminal behavior provides to many. The third category encompasses crimes committed by addicts who do not seem driven by addiction, but who may or may not be influenced by an addiction-related milieu or lifestyle. The relation in such cases is quite indirect. For example, addicts who are part of an addiction-related gang may opportunistically or premeditatedly commit crimes to protect turf rather than directly to support their habits.

The reason to establish this categorization is that on both desert and consequential grounds, the law might well treat the responsibility of the addict differently depending on the type of crime committed.

Responsibility for Becoming Addicted

No matter what answer we may obtain after considering whether an addict is responsible when his actions are motivated in part or wholly by his addiction, if the addict is responsible for being in that state, it is possible that analysis of responsibility need go no further.

Let us start with preaddiction use. Before they reach the age of reason, some children and many early and middle adolescents have substantial experience with alcohol, nicotine, and other drugs, and a small number of them become problem users. Moreover, early experimentation with substances such as nicotine is highly predictive of later behavior that risks health. Still, the simplifying assumption will be made that virtually all people do not have their first substantial experience with potentially addicting substances until they are mid- to late adolescents, an age at which there is reasonable evidence that adolescents are in general formally cognitively indistinguishable from adults, but are nonetheless on average psychosocially less mature, including more willing to take risks (Morse, 1997; Steinberg, Cauffman, Woolard, Graham, & Banich, 2009a). There has been criticism of the findings and ecological validity of the studies purporting to demonstrate such differences (Fischer, Stein, & Heikkinen, 2009), but let us assume that they are reasonably valid (Steinberg, Cauffman, Woolard, Graham, & Banich, 2009b). Nonetheless, the differences are not so large as to preclude responsibility. For example, mid- to late adolescents can be held criminally responsible either through the juvenile court's delinquency jurisdiction or if they are tried as adults.

By the age of reason any competent person, presumably including most mid- and late adolescents, knows generally about the dangers of addicting substances. Most people who use potentially addicting substances do not become addicts, but between 15% and 17% do (Deroche-Gamonet, Belin, & Piazza, 2004). Whether one considers this a high or a low risk is a normative question. On the other hand, people may overestimate the benefits of drug use and underestimate the risks of becoming addicted, especially how bad it will feel to be addicted (Elster, 1999). Experience with and empathy for those already addicted are simply no substitutes for the real experience. Consequently, perhaps addicts are not fully responsible for their addictions because they operate with insufficient information.

This claim appears plausible and not unlike one objection to advanced directives for health care. For example, if one has never faced death or has never faced it while fully competent, how does the person know what he would really want under the circumstances? Although plausible, the claim that nonaddicted drug users have insufficient information about the dangers of drug use seems too strong. There is sufficiently good information as a result of both observation and indirect sources about the perils of addiction to warrant the conclusion that those who take drugs understand the risks sufficiently to be held responsible if addiction ensues. After all, as long as people have general normative competence, including the ability to gather relevant information, perfect information is hardly required for responsibility.

One can deny that any drug use is rational because all drug use is immoral and choosing immorality is always irrational. Claiming generically that immorality is irrational is philosophically controversial, of course, and in this specific context it suggests a highly moralistic, virtue ethics. Why, precisely, is limited experimentation with drugs or more general recreational use immoral? (Husak, 1992; Hough, 1994). Because it feels good? Does all such use degrade the moral personality? Perhaps so. But, after all, limited initial experience genuinely hooks almost no one—

even if the experimental or recreational user is a member of a genetically or socially at-risk population and especially if the diagnostic brain changes almost always require repeated use (Kalivas & Volkow, 2005).

The usual response to claims that experimentation or recreational use is not necessarily irrational is that the process of addiction is insidious. No single instance of use seems to cross a threshold; the process is instead stealthily additive, a slippery slope. At some point, however, the addict is hooked without realizing it. Because no initial user can predict whether and when he specifically will become addicted, it is always irrational to start or to continue, even if one is not yet hooked.

There is truth to this response, but the insidiousness of the addiction process is well known generally and proto-addicts are usually aware that they are developing a problem before the problem becomes a diagnosable addiction. They may, of course, be "in denial" or using other defense mechanisms, such as rationalization, to avoid insight into their own conditions, but the use of defense mechanisms—an imperfect shield at best—is not an excusing condition that morality and law will recognize when serious harms occur. Again, one need not act on perfect information to be responsible. It is difficult to resist the conclusions that most and perhaps all users prior to addiction have some awareness of the risk of potential addiction and that preaddictive use is conduct for which the user is responsible. Consequently, it is also difficult to resist concluding that most addicts are responsible for becoming addicted.

Most addictions probably occur as a result of conscious and not-so-conscious indifference to the risk of becoming addicted, but plausibly it may be rational in some cases to choose intentionally to become an addict and to enter the addictive "life." This claim should be distinguished from the controversial arguments made by Gary Becker and others that addiction is itself rational (Becker, 1996; Leitzel, 2008). My argument is that it can be rational to choose to become irrational, assuming, *arguendo*, that at least some addicts are irrational about their lives when they are addicted.

Imagine a young person who has lived an extraordinarily deprived life and who therefore has little human capital and few prospects. It is possible that the person could acquire the life skills and education needed to beat the odds, but rational calculation would suggest that the odds are overwhelmingly against success. In such circumstances one can easily imagine that a life of intermittent "highs" or oblivion, for example, would be preferable to a clean, straight life, despite the threats of poverty, disease, and prison. Such a life would be limited but made manageable with the use of substances to help ignore or alleviate the misery of existence. Choosing such a life would be quite rational (although society should do all it can to change the odds for those in such situations). On the other hand, many addicts do not enjoy the high and oblivion that drugs produce, and one cannot know in advance what kind of addict one will be.

Even if consciously risking or intentionally choosing to become an addict is not rational behavior, responsibility for conduct does not require acting for good, rational reasons. It is sufficient that the agent retain the general capacity for rationality, the capacity to know the facts and to grasp and be guided by the relevant reasons that pertain in the situation. Some addicts may lose this capacity after becoming addicted, but that is a different issue that is addressed below. Until addiction occurs, and perhaps thereafter, there is little reason to believe that otherwise responsible agents do not retain this general capacity.

Finally, few people are compelled to become addicted. Peer pressure to experiment may be common in adolescence and early adulthood, but it seldom takes a form that would justify a compulsion excuse. Initial use is almost always intentional and in most cases rational because virtually no one is immediately hooked or harmed (and most people who use frequently are not addicts [Warner et al., 1995] or generally endangered). The user tries the substance to please friends, for the thrill of experimenting or being on the edge, for the pleasure or arousal the substance produces, and for a host of other reasons that do not suggest excusing irrationality. Moreover, almost no one is literally forced to become an addict by the involuntary administration of substances. In conclusion, most people who become addicts may fairly be held responsible to a substantial degree for becoming addicted.

To the extent that addicts seek to use their addiction as a mitigating or excusing circumstance when they are charged with crimes related to the addiction, they become vulnerable to the claim that they have caused the condition of their own excuse and, therefore, should not be excused. This is a form of strict liability, however, and becoming an addict is distinguishable from committing crimes once one is addicted. Very few would in fact foresee committing specific crimes, although they may be aware that the addicted life poses risks of illness, poverty, and criminality. The only crimes one may specifically foresee would be crimes of buying, possession, and use in the case of people addicted to illicit substances. For those addicted to arguably the most dangerous drug, ethanol, there may be no specific awareness of the risk of future criminality, except, perhaps, driving under the influence. Indeed, in some cases, such as adherence to a properly prescribed regime of addictive analgesics, becoming addicted may be entirely lawful. In short, even if addicts are mostly responsible for becoming addicted and may be aware of the general risks that addiction may pose, this responsibility is different from the responsibility necessary to be culpable for specific crimes. As suggested below, the better reason to hold most addicts criminally responsible most of the time, *however* they became addicted, is that most of the time they retain a sufficient capacity for rationality to be held responsible.

Once addicted, should addicts be responsible for use and further drug-related activity? By definition, addicts—or anyway most of them—experience subjective craving and compulsion to seek and use drugs. In some cases withdrawal also might be feared, but most addicts know that the physical symptoms are manageable, and for some of the "hardest" drugs, addicts experience no physical withdrawal or any withdrawal syndrome at all (Greenfield & Hennessy, 2004; Haney, 2004). Does addiction negate action or mental state? More important, if compulsion and lack of the capacity for rationality are the law's primary excusing conditions, as is standardly claimed (Morse, 2007b), do craving and compulsion to use addictive substances or to engage in other addiction-related crimes provide a compulsion or rationality excuse?

Act and Mental State (*Mens Rea*) Requirements for Responsibility

This section first considers in more detail the claim already made that the behaviors of addicts are indeed actions and not mechanisms. Then it turns to the relation of addiction to the criminal law's *mens rea* requirement.

Addiction and Action   Although biological models and the discovery of biological causes imply that the addict's symptomatic behaviors are solely mechanisms, this is not true. Compulsive states are marked by allegedly overwhelming desires or cravings, but whether the cravings are produced by faulty biology, including genetic predispositions or neural defects, faulty psychology, faulty environment, or some combination of the three, a desire is just a desire, and its satisfaction by seeking and using is human action. This is true even if addicts have special difficulty using good judgment to undermine their undesirable desires (Holton, 2009). The addict desires, broadly, either the pleasure of intoxication, the avoidance of the pain of withdrawal or inner tension, or both. The addict believes that using the substance will satisfy the desire and consequently forms the intention to seek and to use the substance.

To attempt to demonstrate that people suffering from compulsive states are similar to mechanisms, the following type of analogy is often used. Imagine that a person is hanging by the fingernails from a cliff over a very deep chasm. The hapless cliffhanger is strong enough to hold on for a while, but not strong enough to save his life by pulling himself up. As time passes and gravity and muscle physiology do their work, he inevitably weakens, and it becomes harder and harder to hang on. Finally it becomes impossible, and the cliffhanger falls to his death. We are asked to believe that the operation of compulsive desires or cravings is like the combined effect of gravity and muscle physiology. At first the hapless addict can perhaps resist, but inevitably he weakens and satisfies the desire for drugs.

Brief reflection demonstrates that the analogy is flawed as an explanation of why compulsive states are "just like" mechanisms. Unlike action to satisfy a desire, the fall is a genuine mechanism. Holding on indefinitely is physically impossible, and the ultimate failure of strength is not intentional. Imagine the following counterexample: a vicious gunslinger trails the addict closely and threatens to kill him instantly if he seeks or uses drugs. Assuming that the addict wants to live as much as the cliffhanger does, no addict would yield to the desire. Conversely, even if the same gunslinger threatened to shoot the cliffhanger immediately if he started to fall, he will fall every time. Of course our liberal society does not force or even permit addicts to employ such a self-management technique. Moreover, ascriptions of responsibility would appear unfair if such powerful self-management techniques were necessary. Nonetheless, the counterexample as in Leroy Powell's case indicates that the addict's behavior is not a mechanism.

An addict is not a cliffhanger, of course, so let us consider some closer analogies, such as a powerful, persistent itch, or an increasingly full bladder, or the motor and verbal tics of those suffering from Tourette disorder. It can be damnably hard not to scratch an itch, even if scratching is contra-indicated. An increasingly full bladder can cause dreadful discomfort and an overwhelming feeling of the need to void. The premonitory buildup of tension that precedes and is relieved by tic behavior among those suffering from Tourette syndrome is usually intense and far more bothersome than the tics themselves. In all cases the "pressure" to satisfy the desire, to end the discomfort, can be immense. But even in such cases the agent will be to some degree reward sensitive or reason responsive. The gun at the head will work again. If people with itches, full bladders, or pre-tic tension satisfy the desire to rid themselves of the itch, discomfort, or tension, surely their behavior will be action and not mechanism. If a full bladder finally simply "overflows" because the pressure prevents the agent from controlling the sphincter muscles, voiding is purely a mechanism. Moreover, in some cases Tourette compulsion may be so extreme that tic-ing is more like a reflex than action, and responsibility would be blocked for the tic-ing because the agent did not act at all. All other cases involve action.

Still, although the addict's behavior is not mechanism, perhaps not seeking and using is as hard as not scratching an itch, voiding one's bladder, or engaging in tic behavior. Is it fair to expect the addict to self-regulate successfully in ordinary circumstances that do not permit brute techniques, such as threatening oneself with instant death, just in case one lapses? Is yielding to the desire an appropriate basis for blame and punishment, especially in extreme cases? Perhaps, after all, drug-related activity is sufficiently analogous to mechanistic movement to qualify for an excuse, but this requires an argument rather than an analogy. If one concludes, as I think one should, that the addict's behavior is clearly action and not mechanism, then one must turn to an excusing condition to respond to the addict's difficulty refraining from criminal conduct.

Addiction and Mental State   The law is generally unforgiving if a defendant lacked a required mental state as a result of voluntarily getting drunk. For example, the Supreme Court upheld the exclusion of all evidence of intoxication in a case in which the defendant was plausibly in a state of alcoholic unconsciousness at the time of killing two companions and had no possible defense to murder other than his resultant lack of intent to kill (Montana v. Egelhoff, 1996). For another example, the influential Model Penal Code (American Law Institute, 1962, §2.08(2)) equates voluntarily getting drunk with a defendant's subjective awareness that his conduct was creating a substantial and unjustifiable risk of a prohibited harm, such as the risk that the defendant's conduct endangered life. It is clear, however, that many people who create grave risk to others without awareness of that risk when drunk were not aware when they became drunk that they would be in this situation while drunk. These rules are harsh, and many people think that they are unfair, but the usual justification for them is that the defendant was responsible for creating his own potential defense of lacking a required mental state.

The criminal law is far more forgiving, however, if the defendant was "involuntarily intoxicated." The kinds of cases envisioned are those in which the defendant does not seem responsible for being intoxicated, such as if someone else by deceit causes the defendant to be drunk, or if the defendant has a "pathological" response to an intoxicant by becoming vastly more intoxicated than a reasonable person could foresee. In such instances, a defendant can plead "involuntary intoxication" and will succeed with a complete defense if he can show that he did not know what he was doing or could not control himself. Even if the involuntarily intoxicated defendant's capacities are not so severely undermined, he may use evidence of his intoxication to show that he did not have a required mental state, such as purpose or awareness of a risk.

In most cases an intoxicated person, whether or not he is an addict, will possess the mental state required by the definition of the crime. There are exceptions, however, especially in some cases in which the defendant claims he was not aware of a prohibited risk he was creating. For example, an extremely drunk driver may not be aware of the magnitude of the danger he creates, or a drunk undergraduate may not be consciously aware of the risk that his companion is not consenting to his sexual advances. The question regarding addicts in such cases, however, is whether their intoxication is legally voluntary. Addiction is not one of the criteria for involuntary intoxication, so the addict's intoxication is considered legally voluntary, but should it be?

Simply noting that use is a sign of the disease labeled addiction does not answer the question. We need an analysis about the relationship of use to legal criteria. Recall the testimony about Powell. Even if he had some control over whether he began to consume, once he began, he allegedly could not stop. Control capacity, then, seemed to be the issue, not lack of *mens rea*. Most addicted criminals are probably not intoxicated when they commit their crimes (other than use itself), but whether intoxicated addicts should be treated differently from intoxicated nonaddicts for the purpose of negating *mens rea* is a more general responsibility question about whether addicts should be excused whether or not they use to the point of intoxication. Let us therefore turn to the more general question.

Excusing Theories

This section considers the two prime candidates for excusing addiction-related actions: the internal coercion theory and the lack of rational capacity theory. It concludes that the latter is preferable on conceptual and empirical grounds. It then suggests that the possibility of *diachronic responsibility* may decisively bar most addicts from claiming an excuse to crime on either theory.

The Internal Coercion–Lack of Control Theory   Too often we are seduced by medical metaphors that strongly suggest mechanism (Morse, 2002). Nevertheless, the disease model and ordinary language—the addict allegedly "can't help using," or is "impelled to use," or, more bluntly, is "compelled to use"—suggest that addiction primarily produces a control or volitional problem.

Volition is a vexing foundational problem for philosophy, psychology, and law (Behr, 1993). Even if "black box" models of control problems seem to explain the phenomenon deemed addiction, the law's concept of the person as a conscious, intentional agent implies that such models cannot provide the law with adequate guidance to decide if an excuse is warranted either in general or in individual cases. Any model must translate into terms of human agency.

Consider some alternatives. If one adopts Professor Michael Moore's influential, widely noticed contention that volition is a functional mental state of executory intention (Moore, 1993), the problem of volition disappears because virtually no addict has a volitional problem. Rather, addicts' wills translate their desires for the drug into the necessary action quite effectively. On this account of the will, almost no intentional conduct will raise a problem of volition. Moore's account is persuasive to many, but like all accounts of the philosophical foundations of action, it is controversial. Some competitors that consider volition a species of desire, a view that Moore and others reject (Strawson, 1986), may raise volitional problems in the case of addicts (Wallace, 1999). Unless these alternatives can be reduced to ordinary language concepts that apply to human agency, however, it will be impossible for legislatures and courts to resolve disputes about the metaphysics of mind and action rationally.

An "internal coercion" model is one possible explanation of a control or volitional excuse based on "disorders of desire." The model employs a moralized, commonsense approach that is analogous to the criminal law excuse of duress (Wertheimer, 1987) and that requires no implausible, unverifiable empirical assumptions about how the mind works. Consequently, the criteria for duress will be considered before turning to whether the model can be applied to addictions.

Duress obtains if the defendant is threatened with the use of deadly force or grievous bodily harm against himself or another unless the defendant commits an equally or more serious crime, and a person of reasonable firmness would have been "unable to resist" the threat (American Law Institute, 1962, §2.09). In other words, an agent faced with a particularly hard choice—commit a crime or be killed or grievously injured—is legally excused if the choice is too hard to expect the agent to buck up and obey the law. The defense, however, is not based on empirical assumptions about the subjective capacity of an individual agent to resist threats; it is moralized and objective. Using the term "objective" does not mean to suggest that the "person of reasonable firmness" criterion has a reality independent of our practices that can be discovered by reason or empirical investigation. It is meant to be a thoroughly normative standard that expresses what we all expect of each other in our legal and moral culture. For example, the defense is not available to a defendant allegedly "unable" to resist if the threats were less than death or grievous bodily harm or if a person of reasonable firmness would have been able to resist.

The moralized criterion of the person of reasonable firmness necessary to support the excuse of duress appears to risk unfairness. Suppose a person would find it extraordinarily difficult to resist threats that a person of reasonable firmness could resist. Under such conditions, criminal penalties would be retributively unjust because a person does not deserve punishment for conduct that is so difficult for that agent to avoid. Moreover, specific deterrence is bootless in such cases. A purely consequential view might justify punishment to buck up the marginal people—but only at the cost of injustice to those who find it supremely difficult to resist. Because fault is a necessary condition for blame and punishment in our system, denying the defense would be unjust. Those who take this position should argue for a purely subjective view of the duress excuse, which would require difficult empirical assessment of the defendant's capacity to resist. This standard would be a nightmare to adjudicate but worth the effort if it were necessary to avoid injustice.

There is a good argument, however, that the moralized, objective standard that uses the person of reasonable firmness as the criterion is not unfair. If a person is threatened with death, for example, the defense of duress should be potentially available unless the balance of evils is so remarkably negative that every person would be expected to resist. In all other cases, the question would at least go to the jury. Thus, there will be few cases involving sufficiently serious threats in which the person incapable of resisting would lose the potential defense. The person who genuinely finds resisting extremely difficult even when the threats are relatively mild— say, kill or be touched—will almost certainly be a person with irrational fears who will qualify for some type of irrationality defense. Duress might not obtain, but exculpation will be available on other grounds.

The formulation "unable to resist" has the unmistakable implication of mechanism. Unless *force majeure* or genuine mechanism is at work, we virtually never know whether the agent is in some sense genuinely unable or is simply unwilling to resist, and if the latter, how hard it is for the agent to resist. In the present state of knowledge, research evidence concerning the characteristics that help people maintain control when faced with temptation or experiencing impulses is no more than a general guide (Baumeister, Hetherton, & Tice, 1994). Even if "willpower" is an independent human ability and there are individual differences in self-control (Tangney, Baumeister, & Boone, 2004), no sufficiently valid metric and instrumentation can accurately resolve questions about the strength of craving and the ability to resist. This was in large part the reason that both the American Psychiatric Association and the American Bar Association recommended the abolition of the control or volitional test for legal insanity in the wake of the ferment concerning the defense of legal insanity following the *Hinckley* verdict (American Bar Association, 1989; American

Psychiatric Association, 1982). Moreover, courts faced with deciding whether to adopt a volitional test after *Hinckley* refused to do so for the same reason (United States v. Lyons, 1984). If strength of craving or of resistance are to be the touchstones, legal decision makers will have to act with little scientific guidance and lots of common sense (Blume, Morera, & Garcia de la Cruz, 2005; Cooney, Kadden, & Steinberg, 2005; Donovan, 1988). Moreover, as the next subsection claims, the psychological processes that explain lack of control are better understood as processes that undermine rationality.

The analogy often used to demonstrate that craving is like duress is that the intense cravings or desires of compulsive states are like an internal gun to the head. The sufferer's fear of physical or psychological withdrawal symptoms and of other dysphoric states is allegedly so great that it is analogous to the "do-it-or-else" fear of death or grievous bodily injury that is necessary for a duress defense. Yielding to a compulsive desire, a craving, is therefore like yielding to a threat of death or of grievous bodily harm. The argument is that we cannot expect a person of reasonable firmness not to yield in the face of such an internally generated hard choice, much as we cannot expect such a person not to yield in the face of an external threat of death or grievous bodily harm.

The analogy is attractive, but it is theoretically and practically problematic. First, the analogy suggests no problem with the defender's will, which operates effectively to execute the intention to block or to remove the dysphoria (Fingarette & Hasse, 1979). Further, it is entirely rational, at least in the short term, to wish to terminate ghastly dysphoria, even if there are competing reasons not to, such as criminal sanctions or moral degradation. And it is simply not the case that addicts always act to satisfy their cravings because they fear dysphoria. Many just yield because it is unpleasant to abstain, not because they substantially fear dysphoria. In addition, the phenomenology of the sufferer's response to craving, unlike the phenomenology of the victim threatened by death, often is not, and perhaps never is, clear or the product of unitary, simple causes. Suppose, for example, that the primary motive is the pleasure or satisfaction of yielding or that such pleasure is an important, additional motive. The possibility of pleasure seems more like an offer than a threat, and offers expand rather than contract freedom. The strong desire for pleasure is not a hard-choice excusing condition in law or morals.

Assuming that fear of dysphoria is a sufficient motive and that the analogy to the fear of death or grievous bodily harm is initially plausible, two problems remain: assessing the strength of the fear and deciding what degree of fear of dysphoria is sufficient to excuse what types of conduct. Based on ordinary experience and common sense, the criminal law uses threats of death or grievous bodily harm as objective indicators of the type of stimulus that would in ordinary people create sufficient hard choice to justify an excuse. Of course, people subjected to such threats will differ markedly in their subjective fear responses and in their desires to live or to remain uninjured, but ordinary, average people will have very substantial fear and find the choice to resist very difficult. Even if they do not have great subjective fear, they will still find it difficult to resist.

We have all experienced dysphoric states, and many have experienced intense dysphoria, but dysphoria as a source of present and potential pain is more purely subjective than death or grievous bodily injury. Consequently, assessing the average or ordinary intensity of craving or inner tension, including seemingly strong states, is simply more difficult than assessing the fear of death or grievous bodily injury. Focusing on more objective markers of compulsive states, such as physical withdrawal symptoms, will surely help, but fear of such symptoms is unlikely to support an excuse.

Fear of the physical symptoms of withdrawal from most drugs is not likely to be as intense as the fear of death or grievous bodily harm because in most cases withdrawal is not terribly painful—withdrawal from heroin is often likened to a bad flu—and can be medically managed to reduce the discomfort (Kaplan, 1983). Withdrawal from alcohol dependence can be extremely severe, but it, too, can be medically managed, and because alcohol is freely and inexpensively available for adults, those who fear withdrawal and do not want treatment seldom need to commit crimes or other wrongs to obtain alcohol to avoid withdrawal.

Dysphoric mental or emotional states are surely undesirable, but does their threat, especially if medical management is available, produce a sufficiently hard choice to warrant an excuse? The answer to this question is not obvious, but perhaps at the extreme, they do. People suffering from severe depressive disorders, for example, report subjective pain that is apparently as great and enduring as the reported pain from many forms of grievous bodily harm, and sometimes depressed people kill themselves to avoid the psychological pain. For another example, some people addicted to alcohol who are being treated with a drug that makes them dreadfully sick if they ingest any alcohol, including trace amounts, will "drink through" the miserable sickness (Ludwig, 1988).

These examples and common sense suggest that fear of or aversion to psychologically dysphoric states may be very strong indeed. But is it as strong as the fear of death? Even assuming that the feared dysphoria of unconsummated cravings can be substantial, it will likely seldom be as severe as the fear of death or grievous bodily harm. If this is right, and assuming, too, that we could reliably assess the fear of dysphoria, few addicts would succeed with a hard-choice excuse. On the other hand, if the drug-related activities were solely possession for personal use and use itself, then perhaps the justification of necessity should obtain (American Law Institute, 1962, §3.02). Even if the harm of such activity is less than the harm of dysphoria, however, the law would hold most addicts responsible for becoming addicted and thus for placing themselves in the situation that created the need for the defense. The law disallows the justification in such cases. Finally, even if addicts were not responsible for becoming addicted, all legislatures would today resist permitting a justification for possession and use on policy grounds and would surely reject an excuse for other, possibly related crimes, such as theft or robbery, to pay for drugs. The disease model is powerful, but the moral-failure model is resilient.

In sum, the internal coercion or duress approach uses understandable terms and has a moral basis derived from a defense that the criminal law and ordinary morality already accept. Nevertheless, currently insurmountable practical problems beset attempting to assess the appropriateness of an excuse in individual cases. What is more, thinking about excuse in terms of control difficulties inevitably will invite misleading metaphorical thinking about mechanism and expert testimony that is little more than moral judgment wrapped in the white coat of allegedly scientific or clinical understanding. The law should not adopt an internal coercion excuse.

The Irrationality Theory Irrationality is the most straightforward, persuasive explanation of why some addicts should perhaps be excused. Moreover, irrationality will excuse any addict who may apparently qualify under the internal coercion theory. If craving or other mental states related to addiction sufficiently interfere with the addict's ability to grasp and be guided by reason, then a classic irrationality problem arises, and there is no need to resort to compulsion as the ground for excuse. Finally, it is simply more practicable to assess rationality than to assess the strength of compulsive desires.

How does it feel to crave intensely? The subjective experience of addicts is diverse, but a modal tale about severe addiction may be useful. Despite different historical pathways to addiction, descriptions of the subjective experience are broadly of a piece (Donovan, 1988), although different descriptors and metaphors are and could be used. The story is not meant to include all the features of the addictive process; rather, it is an approximation of the subjective experience preceding use that may bear on responsibility.

Between episodes of use of the substance, the addict commonly experiences a buildup of tension, irritation, anxiety, boredom, depression, or other dysphoric states. As time passes since the last use, these dysphoric states typically become stronger, more persistent, more intense, and more demanding. In some cases, the buildup is described as sheer desire, sheer wanting. As the wanting remains unsatisfied, increased dysphoric states or, in some cases, excitement, accompany the wanting. For illicit drug addicts, anxiety or fear about obtaining the substance often adds to the dysphoria.

At some point, the addict metaphorically, and in some cases literally, can think of nothing but the desire to use the substance. One informant described the desire like "a buzzing in my ears that prevents me from focusing." It is like an extreme version of being dehydrated or starved: the addict can ordinarily think of nothing except getting and using the stuff. It is like the moment just before orgasm during an episode of exceptional excitement, but usually without the pleasurable feeling of sexual excitement. There is only one tune or story in the addict's head, and nothing else drives it out.

When the addict cannot get the tune out of his head, it is very difficult to concentrate the mind on the good reasons not to use, especially because, in almost all instances, there is no police officer at the elbow or other available "self-management technique" sufficiently powerful to motivate the addict to think clearly about drug-related activity. Fundamental components of rationality—the capacities to think clearly and self-consciously to evaluate one's conduct—are compromised. The agent may not recognize or be able to attend to the various options at all or may not be able coherently to weigh and assess those that are recognized. Attention is captured and narrowly focused; judgment and motivation may be disconnected (Holton, 2009). For moral and legal purposes, however, the precise mechanisms by which addiction can compromise rationality are less important than the clear evidence that it can do so (Elster, 1999; Kalivas, 2004; Redish, Jensen, & Johnson, 2008; Vanderschuren & Everitt, 2004). On the other hand, the addict's characteristic ambivalence about addiction suggests that addicts recognize that they have good reason to stop, at least during lucid or interuse intervals.

The degree to which the general capacity for rationality is compromised can vary widely among addicts. The modal tale is told as an extreme case and is anyway only an approximation. Still, addiction can compromise rationality and therefore can potentially excuse drug-related activity, especially for those most severely affected. Thus, the question remains whether the law should consider addiction as a potential excuse. This is an important question for social and legal policy because drugs are a factor in much criminal conduct. Possession and use offenses are rampant, and in most big cities, well over half of all people arrested for felonies test positive for addictive substances (Harrison & Beck, 2003). Many of these are surely addicts. Society may believe that it is fair to blame and punish them, but is it?

Whether or not addicts were responsible for becoming addicted, they will not lack *mens rea* for their substance-related criminal activity. The major exception will be cases in which the addict offends while in a state of unconsciousness or blackout induced by substance use. Most jurisdictions would permit only limited use of such evidence to negate *mens rea,* and some would not permit it at all. Virtually all potential addicts are consciously aware of the risk that if addicted they will persistently and intentionally seek and use substances. Nevertheless, the previous conscious awareness of this risk is distinguishable from forming the intention preaddiction to seek and use after becoming addicted. For most addicts, however, there will be no *mens rea* problem when they seek and use. They are not automatons, and they do form the intent to buy, possess, and use. In most cases of serious criminal wrongdoing, the potential addict may be unaware of the risk of committing such offenses unless the addict has a history of such wrongdoing. Even if this is true, however, there still will be no *mens rea* problem. An addict who burgles, robs, or kills surely forms the intent to do so. In the narrow legal sense, most addicts have the true purpose to engage in their drug-related conduct. If they deserve mitigation and excuse, it is because they are not fully rational, not because they lack the mental state required by the definition of the offense.

Responsibility despite the Presence of an Excusing Condition at the Time of the Crime? Assume that as a result of addiction some addicts are sufficiently irrational or are so "internally coerced" as to warrant mitigation or excuse at the time they commit their substance-related crimes. Should they be held responsible nonetheless? Two theories suggest in general that virtually all should be. The first is that by experimenting with drugs, the addict knowingly took the risk that he would become irrational, including the possibility that the irrationality would operate specifically in contexts involving substance-related behavior. This theory comes dangerously close to strict liability in many instances, however, because most people who experiment with drugs probably are not consciously aware that they might become involved in criminal behavior beyond buying, possessing, and using drugs. And buying, possessing, and using are not illegal in the case of licit addictive drugs such as ethanol.

The second and more convincing theory is that almost all addicts have lucid, rational intervals between episodes of use during which they could act on the good reasons to seek help quitting or otherwise to take steps to avoid engaging in harmful drug-related behavior. This has been termed a case of *potential diachronic self-control* because the person knows that at a later time he will be in a state of nonresponsible irrationality (Kennett, 2001). Again, the ambivalence about addiction that characterizes addicts implies that they are capable of and do recognize these good reasons during their lucid intervals. Even if some addicts are unable to think rationally when they are in a state of intense craving, they are capable of rationality in refractory periods and have a duty to take steps to avoid future offending.

Consider the following analogy. If a person knows that he is subject to psychomotor epileptic seizures that cause blackout, then he will be held responsible if he blacks out while driving and kills someone. Although when he killed he was in a blacked-out state that would otherwise defeat liability, he will be guilty of creating an unreasonable risk of death simply by driving with knowledge that he might black out. The question for addicts would be with what mental state they commit their crimes while they are not fully rational. In virtually all cases, they would commit their crimes intentionally, and the law would not provide an excuse for their culpable lack of rationality. A sentencing judge might consider this a mitigating factor as a matter of discretion.

Both theories for holding addicts responsible are potentially subject to the same objection, however. Addiction can become an entire lifestyle, and the consequences of prolonged use of substances can so debilitate some addicts physically and psychosocially that this group has exceptional difficulty at all times exercising substantial rationality concerning their status and behavior. Although potential addicts may be aware of the risk of irrationality, they may not be fully aware of the risk of extreme irrationality that can arise in some cases. In such instances, perhaps, one cannot find responsibility for extreme irrationality by referring back to preaddiction, knowing conduct, or by considering quiescent intervals. In cases of extreme debilitation, the intervals between episodes of use may not be fully rational.

The foregoing objection does not seem decisive, however. In those few cases in which prolonged drug use produces a permanent, major mental disorder that compromises rationality at the time of criminal conduct, the addict will have available a traditional insanity defense based on *settled insanity* resulting from the use of intoxicants (La Fave, 2003). But except in such rare cases, most addicts' rational intervals are probably sufficiently rational to hold them largely or fully responsible for diminishing their own rationality at the time of use or of other drug-related crimes. In addition, as a result of both street wisdom and personal history, experienced addicts typically know during these intervals both what treatment alternatives are available and the type of criminal behavior beyond seeking and using in which they are likely to engage. Indeed, much of the further criminal activity probably takes place during the rational intervals and involves harm to others, which carries greater criminal penalties, giving the addict even stronger self-regarding and other reasons not to offend than in the case of personal possession and use.

Finally, suppose one concludes that some addicts deserve mitigation or excuse for at least some criminal conduct. The discussion of the internal coercion theory suggests that irrationality would excuse any addict that the internal coercion theory might fairly excuse. The argument, in brief, is this: a person driven crazy by fear is crazy. Or, in the alternative, people so fearful of mild dysphoric states that they appear incapable of bucking up when reasonable people would are irrationally fearful. Any plausible story about allegedly compulsive cravings motivating the criminal conduct, especially in cases of serious crime, also will be a story in which the addict is less than fully rational or not rational at all. In such cases, irrationality would be the appropriate excusing claim; there would be no need to resort to problematic internal coercion.

The conclusion is that most addicts are responsible for seeking and using and almost none should be excused for further criminal activity and especially not for serious wrongdoing. There are simply too many periods of rationality, and there is simply too much awareness of alternative possibilities to permit excuse in more than a small number of cases unless, perhaps, the law were to expand doctrines of mitigation (Morse, 2003).

Social Responsibility

Socioeconomic arrangements, culture, life stories, legal regulation, and other external causal variables can seem much to blame for addiction and its consequences. Even if most addicts are personally responsible for becoming addicted and for their behavior while addicted, whether one becomes an addict and how one lives as an addict are not solely due to the intentional conduct of an agent who becomes an addict.

Consider the following examples. It is entirely understandable that people living in communities of deprivation, with few life chances, may find a life of addiction preferable to the misery of an impoverished straight life. Some subcultures particularly encourage and celebrate the use of potentially addictive substances, increasing the risk of addiction among members of that subculture. For those who have lived lives of desperation or who suffer from psychological miseries for any reason, substance use can be a welcome escape. Finally, legal regulation can affect the probability of addiction, the lifestyles of addicts, and the further behavioral conse-quences of addiction. It is more difficult to bum a dime bag than to bum a smoke or to cadge a free drink, even from friends, and the addict can never be sure that a dealer is not an undercover narc, an informant, or cutting the dope. Lawful availability and price affect all of the following:

rates of consumption; the development of informal customs and conventions for controlled use; the health, safety, and legal dangers of seeking and using drugs; and the probability that other criminal behavior beyond possession and use will occur as a result of addiction. Explanations such as these, especially when considered in the context of a sympathy-arousing life history, can tug at our hearts and influence our responsibility attributions. As Gary Watson concluded in his discussion of the case of a murderer who had suffered a dreadful childhood, in many cases our reaction will be, "No wonder" (Watson, 1987, 275).

How should we respond to powerful social explanations? Social variables account undeniably for a great deal of the variance in addictions and related behavior, and many of these variables are potentially modifiable by sound social policy. For example, millions of lives will be affected by resolution of the current debates concerning decriminalization of illicit drugs, by differential penalties for essentially similar substances such as crack and powdered cocaine, by the propriety of needle exchanges, and by whether nicotine should be regulated by the Food and Drug Administration. A just society should try to minimize the inevitable ill effects of its policies (see generally, Leitzel, 2008). Nonetheless, crimes and moral wrongs are ultimately committed by individual agents, and social causal variables, or any other kind of causal variable, cannot excuse addicts who are individually responsible without threatening all individual responsibility (Morse, 2000).

All behavior is caused by innumerable variables over which we have no control. Some causal stories surely arouse more sympathy than others, but sympathy and an unfortunate life history are not excusing conditions per se. One may wish to consider such variables for disposition on consequential grounds or as an expression of mercy, but they do not excuse unless they produce sufficient irrationality or a sufficiently hard choice. Focusing on individual responsibility should not blind us to the remediable causes of wrongdoing and should not diminish justifiable sympathy for wrongdoers, but neither should explanations and sympathy undermine our view that most wrongdoers are responsible agents.

Conclusion: Sensible Criminal Justice Policy

Most addicts most of the time can fairly be held responsible for the crimes they commit, including those such as buying and possessing controlled substances that are criteria for their disorder. This does not mean, however, that the criminal justice policies our society pursues toward addicts and other users are wise. Indeed, I firmly believe that society should decriminalize purchase and possession for personal use and using itself (Morse, 2009). Political liberalism and public health considerations suggest that criminal justice is not the optimum or even a sensible means to address buying and using substances. Indeed, using criminal justice in such cases may be simply cruel. Moreover, doctrines of mitigation should be expanded to cover some cases when addicts commit other crimes that are not a part of personal use itself (Morse, 2003). Finally, vastly greater treatment ought to be available to those addicts who would benefit, including reducing their risk of criminal behavior. Until discoveries about addicts convince us that they are nonresponsibly out of control or irrational, however, they may be held criminally responsible in most cases.

References

American Bar Association. (1989). *ABA criminal justice mental health standards*. Washington, DC: American Bar Association.

American Law Institute. (1962). *Model penal code*. Philadelphia: The American Law Institute.

American Psychiatric Association. (1982). *Insanity defense: position statement*. Washington, DC: American Psychiatric Association.

Baumeister, R. F., Hetherton, T. F., & Tice, D. (1994). *Losing control: how and why people fail at self-regulation*. San Diego: Academic Press.

Becker, G. S. (1996). A theory of rational addiction. In *Accounting for tastes* (pp. 50–76). Cambridge, MA: Harvard University Press.

Behr, B. J. (1993). Why volition is a foundation problem for psychology. *Consciousness and Cognition, 2* (4), 281–309.

Blume, A. W., Morera, O. F., & Garcia de la Cruz, B. (2005). Assessment of addictive behaviors in ethnic-minority cultures. In D. M. Donovan & G. Alan Marlatt (Eds.), *Assessment of addictive behaviors* (2nd ed., pp. 49–70). New York: Guilford Press.

Camí, J., & Farré, M. (2003). Mechanisms of disease: drug addiction. *New England Journal of Medicine, 349* (10), 975–986.

Cooney, N. L., Kadden, R. M., & Steinberg, H. R. (2005). Assessment of alcohol problems. In D. M. Donovan & G. Alan Marlatt (Eds.), *Assessment of addictive behaviors* (2nd ed., pp. 71–112). New York: Guilford Press.

Deroche-Gamonet, V., Belin, D., & Piazza, P. V. (2004). Evidence for addiction-like behavior in the rat. *Science,* 305 (5686), 1014–1017.

Donovan, D. M. (1988). Assessment of addictive behaviors: implications of an emerging biopsychosocial model. In D. M. Donovan & G. Alan Marlatt (Eds.), *Assessment of addictive behaviors* (pp. 3–48). New York: Guilford Press.

Elster, J. (1999). *Strong feelings: emotion, addiction and human behavior.* Cambridge, MA: MIT Press.

Fingarette, H., & Hasse, A. F. (1979). *Mental disabilities and criminal responsibility.* Berkeley, CA: University of California Press.

Fischer, K. W., Stein, Z., & Heikkinen, K. (2009). Narrow assessments misrepresent development and misguide policy: comment on Steinberg, Cauffman, Woolard, Graham, and Banich 2009. *American Psychologist, 64* (7), 595–600.

Gastfriend, D. R. (2005). Physician substance abuse and recovery: what does it mean for physicians—and everyone else. *Journal of the American Medical Association, 293* (12), 1513–1515.

Greenfield, S. F., & Hennessy, G. (2004). Assessment of the patient. In M. Galanter & H. D. Kleber (Eds.), *The American Psychiatric Publishing textbook of substance abuse treatment* (3rd ed., pp. 101–120). Washington, DC: American Psychiatric Publishing, Inc.

Haney, M. (2004). Neurobiology of stimulants. In M. Glanter & H. D. Kleber (Eds.), *The American Psychiatric Publishing textbook of substance abuse treatment* (3rd ed., pp. 31–40). Washington, DC: American Psychiatric Publishing, Inc.

Harrison, P. M., & Beck, A. J. (2003). *Prisoners in 2002.* Washington, DC: Bureau of Justice Statistics.

Heyman, G. (2009). *Addiction: a disorder of choice.* Cambridge, MA: Harvard University Press.

Holton, R. (2009). *Willing, wanting, waiting.* New York: Oxford University Press.

Hough, S. (1994). The moral mirror of pleasure. In S. Luper-Foy & C. Brown (Eds.), *Drugs, morality, and the law* (pp. 153–182). New York: Garland Publishing, Inc.

Husak, D. N. (1992). *Drugs and rights.* Cambridge: Cambridge University Press.

Kalivas, P. W. (2004). Choose to study choice in addiction. *American Journal of Psychiatry, 161* (2), 193–194.

Kalivas, P. W., & Volkow, N. D. (2005). The neural basis of addiction: a pathology of motivation and choice. *American Journal of Psychiatry, 162* (8), 1403–1413.

Kaplan, J. (1983). *The hardest drug: heroin and public policy.* Chicago: University of Chicago Press.

Kasanetz, F., Deroche-Gamonet,V., Berson, N., Balado, E., Lafourcade, M., Manzoni, O., & Piazza, P. V. (2010). Transition to addiction is associated with a persistent impairment in synaptic plasticity. *Science*, *32*, 1709–1712.

Keller, J. (2005). In genes we trust: the biological component of psychological essentialism and its relationship to mechanisms of motivated social cognition. *Journal of Personality and Social Psychology*, *88* (4), 686–702.

Kennett, J. (2001). *Agency and responsibility: a common-sense moral psychology*. New York: Oxford University Press.

Kosten, T. R. (1998). Addiction as a brain disease. *American Journal of Psychiatry*, *155* (6), 711–713.

LaFave, W. R. (2003). *Criminal law* (4th ed.). St. Paul, MN: West.

Leitzel, J. (2008). *Regulating vice: misguided prohibitions and realistic controls*. Cambridge: Cambridge University Press.

Leshner, A. I. (1997). Addiction is a brain disease, and it matters. *Science*, *278* (5335), 45–47.

Ludwig, A. M. (1988). *Understanding the alcoholic's mind: the nature of craving and how to control it*. New York: Oxford University Press.

Montana v. Egelhoff, 518 U.S. 37 (1996).

Moore, M. S. (1993). *Act and crime: the philosophy of action and its implications for criminal law*. New York: Oxford University Press.

Morse, S. J. (1994). Culpability and control. *University of Pennsylvania Law Review*, *142* (5), 1587–1660.

Morse, S. J. (1997). Immaturity and irresponsibility. *Journal of Criminal Law & Criminology*, *88* (4), 15–67.

Morse, S. J. (1999). Craziness and criminal responsibility. *Behavioral Sciences & the Law*, *17* (2), 147–164.

Morse, S. J. (2000). Deprivation and desert. In W. C. Heffernan & J. Kleinig (Eds.), *From social justice to criminal justice* (pp. 114–160). New York: Oxford University Press.

Morse, S. J. (2002). Uncontrollable urges and irrational people. *Virginia Law Review*, *88* (5), 1025–1078.

Morse, S. J. (2003). Diminished rationality, diminished responsibility. *Ohio State Journal of Criminal Law*, *1* (1), 289–308.

Morse, S. J. (2007a). Voluntary control of behavior and responsibility. *American Journal of Bioethics*, *7* (1), 12–13.

Morse, S. J. (2007b). The non-problem of free will in forensic psychiatry and psychology. *Behavioral Sciences & the Law, 25* (2), 203–220.

Morse, S. J. (2007c). Criminal responsibility and the disappearing person. *Cardozo Law Review, 28* (6), 2545–2575.

Morse, S. J. (2009). Addiction, science and criminal responsibility. In N. Farahany (Ed.), *The impact of the behavioral sciences on criminal law* (pp. 241–288). New York: Oxford University Press.

Nestler, E. J. (2000). Genes and addiction. *Nature Genetics, 26* (3), 277–281.

Pereboom, D. (2001). *Living without free will.* Cambridge: Cambridge University Press.

Powell v. Texas, 392 U.S. 514 (1968).

Redish, A. D., Jensen, S., & Johnson, A. (2008). A unified framework for addiction: vulnerabilities in the decision process. *Behavioral and Brain Sciences, 31* (4), 415–437.

Robinson v. California, 370 U.S. 660 (1962).

Satel, S. L., & Goodwin, F. K. (1998). *Is drug addiction a brain disease?* Washington, DC: Ethics & Public Policy Center.

Steinberg, L., Cauffman, E., Woolard, J., Graham, S., & Banich, M. (2009a). Are adolescents less mature than adults? Minors' access to abortion, the juvenile death penalty, and the alleged APA "flip-flop." *American Psychologist, 64* (7), 583–594.

Steinberg, L., Cauffman, E., Woolard, J., Graham, S., & Banich, M. (2009b). Reconciling the complexity of human development with the reality of legal policy: reply to Fischer, Stein, and Heikkinen (2009). *American Psychologist, 64* (7), 601–604.

Strawson, G. (1986). *Freedom and belief.* New York: Oxford University Press.

Strawson, G. (1989). Consciousness, free will and the unimportance of determinism. *Inquiry, 32* (1), 3–27.

Tangney, J. P., Baumeister, R. F., & Boone, A. L. (2004). High self-control predicts good adjustment, less pathology, better grades, and interpersonal success. *Journal of Personality, 72* (2), 271–324.

United States v. Lyons, 731 F.2d 243 (5th Cir. 1984) (en banc)

Vanderschuren, L. J. M. J., & Everitt, B. J. (2004). Drug seeking becomes compulsive after prolonged cocaine self-administration. *Science, 305* (5686), 1017–1019.

Wallace, R. J. (1994). *Responsibility and the moral sentiments.* Cambridge, MA: Harvard University Press.

Wallace, R. J. (1999). Addiction as defect of the will: some philosophical reflections. *Law and Philosophy, 18* (5), 621–654.

Warner, L. A., Kessler, R. C., Hughes, M., Anthony, J. C. & Nelson, C. B. (1995). Prevalence and correlates of drug use and dependence in the United States: results from the national comorbidity survey. *Archives of General Psychiatry, 52,* 219–229.

Watson, G. (1987). Responsibility and the limits of evil: variations on a Strawsonian theme. In F. Schoeman (Ed.), *Responsibility, character, and the emotions: new essays in moral psychology* (pp. 256–286). Cambridge: Cambridge University Press.

Wertheimer, A. (1987). *Coercion.* Princeton, NJ: Princeton University Press.

8   Grounding for Understanding Self-Injury as Addiction or (Bad) Habit

Nancy Nyquist Potter

There is no doubt that the addiction construct has been seized upon and utilized in popular culture as well as in theology and medicine. The identification of addictive behaviors and full-blown addictions with lack of moderation and too much pleasure seeking has resulted in a proliferation of defined addictions ranging from garden-variety alcoholism and marijuana dependence to gambling, sex, love, shopping, and reading addictions, using the Internet, and role-playing games. It seems that almost anything done to excess and felt to be necessary to manage stress can be conceptualized as an addiction. Although many researchers distinguish between substance addiction and behavioral addiction, even popular culture takes behavioral addictions to be more than simply metaphor.

In this chapter, I focus on self-injurious behavior (SIB). A tendency to be self-injuring is a trademark of many patients diagnosed with borderline personality disorder and is one of the behaviors that clinicians, family, and friends find repugnant and utterly perplexing. This chapter discusses self-injury within the context of this personality disorder and primarily addresses what is called superficial or delicate self-injury. Self-injurious behavior is increasingly characterized as an addiction. I hasten to add that I do not aim to settle questions about the etiology of self-injury or even to unequivocally declare how SIB should be classified. My objective is much more modest: it is to give pause to the culturally prevalent understanding of SIB so as to open up a space for alternative, more patient-generated and patient-friendly, understandings.

Consider Lindsay. As described by an interviewer, cutting behavior led her to decreased ability to tolerate strong negative emotions such as fear and rage. Eventually, just her feeling a twinge of anxiety would be followed by a session of self-injury until many of the normal stressors of life, such as tension with a friend or a lower grade than one hoped for, prompted cutting. Lindsay came to understand her SIB as a way to avoid feelings, but she could not avoid the shame she felt when she saw herself as being out of control: "'It really is like an addiction,' says Lindsay" (Strong, 1998, 57–58).

The language used to describe Lindsay's experience is encumbered with a particular way of explaining and evaluating her SIB, the language of addiction. Yet it is a mistake for clinicians to assume that SIB necessarily is a form of addiction. The addiction trope is powerful in American society, and it may be functioning as what Ian Hacking calls an "interactive kind," a kind that bridges the conceptual gap between natural kinds (what Hacking calls "indifferent kinds") and socially constructed kinds. Quarks are indifferent kinds, according to Hacking, because "calling a quark a quark makes no difference to the quark" (Hacking, 1999, 105). Hacking argues that some mental disorders—autism, for example—are interactive kinds in that being diagnosed with some mental disorders changes the self-conception, behavior (and symptoms) of the person diagnosed. If we apply the concept of interactive kinds to SIB, it may be the case that people who self-injure and whose behavior is cast as addictive may begin to display symptoms of addiction—or, as I believe in this case, to use the language of addiction—in response to social cues as to how their behavior should be understood and addressed. But an analytically distinct question also arises about what Peter Zachar calls "practical kinds"—a way of sorting through the entities we take to be part of the scientific world so as to understand the role of such classification (Zachar, 2000). I show how cultural norms of making sense of and explaining the world drive people to draw on what are called *master narratives* to understand why some people self-injure. Many master narratives are domain specific (e.g., see Nelson, 2001, on the clinically correct narrative for transsexual identity).

It is my view that the master narrative in place is the addiction narrative and, more specifically, the disease model found in Alcoholics Anonymous (AA). Self-injurious behavior, then, is cast as a subgroup of the domain-specific master narrative for addiction. I think this is a mistake. First I will set out the idea of master, or grand, narratives, and then I will apply that notion to the 12-step recovery process. Ultimately, I argue that the master narrative of SIB as an addiction is not accurate or helpful to those who self-injure. This will lead me to a brief consideration of SIB as a practical kind of problematic behavior best understood through a pragmatic lens.

Master (or Grand) Narratives and Hegemonic Cultures

Vilma Hänninen and Anja Koski-Jännes say that two modes of cognitive functioning exist, one the logical and scientific reasoning process and the other a narrative telling of events (Hänninen & Koski-Jännes, 1999, 1837). The latter mode views stories as cultural products; narratives from AA are examples (Hänninen & Koski-Jännes, 1999, 1838). A narrative is a way that people make meaning of their lives and focuses not only on past events but on the future. Hence, people draw upon a "cultural stock of narratives and myths" to make sense of their lives (Hänninen & Koski-Jännes, 1999,1838).

Western culture supplies its population with the "grand narratives"[1] of the Enlightenment period. Such narratives are explanatory and global; their function is to give us a manageable way to understand how disparate aspects of the world fit together. Science presents a grand narrative of evolving creatures making progress and advancing from simpler to highly complex technocultures. Shannon K'doah Range frames master narratives in terms of "familiar rhetorical scripts" and "cultural codes" (Range, 2008). She argues that when a person or group deviates from the scripts and codes of dominant culture (by "dominant culture" I mean the cultural beliefs, myths, practices, and ideologies that hold most sway over time), that individual or that group of people may be delegitimized. One way to delegitimize those who defy a master narrative is to force a categorical dichotomy between "mad" and "bad" behavior (or people). This dichotomy points to a way of classifying behavior into a mutually exclusive disjunction in which a person's behavior is either viewed as psychiatric in character or judged according to moral values of social or cultural disapproval. The issue is what degree of social deviance or unconventionality is enough to count as a mental disorder or as criminal or wrongful behavior, assuming that, for some behaviors, we must choose between those two alternative categories (cf. Sadler, 2005, ch. 6).

Master narratives organize societal beliefs, values, and aims in an apparently logical fashion. They also are little questioned; instead, they are unwittingly taken as true, reproducing dominant themes of everyday living and marginalizing the voices that are less coherently woven in or that lack fitness.

The work of Hilde Lindemann Nelson (2001) as well as that of Range (2008) calls attention to the stratified way that master narratives operate within society.

Master narratives are often archetypal, consisting of stock plots and readily recognizable character types, and we use them not only to make sense of our experience . . . but also to justify what we do. . . . As the repositories of common norms, master narratives exercise a certain authority over our moral imaginations and play a role in informing our moral intuitions. (Nelson, 2001, 6)

The master narratives shape interpretation, causality, responsibility, and future expectations—all from a dominant and privileged position. Nelson argues that master narratives, because they carry values, explanations, and choices, can distort the identities of those who do not fit comfortably within the dominant story. That is, master narratives are epistemically, psychologically, and morally bad for members of oppressed groups.

For example, the American master narrative tells us that the hard-won efforts of the civil rights era resulted in greater freedom for women and significantly more equality with men. Young women in American culture, then, have come to believe that "women's rights" have been achieved; when activists and scholars correct that story (women still earn between 75 and 78 cents to the dollar compared to men; women are still working the "second shift"—a full day's work on the job and then the majority of work again at home, cf. Hochschild 2003), the young women think their elders are just stuck, harping on old themes.

As another example of a master narrative, consider the dominant response to the 9/11 attacks in the United States. The master narrative, in which the language of "us" and "them" was used to mark patriotism pitted against Saddam Hussein and Islamic terrorists, quickly morphed into sweeping anti-Muslim rhetoric and the "moral righteousness" of Americans to go to war. This master narrative fuels hostility, often resulting in persecution and, sometimes, hate crimes against "Muslim-looking" people (Kwan, 2008). Mei-Po Kwan argues that the "anti-Muslim master narrative" allows non-Muslims to conflate the distinction between the faith of Islam and the violence of terrorism. Thus, the dominant narrative encourages non-Muslims to see all "Muslim-looking" people with suspicion and persuades many Americans that all Muslims are dangerous. This master narrative allowed the previous administration to link patriotism with hatred for Muslims and to demand that its citizens declare whether they are "for or against" freedom and democracy. And it justified torture (by calling it "enhanced interrogation techniques") of any person who was suspect—which meant all Muslims.

Nelson argues that, in developing and creating our identities, we draw on culturally embedded familiar stories that we share with others (Nelson, 2001, 71). Master narratives, however, falsify many people's experience and identity because master narratives are ones promulgated by oppressive structures. They tell members of dominant (meaning, more powerful and oppressor) groups and members of disenfranchised or oppressed groups how the dominant group conceptualizes and evaluates those in oppressed groups, and those ideas are, to some degree, successful in being internalized by those others. María Lugones, for example, discusses ways in which she cannot animate playfulness in some constructions of herself (Lugones, 1987). Nelson argues that "the master narratives used by a dominant group to justify the oppression of a less powerful group distort and falsify the group's identity by depicting the group—and therefore also its members—as morally subnormal" (Nelson, 2001, 106). She suggests that narratives are, in many ways, central to moral philosophy: for example, in the kinds of identity that a culture makes possible for members of various groups, in the evaluations of moral damage to identity, or in the ascertaining of moral responsibility. Most cultures have master narratives (I leave open the possibility that a culture might exist whose dominant stories are not particularly oppressive) that have a tenacious hold on them and are very difficult for their members to resist. Nelson explains why these are so prevalent and durable:

> . . . they are organic ensembles that grow and change, they constitute a world view, and they assimilate opposition. In addition oppressive master narratives are often epistemically rigged. Taken in combination, these features produce a formidable resiliency, and it's this, as well as their prevalence, that makes them so hard to uproot. (Nelson, 2001, 157–158)

However, not all master narratives are equally pernicious; some have weaknesses and fault lines that make possible stories of resistance—and some "counterstories," as Nelson calls them, are bad ones but better than nothing. As Nelson says, "If the counterstory concedes too much [to the master narrative] it might nevertheless be better than no counterstory at all. Sometimes a local repair job is the best that a person can do" (Nelson, 2001, 178). So, some counterstories are more liberating than others, but also, some master narratives are more oppressive than others. In general master narratives are psychically and morally damaging and ought to be challenged and resisted. I argue that the addiction narrative is one such master narrative.

Story Hour for Addicts

Hänninen and Koski-Jännes (1999) analyzed recovery stories from substance and behavior addictions. They review four kinds of addiction-recovery narratives, aspects of which will resonate with ways we talk about SIB. The AA model draws on a master narrative that is quite rigid (cf. Mitchell, 2006, on rigidity of 12-step programs in general). "Hitting bottom" is key to this kind of story as the person's clear and convincing evidence that her life must change. Humility is necessary because the person must surrender to a Higher Power and must rely on others who have been in recovery longer. Also necessary are the insight that alcoholism is a disease (and all that that means, e.g., absolving the drinker from guilt) and gratitude (as in "gift" or "blessing"). If someone is struggling with a misuse or abuse of a substance or behavior and rejects the idea of a Higher Power, let alone resists the principle that requires him to become willing "to turn his will and his life over to the care of God," he is considered recalcitrant—not fully committed to changing.

A second narrative trope is the personal growth story, whereby the person frees himself from oppressive and/or abusive relationships, learns to accept himself, to develop his own voice, and to trust appropriate others (Hänninen & Koski-Jännes, 1999, 1844). "In the moral sense the growth story releases the protagonist from guilt by seeing oppressive relations as the cause of the problems" (Hänninen & Koski-Jännes, 1999, 1843). Accompanying this understanding comes the recognition that "all forms of dependence had been parts of the same problem, the denial of one's emotions" (Hänninen & Koski-Jännes, 1999,1844).[2]

A third narrative trope is the "love story" in which the sufferer transforms herself from an attention-seeking, desperately needy person who is filled with self-criticism and self-doubt to someone with self-worth and self-confidence who is able to develop intersubjective relationships. This transformation comes about through the love and care another gives her who accepts her as she is.

The mastery (not "master") story is the fourth recovery story that Hänninen and Koski-Jännes researched. In mastery, people aim to have mastery over their own behavior; this theme strongly implies that overcoming troubles with substances is a matter of character through which one defeats the "enemy." This story form has given rise to metaphors such as the Beast, or the Monkey on the Back. It also highlights the fact that an activity that is begun in order to gain control over one's life can turn into a dependence that compromises that control (Hänninen & Koski-Jänne, 1999, 1846).

It is important to note that all these stories emerge out of models of addiction and, to some degree, have incorporated elements of the AA model. For example, for AA members the love story is a story of God's redemptive love (or that of one's Higher Power). And in each type of story, the narrative explains and evaluates past, present, and future behavior in terms of a person's recovery from addiction. Recovery involves different meanings in different narratives; for instance, powerlessness over the addiction, a recognition that one could not sink any lower in behavior than one has now sunk, and a need to depend on others, especially God or a Higher Power, to shift attention and relief from one's poor management of pain to an ability to face anguish without depending on a substance or addictive behavior. The way that recovery narratives are told has moral consequences, and a narrative can emphasize the power or powerlessness of the narrator, thus excusing behavior or laying blame (Hänninen & Koski-Jännes, 1999, 1839). I discuss behavior and responsibility in further detail below.

The mastery story has some of the elements identified in the previous paragraph but tends to emphasize the impression or experience that part of oneself is self-destructive and another part is longing for healing and peace; hence, one must become embroiled in a battle, fight the Enemy within (e.g., the Beast that needs to be "fed" to keep it alive), and emerge triumphant, having succeeded in reducing the Beast to a background whine. This last story teaches people about "disease-*thinking* patterns" and ways to override or correct for them. In Rational Recovery (<http://www.rational.org>) for example, one learns to consider such thinking patterns as *stupid* and simply to stop "feeding the Beast" *right now*. The approach used in Rational Recovery claims that it does away with the need for recovery groups because one can will oneself to stop if one can just understand what the disease needs and understand that it is only kept alive by one's own behavior. Rational Recovery emphasizes reason over emotion and is, perhaps, the clearest framework for thinking of addiction as an individual choice that has been obscured by the more prevalent AA models. The Rational Recovery model frames problematic use of substances or behaviors in terms of faulty thinking and bad habits, thereby moving addiction from the medical to the moral domain. I return to this point later.

Addiction Language by Sibbers

Those who self-injure ("sibbers") are vulnerable to the "mad or bad" trope in psychiatric and legal literature. This trope is extremely forceful in clinician attitudes toward patients diagnosed with borderline personality disorder (BPD), where having a personality disorder (being "mad") ought to evoke sympathy in carers but, instead, evokes strong negative feelings of blame toward those patients (being "bad") (cf. Potter, 2009). But because most lay people and many clinicians find self-injury to be totally bewildering and repulsive, we are more likely to find people who self-injure to be classified as symptomatic of a pathology. Most often they are diagnosed with BPD instead of being conceptualized as having a bad habit (and it is not clear that the latter would be an improvement, since bad habits are framed as moral flaws and thus blameworthy—a particular problem for clinicians who deal with patients who self-injure in that when such behavior is viewed as blameworthy, it reduces empathy (cf. Potter 2009)). Part of the reason for this diagnostic classification is that, unlike addictions, SIB lacks the social approbation that more benign forms of substance abuse offer. It is easier to see how something pleasurable in moderation can become a habit and then a use/abuse problem, harder to see why someone would even think of deliberately hurting herself let alone developing that hurting into a use/abuse problem. But Whitlock, Powers, and Eckenrode (2006) analyze the use of the Internet to bring people who self-injure together in cyberspace where individual sibbers are less isolated. These researchers report postings that illustrate the way the addiction narrative relies on the most prevalent addiction model, the disease model where, it is thought, some people's biologies are such that they cannot avoid getting hooked on a substance or behavior and cannot escape the yearning and desire for that substance or behavior without intervention of some sort. The disease model of addiction draws on a discourse of biological vulnerability and inevitability, powerlessness over particular desires, and a prayerful wonder when one manages, through intervention, to—for the time being—triumph over the influence of the disease. (One must always be vigilant over the disease because one never is completely cured of it.)

Typical examples of these postings include "It just haunts me and I don't think I'll ever get away from it" and "I may try and quit, but even if I succeed, I'll always dream of razorblades and blood." Observations starting with the phrase "I've been cutting free for [length of time]" accounted for almost half of posts coded with addiction elements. References to stable patterns of self-injury, tendency to minimize the problem, similarities to other drugs, multiple quit attempts, the need to self-injure more or more deeply because of increased tolerance for effects of self-injury, and relapse after quitting were all areas discussed within this category (Whitlock et al., 2006, 412).

These researchers note that, accompanying many of the posts is the refrain that others do not understand the addictive quality of self-injury (Whitlock et al., 2006, 412). As I have indicated, it is my contention that the cultural lexicon and discourse available to sibbers pushes them toward a particular conception of themselves and their behaviors that does not serve them well. (I leave open the possibility that an individual might find aspects of the dominant clinical discourse useful at least for a time. For example, a person who is distressed and afraid of the effects of her own behaviors might find the diagnosis of BPD helpful because it provides an explanatory framework she can relate to. But given the myriad problematic values and assumptions that undergird the current BPD diagnosis, I am skeptical that it can serve people well in the long run. See my *Mapping the Edges and the In-Between* [Potter, 2009]). Note the addiction ideology that Whitlock, Powers, and Eckenrode report: multiple quit attempts, always an addict, increased tolerance, minimizing the problem, and relapses. But it is an open question whether or not the subjects in this study themselves came up with the addictive model independent of cultural stories of addiction or whether the subjects (unconsciously) framed their answers in ways they believed were most understandable to listeners. When one's behavior is seemingly inexplicable to others, one casts about for an explanation that might make more sense to others; the addiction model may function this way for SIB—but that in itself does not indicate that it is the most apt explanation.

I am pointing to a way discourse works such that cultural norms interact with both subjects and researchers to reinforce a master narrative that then seems accurate and does not make much room for alternatives. A related problem can be seen when researchers are influenced by a master narrative to such a degree that they project it onto their subjects even when the subjects themselves protest such an interpretation. This sort of problem (drawing upon a dominant lexicon without good reason for doing so) is discussed by Lawrence Langer (1993), who analyzes interviews with Holocaust survivors and finds that interviewers persistently try to reformulate survivors' stories into a moral lexicon of heroes and courageousness despite evidence from the survivors themselves that would reject such interpretations. It is hard to imagine that people in North America—both subjects and researchers of studies on SIB—could be uninfluenced by the master narrative of addiction in their interpretations of behavior, given the dominant role that that narrative plays in North America. This is, of course, the way of cultural stories and of ideologies, but it should give us pause in our attempts to understand a phenomenon that has virtually no social approbation.

Conceptual Issues: Is SIB an Addiction or Not?

Addictions cannot accurately be lumped together, and Elizabeth Gifford and Keith Humphreys caution against "equating long days working at the office, [searching out] discounts at Sainsbury's, and [continually watching] reruns of Star Trek episodes with nicotine, heroin and alcohol" (Gifford & Humphreys, 2007). Nevertheless, according to these researchers, the different kinds of addiction seem to share some common features:

> . . . addictive behavior is reinforcing, chosen behavior; emerges gradually and occurs along a continuum; does not occur in isolation but as part of behavior clusters; occurs within a family context; responds to changes in reinforcement; is affected by a larger social context; has identifiable risk and protective factors, tends to become self-perpetuating once established; is motivated behavior; and is influenced by the therapeutic relationship. (Gifford & Humphreys, 2007, 357)

Similarly, Constance Holden remarks that several different kinds of disorders are classified in a "grab bag" of addictions, compulsions, and obsessions—"all related to loss of voluntary control and getting trapped in repetitious, self-defeating behavior" (Holden, 2001, 980). This description might fit sibbers, but it can do so by conceptualizing SIB as a habit, as well. The question I am posing is whether it is accurate to include SIB as falling under the description of addiction, compulsions, and obsessions. To do this, I first raise some conceptual questions that would need to be addressed before we can settle such questions; then, in what follows, I further develop the discussion of habit as contrasted with addiction.

Explanation and Prediction

To clarify how best to conceptualize SIB, one thing we need to consider is the more general question of how behavior shifts from benign pleasure to problematic drivenness and then whether or not the answer applies to SIB. "The presence of cues associated with the availability of learned reinforcers such as alcohol or other drugs will increase behavioral responding for these rewards. . . . These studies [provide] important information on how alternate behaviors can be produced even when a given response has become 'automatic' and favored" (Gifford & Humphreys, 2007, 355). Likewise, Pallanti, Bernardi, and Quercioli frame addiction as a disturbance in reward motivation. They cite research that suggests that immature neurodevelopment in adolescents is the foundation of disorders involving such a disturbance (Pallanti, Bernardi, & Quercioli, 2006, 968). (This view draws on the medical model's notion of disease.) Certainly, a reward system is key to a person's desire and motivation to return to an activity; its short-term pleasant effects provide a reinforcement of that behavior. The problem arises when the agent is unable or unwilling to identify a significant gap between short-term rewards and long-term dysfunction and to act in one's best interests in aiming for longer-term rewards. Pallanti, Bernardi, and Quercioli's interest is in assessing the extent to which Internet users are addicted to Internet usage. They define Internet pathology as "the individual's inability to control his/her use of the Internet, with related marked distress and/or functional impairment" (Pallanti et al., 2006, 967). And, they write, "The symptoms of Internet-addicted adolescents usually reported were lying, difficulty in stopping Internet use, irritation and anger, increasing time invested in Internet use, difficulty in maintaining steady study habits or everyday functions, and the occurrence of health problems" (Pallanti et al., 2006, 971).

True to the DSM's (*Diagnostic and Statistical Manual* of the American Psychiatric Association) commitment to emphasize symptoms at the expense of attending to etiology, those working on nosology are able to group symptoms in, say, alcohol or drug abuse with "symptoms" of Internet abuse. In addressing self-injury, Marilee Strong argues that cutting develops out of a conditioned response to stress. The patient discovers that she feels better after self-injury, and Strong reports research that suggests that stress elevates opiates in the brain that, in turn, produce numbing. In times of less stress, then, the patient experiences a lower presence of opiates that starts to feel bad. Patients may experience the lowered opiates as a kind of withdrawal and show symptoms of anxiety, aggression, and other behaviors associated with withdrawal (Strong, 1998, 107).

Strong reports that:

after cutting, [patients] feel calm, reintegrated, "real" again, and often fall into restful sleep. However self-destructive the act may seem, they have moved from a place of passive helplessness to active control. Some look upon their wounds with pride as true battle scars, tests of their strength, courage, and survival. More often, though, when the peace and euphoria recedes [*sic*], they are filled with shame and regret. They hate that they seem to need it so much, that they can't stop, that they feel addicted to a behavior others would consider crazy and grotesque. (Strong 1998, 57)

And she notes that symptoms that sibbers exhibit, that seem akin to addictions in the AA model, are behavior that is progressive and that escalates in frequency and intensity over time. If they are unable to self-harm, they have cravings and experience withdrawal symptoms (Strong, 1998, 58). In the prevailing domain-specific master narrative, addiction—whether in the form of substance abuse or SIB—follows the progressive and deteriorating pattern of a disease. Thus, SIB is interpreted as an addiction in part because it seems to exhibit patterns, symptoms, and processes similar to those found in addictions of various sorts (such as learned reinforcers and disturbances in reward motivation). But it is not clear that the explanation of how behavior shifts from benign to problematic is correct in general, let alone that such a pattern applies to SIB. Those are assumptions made, assumptions that are difficult to disentangle given dominant cultural tropes. Furthermore, the decontextualized nature of the DSM leads to an ease of generalizing across symptom sets that may not be clinically appropriate for SIB.

Disease

The master narrative for addiction casts addiction as a disease. The concept of disease, however, is fraught with ambiguity and difficulty. Other chapters address this aspect of addiction, so I will only note a few of the main views. The aim here is to begin to clarify further key aspects of the master narrative of addiction to help with the question of whether or not SIB is best conceived as an addiction.

George Agich argues that disease talk should be considered one kind of response to illness—a response that is committed to scientific method; disease language includes sickness, illness, and disease but also suffering, disability, and incapacity (Agich, 2002, 105, 106). Agich says that disease language is evaluative; it carries meanings of illness and harm (Agich, 2002, 107). But it does provide a scientific basis for taking care of the sick (Agich, 2002, 107). Similarly, Andreas Gerber, Frieder Hantzelt, and Karl Lauterbach argue that the constantly shifting core concepts of evidence-based medicine require that not just one concept of disease will do (Gerber, Hentzelt, & Lauterbach, 2007, 395). However, they, too, suggest that however we conceptualize disease, the concept of disease will be inescapably normative (Gerber et al., 2007, 398).

Paul McHugh and Phillip Slavney frame diagnosis in terms of disease *reasoning*, which reasoning is a combination of drawing on categories that have distinct underlying abnormalities and of a clear pathway to discover causes (McHugh & Slavney, 1998, 45). That is, this kind of reasoning is categorical and explanatory. Simply put,

[d]isease denotes disruptions of the organism and of some part of it in particular. . . . In psychiatry the construal of a disease is prompted by evidence of the breakdown of normal capacities, such as intelligence and consciousness, or by the appearance of new forms of mental phenomena, such as hallucinations (perceptions without stimuli) or delusions (fixed, false, idiosyncratic beliefs). (McHugh & Slavney, 1998, 63–64)

However, that approach seems to have led us to the proliferation of addictions. Edmund Pellegrino states that, in the last twenty-some years, the conceptualization of disease has become such that "every disturbance of function, imperfection, or threat to life's 'quality' becomes a disease, a problem for resolution by the technological prowess of medicine. Imperfections, limitations of any kind, and gaps between expectations and capabilities are no longer tolerable" (Pellegrino, 2004, xii). For example, Arthur Caplan argues for the conclusion that aging is a disease by noting that "[t]he presence of symptoms and an underlying etiology closely parallels the standard paradigmatic examples of disease" (Caplan, 2004, 123). Caplan cites five characteristics that a disease is likely to have, although they should not be thought of as necessary and sufficient conditions: (1) the condition produces distress or suffering; (2) that condition can be traced to a specific and identifiable trigger; (3) clear-cut, uniform, and sequential changes can be expected; (4) a set of clinical symptoms are commonly associated with that condition; and (5) some functional impairment is exhibited or felt. Based on those criteria, Caplan argues, aging is a biological process that should be viewed as a disease (Caplan, 2004, 124). A central benefit of thinking this way about disease is that it situates researchers to look for a cure for aging. As Caplan argues, once we understand what aging is, we see that there is nothing inherently wrong with searching for a cure or a reversal of the aging process (Caplan, 2005, 75).

The combination of the evaluative features of the disease concept with the broadening of the notion of "disturbance" to include challenges to our quality of life implies that we can categorize as addictions everything from cigarette smoking to gambling to shopping to reading in bed to falling in love, and to getting post–secondary education degrees. Surely such a watered-down version of "addiction" calls for critique.

But even if that addiction model is accurate, it does not settle the question of whether or not SIB is a disease. This investigation leads to the question—especially if we accept the fuzziness of the categories of addiction and disease—of what work such a classification is expected to do. How is it useful to conceptualize SIB as an addiction in the disease sense? One answer might be in the ways we understand moral responsibility for addiction. Thus, I am arguing that at the heart of the addiction concept is a disease concept that is highly inclusive, which inclusivity leads to an overly broad addiction category. This nosological problem calls for a critique. But even if we narrow down and clarify what belongs in the concept of addiction, we still are left with the question of whether or not SIB is best characterized that way. One way to address that further question is to inquire into whether or not such a conceptualization (the addiction conceptualization) would serve important purposes. We might, for example, consider determinations of responsibility as one potentially useful purpose that categorizing SIB as an addiction would serve. That is, the disease model of addiction (arguably at least) partly mitigates against evaluations of moral blame. Do pragmatic reasons exist to exculpate people (for some behavior and to some degree) such that it is, practically speaking, better to think about them as addicted to that behavior? And do those reasons apply to SIB? The discussion directly following takes up this issue.

Becoming and Being Morally Responsible

Steven Hyman (2007) discusses one of the central questions that arise when talking about addiction: should it be conceptualized as a brain disease, as a moral condition, or both (8)?[3] The way this question is answered is important to questions of moral responsibility. According to Hyman, "modern definitions of addiction focus squarely on the issue of voluntary control. The current medical consensus is that the cardinal feature of addiction is compulsive drug use despite significant negative consequences" (Hyman, 2007, 9), where "compulsion" is understood as a diminished ability to control drug use. Hyman also points out, though, that none of the current views of addiction holds that a person with an addiction is entirely without the ability for voluntary self-control—which means that none of those views considers addictive behavior to be wholly excused or excusable (Hyman, 2007, 9). The disease model thus holds both that the person has diminished capacity to control herself and that she nevertheless has not lost her autonomy totally and so must be held accountable for continued harmful behavior. Karl-Ernst Bühler also characterizes dependence (on substances) as an increasingly impaired freedom of choice (Bühler, 2005, 81).

So, categorizing behavior as addiction, and therefore a disease, doesn't entirely eliminate a person's moral responsibility; typically, addiction stories encourage the person to have compassion for her disease (something she cannot help once it is "contracted") but also to take responsibility for caring properly for her diseased self—namely, by not exacerbating it—just as one has to care for one's diabetes by diet and insulin control. Nevertheless, addiction stories do garner sympathy from others because the bearer suffers tremendously from losses due to the addiction. So, the story exonerates a person for being addicted to some entity, E, even as it holds her responsible to change her behavior and eventually to make amends for bad behavior that was done in the throes of the addiction.

A central tenet of addiction narratives is that addiction threatens and eventually decreases autonomy. To regain one's autonomy, the person must turn her will and her life over to a Higher Power as advocated by AA. (I do note, however, that it does seem a similar process: instead of surrendering to drugs or addictive behaviors, one surrenders to a Higher Power. Given such a view, surrender, then, is not unequivocally bad.)

Neil Levy states that "addiction is universally recognized as impairing autonomy"—where autonomy is understood to include not only present choices but future ones as well. That is, having and exercising autonomy is not only important in the here-and-now but also in shaping one's future or what Levy calls "extended agency" (Levy, 2006, 427). Thus, "[a]n agent adopts a personal rule when she bunches the rewards of future abstention together, seeing her current decision to abstain as setting a precedent for her future behavior; for such a rule to work, she must value future abstention even as she is tempted to consume" (Levy, 2006, 435). He defines basic autonomy as "self-government" where one's choices and will are reasonably stable in acquisition and expression (Levy, 2006, 429).

The question is how to understand the claim that an addict acts against her own will. Levy argues that addicts do, in some sense, choose to use the drug, or gamble the house, so the person does not entirely lack agency. The central issue is that the addict's preferences at $time_n$ alternate with preferences at $time_{n+1}$, and so what was decided against at one time seems reasonably attractive at another time. The addict "changes her mind" about which desires she wants to move her to action. Levy identifies the problem as being unable to imaginatively project one's proximal actions into a future one genuinely wants. "A basically autonomous agent is self-governing, and a necessary condition of self-government is the ability to extend one's will across time. The agent who is unable to exert control over her future behavior by shaping her desires and her actions lacks the capacity for self-government" (Levy, 2006, 440).

Some researchers posit that evidence of addiction is not to be found in a person's increasing tolerance or withdrawal; it is found in the person's continued pursuit of an activity that has high costs to him or her. Why does the addict persist in seeking immediate rewards even when that seeking flies in the face of longer-term aims and goals (cf. Gifford & Humphreys, 2007, 353)? Because they conceptualize addiction as always embedded in social contexts, Gifford and Humphreys argue that social factors are both the source of elevated risk and a source for aid in recovery. So, they claim that associating with others who are or may be addicts is a major risk factor (Gifford & Humphreys, 2007, 353). Contradictorily, researchers also claim that participation in a 12-step program helps people to recover (Gifford & Humphreys, 2007, 353), but, especially with respect to sibbers, the risk is great that self-injury techniques will be shared.

As discussed above, people who self-injure are typically ashamed and secretive about their cutting or burning (except when it comes to clinicians and other mental health workers). Internet chat rooms can decrease isolation, but they also provide a means for self-injurers to advise one another and offer techniques. Whitlock, Powers, and Eckenrode cite examples of postings that discuss techniques:

Poster 1: Does anyone know how to cut deep without having it sting and bleed too much?

Poster 2: I use box-cutter blades. You have to pull the skin really tight and press the blade down really hard. You can also use a tourniquet to make it bleed more.

Poster 3: I've found that if you press your blade against the skin at the depth you want the cut to be and draw the blade really fast it doesn't hurt and there is blood galore. Be careful, though, 'cause you can go very deep without meaning to.

Poster 1: Okay, I'll get a Stanley blade 'cause I hear that it will cut right to the bone with no hassle. But I'll be careful if I do use a tourniquet and I won't cut that deep. (Whitlock et al., 2006, 413)

Thus, for sibbers, the Internet is not unequivocally beneficial. That is, although the Internet may provide a social context for daily life, it also plays a dual negative role in entrenching SIB as an addiction through addiction language and as an undesirable, or bad, learned activity through the posting of techniques. Examining SIB in light of Internet chat rooms, then, highlights some of the problems in assessing moral responsibility when a person's behavior calls for explanation but when the classification of addiction is not (or not obviously) appropriate. Evaluations of moral responsibility are particularly messy here when we attempt to sort out degrees of autonomy, explanations for the continued pursuit of high-cost activities, and the social dimensions of sibber interactions and advice giving. As things stand, my view is that we need to analyze and then tease apart the constructs of will, desire, impulsivity, and choice as they function (or fail to function) in SIB, but a full treatment of those tasks is beyond the scope of this chapter. My aim has been, instead, to raise questions about what I take to be underlying assumptions in the master narrative on SIB that need to be pressed before we can be clear on the usefulness of classifying SIB as an addiction (and therefore a disease) rather than classifying it as a habit.

The Habit of Self-Injuring

I am not persuaded that the addiction model is accurate for most SIB. My reservations are that, first of all, the typical clinical picture is that behaviors done in moderation may, for some people, become addictions. But there seems to be no moderate position on self-injurious behavior. It is unlike the difference between having a glass or two of wine and having a bottle and then some; even occasional, superficial self-injuries are considered symptoms, not a moderate approach to a normal human activity. Second, SIB is particularly secretive and shameful. One may be a "closet drinker" or a secret junkie, but others are at least implicated as the supplier. One may gamble away the house, but it takes more than one person to play the game. One may charge credit cards to the maximum limit, but doing so takes the cooperation of banks and stores. Self-injury, however, is a mostly private activity, except for contact with other self-injurers or in the talking about it with one's therapist. Third, if self-injury as an addiction is an accurate diagnosis or classification, it should result in treatment protocols that are similar to other addiction treatments—12-step programs, surrender, mastery, and so on. But I do not see evidence that those treatment programs are applicable to SIB. Such an absence of evidence does not mean that these protocols are not helpful, but it should remind readers of the theory-driven quality of domain-specific master narratives of addiction or Hacking's interactive kinds. Note that a diagnosis can be an interactive kind and nevertheless capture something "real" about a person's behavior and symptoms of distress; but being an interactive kind does mean that the looping effect of interaction between category and person makes it possible for the category to *lead* the interpretation beyond what a particular person exhibits. These three reasons should give us pause when contemplating classifying SIB as an addiction. The question then is, how else should it be classified? And are there pragmatic considerations for thinking that SIB is a habit instead of an addiction?

Not all problem behavior should be thought of as addictive. Sometimes we just develop bad habits. And not all habits are bad; we might train ourselves to form a habit of rising with the sun every morning, and becoming habituated to early rising offers us quietude and time for meditation. Habits are dispositions to behave in particular ways that are instilled from an early age (Burkitt, 2002, 219). Burkitt argues that habits are what constitute the self, "that we are forced to partially reflect upon whenever we want to refine or reconstitute the self" (Burkitt, 2002, 219). (I disagree with Burkitt if what he means is that *only* habits constitute the self, but that should not obscure the point of Burkitt's claim that the sort of person we become is, to some degree, up to us (cf. Potter 2002 for an Aristotelian analysis of that idea).

Theories of the self, Aristotle's included, tend to focus on conscious, reflective, and meaningful aspects of the self and give insufficient attention to the role that habits play in our lives (Burkitt, 2002, 220). According to Burkitt, a crucial moment in our lives is when a habit breaks down or clashes with other modes of being, and we find ourselves thinking reflexively about things we formerly did not notice or that we took for granted. For example, Marcus Credé and Nathan Kuncel's (2008) research suggests that poor study habits are a predictor of students' academic mediocrity, and they urge educators to take more seriously the need to inculcate good study habits at a young age so that these become "second nature" to students by the time they are of college age. Or consider a study by Christina Knussen and Fred Yule on recycling habits within households. They define habit as "learned, goal-directed acts that become automatic responses in specific situations" (Knussen & Yule, 2008, 684). The aspect of one's behavior that is automatic indicates an action that is not, at the moment, consciously decided on. Research on the environment investigates habits because of the important effect our behavior has on it. Knussen and Yule found that "lack of recycling habit" significantly contributed to past failure to recycle; if our leaders want us to recycle, they need to find ways for us to cultivate good recycling habits.

Habits are grounded in activities and behaviors that we do with some degree of dissociation—for example, always taking a particular exit on the freeway and then realizing that you are not, in fact, going that direction this time, or turning on the radio for companionship without listening. And habits are not necessarily benign. One could have a habit of shouting and throwing things when angry, for instance, and a settled disposition to act violently due to a bad habit may be categorized as a vice. Vices are moral kinds, and although being a moral kind does not preclude theorizing self-injury as habit instead of addiction from also being a medical kind, such theorizing does seem to present exactly the problem that a disease model of addiction is meant to avoid—namely, that one is a bad person for having a character such that one does such-and-such a bad thing under stress.

I am not much more enthusiastic about labeling sibbers as bad or vicious than I am about labeling them as addicts. As I understand the testimonies of people who self-injure, such behavior—not always, but often—is borne out of experiences of suffering that sometimes defy expression in language. Charges that blame the self-injurer for engaging in bad habits suggest a lack of empathy for a complex kind of suffering that in fact ought to evoke compassion rather than blame or pathologizing. Neither the "habit" nor the pathology conceptualization of SIB seems helpful.

What Should the Cultural Narrative of SIB Be?

Underpinning this analysis is a debate about what kinds of things addiction and disease are. As noted at the beginning of this discussion, they might be indifferent, or natural, kinds (meaning that they exist in nature independently of our beliefs about them and that they have distinct and discernable boundaries that mark off their essence from other entities). They could be interactive kinds, things that affect and are affected by the identification of persons with that kind. Or, they could be practical kinds. Zachar (2000) argues that psychiatric disorders are practical, not natural or artificial (or interactive, I take it), kinds in that the properties of a disorder are not fixed and immutable but are more or less present, having fuzzy boundaries. In understanding nosology, Zachar argues, we need to think in terms of the benefits and burdens that attend a particular way of categorizing various disorders. If we theorize in terms of practical kinds, we eschew the search for necessary and sufficient conditions, a move Zachar wholeheartedly supports.

McHugh and Slavney (1998) seem to endorse the idea of practical kinds. They argue that alcoholism is a disease only in the metaphorical sense, and "disease" is not a useful way to think about alcohol addiction, as it narrows the availability of other ways of understanding it (including creatively developed narratives). Perhaps this is the best conclusion I can arrive at for the time being. I suggest that the focus of inquiry should concern how useful it is to people who self-injure to think of them as addicted or diseased or having bad habits. Further, I suggest we need ask to whom it would be useful. Who benefits, and what treatment regimes are indicated if we ditch current master stories? To dodge the "mad or bad" problem, we need to decouple the power of the domain-specific master narrative of addiction from acts of SIB. We need to loosen our grip on the prevailing lexicon of addiction, and we must listen openly to what sibbers tell us about their experiences and motivations. As I argue elsewhere (Potter, 2009, chs. 5 and 8), being open is both an epistemic and a moral requirement in order to do good clinical work; it involves attending to the particular perspective, context, and features of the individual in building a narrative that is useful for a specific person, in a specific context, from that individual's point of view. Of course, a person's narrative is not entirely up to that individual. Narratives emerge out of cultural and historical contexts as well as social identities and contested experiences. But this messiness just makes it more important that we approach the person who engages in SIB with what I call "the virtue of giving uptake" (Potter, 2009, ch. 8). My less-than-definitive answer, therefore, is that we must not let master narratives and conventions in speech acts close off the possibility that new understandings and interpretations of self-injury might emerge with patients diagnosed with BPD. I advocate an ethic of openness in communication, where giving play to words and phrases expands the repertoire between patients and clinicians (cf. Lugones, 1987; Potter, 2000, 2003a, 2003b).

Acknowledgments

I want to thank Jeffrey Poland and George Graham for their extremely helpful advice on how to improve this chapter. I am indebted to Christian Potter and Kim Baker for their willingness to explore these issues with me early on and, especially, for Christian's insightful and passionate way of looking at these questions.

Notes

1. Grand narrative or "master narrative" is a term introduced by Jean-François Lyotard in *The Postmodern Condition: A Report on Knowledge* (Lyotard, 1984/1979). He also referred to them as "meta-narratives."

2. Now that might be the case for substance abuse, but it is not clear that it applies to sibbers; sibber patients sometimes say they want to feel pain, meaning that they want to transform emotional numbness into physical sensations or, as Susanna Kaysen says, "Oh God, there aren't any bones in there, there's nothing in there. . . . 'I just want to see them,' I said. 'I just have to be sure'" (Kaysen, 1993, 102–103).

3. An analogous question and discussion of the distinction between medical and moral kinds in the context of personality disorders can be found in Zachar and Potter (2010).

References

Agich, G. (2002). Implications of a pragmatic theory of disease for the DSMs. In J. Sadler (Ed.), *Descriptions and prescriptions: values, mental disorders, and the DSMs* (pp. 96–113). Baltimore: Johns Hopkins Press.

Bühler, K.-E. (2005). Euphoria, ecstacy, inebriation, abuse, dependence, and addiction: a conceptual analysis. *Medicine, Health Care, and Philosophy, 8,* 79–87.

Burkitt, I. (2002). Technologies of the self: habitus and capacities. *Journal for the Theory of Social Behaviour, 32* (2), 219–237.

Caplan, A. (2004). The 'unnaturalness' of aging—Give me a reason to live! In A. Caplan, J. McCartney, & D. Sisti (Eds.), *Health disease illness: concepts in medicine* (pp. 117–127). Washington, DC: Georgetown University Press.

Caplan, A. (2005). Death as an unnatural process: Why is it wrong to seek a cure for ageing? *EMBO Reports, 6,* 72–75.

Credé, M., & Kuncel, N. (2008). Study habits, skills, and attitudes: the third pillar supporting collegiate academic performance. *Perspectives on Psychological Science, 3* (6), 425–453.

Gerber, A., Hentzelt, F., & Lauterbach, K. (2007). Can evidence-based medicine implicitly rely on current concepts of disease or does it have to develop its own definition? *Journal of Medical Ethics, 33* (7), 394–399.

Gifford, E., & Humphreys, K. (2007). The psychological science of addiction. *Addiction (Abingdon, England), 102,* 352–361.

Hacking, I. (1999). *The social construction of what?* Cambridge, MA: Harvard University Press.

Hänninen, V., & Koski-Jännes, A. (1999). Narratives of recovery from addictive behaviors. *Addiction (Abingdon, England)*, *94* (12), 1837–1848.

Hochschild, A. (2003). *The second shift.* New York: Penguin Books.

Holden, C. (2001). "Behavioral" addictions: Do they exist? *Science*, *294*, 980–982.

Hyman, S. (2007). The neurobiology of addiction: implications for voluntary control of behavior. *American Journal of Bioethics*, *7* (1), 8–11.

Kaysen, S. (1993). *Girl, interrupted.* New York: Vintage Books.

Knussen, C., & Yule, F. (2008). "I'm not in the habit of recycling": the role of habitual behaviour in the disposal of household waste. *Environment and Behavior*, *40*, 683–702.

Kwan, M.-P. (2008). From oral histories to visual narratives: Re-presenting the post-September 11 experiences of the Muslim women in the USA. *Social & Cultural Geography*, *9* (6), 653–669.

Langer, L. (1993). *Holocaust testimonies: the ruins of memory.* New Haven, CT: Yale University Press.

Levy, N. (2006). Autonomy and addiction. *Canadian Journal of Philosophy*, *36* (3), 427–448.

Lugones, M. (1987). Playfulness, "world"-traveling, and loving perception. *Hypatia*, *2* (2), 3–19.

Lyotard, J.-F. (1984). *The postmodern condition: a report on knowledge.* Minneapolis: University of Minnesota Press. (Original work published 1979.)

McHugh, P., & Slavney, P. (1998). *The perspectives of psychiatry* (2nd ed.). Baltimore: Johns Hopkins University Press.

Mitchell, A. (2006). Taking mentality seriously: a philosophical inquiry into the language of addiction and recovery. *Philosophy, Psychiatry, & Psychology*, *13* (3), 211–222.

Nelson, H. L. (2001). *Damaged identities, narrative repair.* Ithaca, NY: Cornell University Press.

Pallanti, S., Bernardi, S., & Quercioli, L. (2006). The shorter PROMIS questionnaire and the Internet Addiction Scale in the assessment of multiple addictions in a high school population: prevalence and related disability. *CNS Spectrums*, *11* (12), 966–974.

Pellegrino, E. (2004). Renewing medicine's basic concepts. In A. Caplan, J. McCartney, & D. Sisti (Eds.), *Health disease illness: concepts in medicine* (pp. xi–xiv). Washington, DC: Georgetown University Press.

Potter, N. (2000). Giving uptake. *Social Theory and Practice, 26* (3), 479–508.

Potter, N. (2002). *How can I be trusted? A virtue theory of trustworthiness.* Lanham, MD: Rowman-Littlefield.

Potter, N. (2003a). Commodity/body/sign: borderline personality disorder and the signification of self-injurious behavior. *Philosophy, Psychiatry, & Psychology, 10* (1), 1–16.

Potter, N. (2003b). Moral tourists and world-travelers: some epistemological considerations for understanding patients' worlds. *Philosophy, Psychiatry, & Psychology, 10* (3), 209–223.

Potter, N. (2009). *Mapping the edges and the in-between: a critical analysis of borderline personality disorder.* Oxford: Oxford University Press.

Range, S. K. (2008). Re-framing progressive education: searching for viability in the marketplace of ideas. *Dissertation Abstracts International, The Humanities and Social Sciences, 68* (9).

Sadler, J. (2005). *Values and psychiatric diagnosis.* Oxford: Oxford University Press.

Strong, M. (1998). *A bright red scream: self-mutilation and the language of pain.* New York: Penguin.

Whitlock, J., Powers, J., & Eckenrode, J. (2006). The virtual cutting edge: the Internet and adolescent self-injury. *Developmental Psychology, 42* (3), 407–417.

Zachar, P. (2000). *Psychological concepts and biological psychiatry.* Philadelphia: John Benjamins.

Zachar, P., & Potter, N. (2010). Personality disorders: moral or medical kinds—or both? *Philosophy, Psychiatry, & Psychology, 17* (2), 101–117.

9 Contingency Management Treatments of Drug and Alcohol Use Disorders

Nancy M. Petry, Sheila M. Alessi, and Carla J. Rash

Colloquially, a substance use disorder is considered to be use of a substance that is "out of control." Persons suffering from drug and alcohol use disorders report a multitude of adverse consequences stemming from their substance use, ranging from employment to legal, family, and health problems. Individuals with substance use disorders often experience intense guilt and regret regarding their use of substances, and many express extreme desire to abstain. Nevertheless, when they encounter the substance itself or a "trigger" for its use, they relapse—time and time again.

Twelve-step fellowships such as Alcoholic's Anonymous have popularized one conceptualization of substance use disorders as a disease or illness. This concept is used primarily to challenge the belief that alcoholics can stay sober by willpower alone. In contrast, the disease concept implies that alcoholics have an "allergy" to alcohol, which triggers a compulsion to continue drinking once a drink is taken. According to this theory, there is no cure for alcoholism, but by complete abstention, an alcoholic can avoid the adverse consequences associated with his or her disease.

Although this concept may be useful in helping some individuals to abstain, others have argued that substance use is better conceptualized as operant behavior. Skinner (Ferster & Skinner, 1957; Skinner, 1974) noted that any behavior that is positively reinforced increases in frequency, and a wide body of laboratory research demonstrates that drugs of abuse are positively reinforcing. For example, any animal can learn to press a lever to obtain the drugs commonly abused by humans. Once the behavior pattern is established, accessibility to drugs of abuse will maintain substantive behavior, such that animals will lever-press hundreds and even thousands of times to obtain drug infusions, even to the point of death (Johanson, Balster, & Bonese, 1976).

Thus, environmental contingencies have strong impacts on establishing substance-using behaviors. The positive or reinforcing effects of drugs include the pleasurable effects of the drug itself, such as the high or rush. In humans secondary reinforcers, such as social benefits of feelings of fitting in with others, can also increase drug-using behaviors, and negative reinforcers, including reductions in anxiety or boredom, maintain drug use as well. Once physical dependence occurs, use of many substances has an additional benefit of alleviating withdrawal symptoms.

Although these reinforcing effects of drugs perpetuate their use, environmental contingencies can be invoked to reduce substance-using behaviors. In the treatment of substance use disorders these interventions are termed "contingency management." The remainder of this chapter describes the background and efficacy of contingency management (CM) treatments for substance use disorders, with an emphasis on how environmental contingencies can decrease drug use. Although CM is highly efficacious in treating substance-using behaviors, these interventions are rarely adapted in clinical settings. This disconnect between research and practice is in part related to practical barriers, but it is also reflective of a philosophical schism. The final part of the chapter discusses commonly invoked objections to CM techniques and how such concerns may be hindering adoption of effective treatments for this significant public health issue.

Contingency Management Treatments

Contingency management is a form of behavioral therapy that has been widely applied to substance abusers in the context of research studies. The basic premises of these interventions are to (1) frequently monitor whatever behavior one is trying to impact, (2) provide a tangible reinforcer each time the desired behavior occurs, and (3) remove the reinforcer when the desired behavior does not occur.

Higgins and colleagues (Higgins, Delaney, Budney, & Bickel, 1991; Higgins et al., 1993) developed a voucher-based CM approach. Voucher CM treatments provide points worth a specific amount of money each time a patient submits a scheduled urine sample that tests negative for cocaine. Typically, patients submit samples thrice weekly, for example, Monday, Wednesdays, and Fridays, and the samples are tested immediately using onsite testing technology that can detect any use of cocaine over the past 3-day period. When cocaine-negative samples are submitted, the patients receive a piece of paper listing the voucher amounts earned. Vouchers can then be exchanged for monetary-based products, such as restaurant gift certificates, clothing, or electronics. The patient simply makes a request for specific items, and staff purchase them by the next clinic visit. The amount of vouchers earned increases with each consecutive instance of drug abstinence, such that the first negative sample results in a $2.50 voucher, the second negative sample earns a $3.75 voucher, the third negative sample a $5.00 voucher and so on, with a $10 bonus voucher for every third negative sample in a row. Voucher values reset to a low value (e.g., $2.50) if any cocaine use occurs or if a patient fails to submit a scheduled sample.

The initial study of voucher-based CM (Higgins et al., 1991) compared CM combined with a complementary behavioral therapy—the Community Reinforcement Approach (CRA; Hunt & Azrin, 1973) to 12-step–oriented drug abuse counseling. The first 13 patients entering treatment received the combined behavioral therapy, and the next 15 consecutively admitted outpatients received the 12-step counseling. The proportion of patients who remained in treatment differed significantly between the groups, with 85% of those receiving CM+CRA, versus only 42% of those receiving 12-step therapy, staying in treatment for 12 weeks. Patients receiving the CM+CRA also achieved significantly longer periods of objectively verified continuous cocaine abstinence. Seventy-seven percent of those receiving CM+CRA attained four or more weeks of continuous cocaine abstinence compared to 25% in the 12-step group.

Higgins et al. (1993) subsequently conducted a randomized study comparing the same two treatments in a sample of 38 cocaine-dependent patients. Fifty-eight percent of patients randomly assigned to CM+CRA remained in treatment for the full 24 weeks versus only 11% of patients assigned to 12-step counseling. Moreover, 68% of those receiving CM+CRA achieved eight or more weeks of continuous cocaine abstinence; only 11% of those receiving 12-step counseling group maintained this duration of abstinence. Differences between patients assigned to the two conditions remained at 6-, 9-, and 12-month follow-ups; patients who had received CM+CRA earlier were more likely to submit cocaine-negative urine samples and to report cocaine abstinence over the past month than patients who had received 12-step counseling (Higgins et al., 1995).

To isolate the unique contribution of CM to these beneficial effects, Higgins et al., (1994) next compared CM+CRA to CRA alone. They randomized 40 cocaine-dependent outpatients to these two conditions and again noted significant differences between groups. Of those assigned to CM+CRA, 75% remained in treatment for 24 weeks versus 40% of those assigned to CRA alone. The two groups also differed significantly with respect to the longest duration of continuous cocaine abstinence achieved. Patients receiving CM+CRA achieved an average of 11.7 ± 2.0 weeks of continuous abstinence, whereas patients in CRA alone condition achieved an average of 6.0 ± 1.0 weeks of continuous abstinence. The average duration of continuous cocaine abstinence was longer in the CM+CRA condition during the first 12 weeks of treatment when they received vouchers, as well as during the second 12 weeks of treatment when they no longer earned vouchers, suggesting that the enhancement of early abstinence associated with the voucher reinforcement contributed to further abstinence even when tangible reinforcements were no longer available.

Silverman, Higgins, et al. (1996) established that it was the contingent nature of the voucher reinforcement, rather than just the availability of vouchers, that resulted in the beneficial effects. They randomly assigned cocaine-dependent methadone patients to a voucher CM condition or a yoked-control condition, in which patients received vouchers at the same rate and magnitude as patients in the contingent condition, but in this case regardless of their urinalysis results. Almost 50% of patients in the CM condition achieved 2 months or more of continuous cocaine abstinence versus no patients in the yoked condition.

This series of studies demonstrated conclusively that voucher-based CM interventions were efficacious in reducing cocaine use. Further, they isolated the efficacy of these techniques to the contingent nature of the relation between the behavior (submission of a cocaine-negative urine sample) and the receipt of the vouchers.

Behavioral Parameters Important in CM Treatments

Several features of CM interventions impact their efficacy. One important aspect of CM treatments, as noted above, relates to the contingent association between the behavior and the reinforcer. A related concept is immediacy of the reinforcement (Lussier, Heil, Mongeon, Badger, & Higgins,

2006). CM studies that provide reinforcers delayed in time are less efficacious than those that apply the reinforcers in more immediate proximity
to the target behavior (Roll, Reilly, & Johanson, 2000). Thus, testing for
abstinence is best done onsite rather than having urine toxicology samples
sent to outside laboratories for testing, which adds days of delay between
abstinence and the provision of the contingencies (Petry, 2000).

Escalating reinforcers for sustained behavior change also appear to be
important to the efficacy of CM interventions. Roll, Higgins, and Badger
(1996) randomly assigned daily cigarette smokers to one of three conditions. One condition involved three times daily breath testing for evidence
of smoking, with a fixed amount of $9.80 in vouchers for each negative
breath test. A second condition was the same breath testing schedule plus
an escalating amount in vouchers for each negative breath test. In that
condition the first smoking-negative breath test was worth a $3.00 voucher,
the second negative test was worth a $3.50 voucher, the third negative test
was worth a $4.00 voucher, and so on, with a $10.00 bonus for every third
negative test in a row. The third condition involved the same breath-
testing schedule, but the amount of vouchers earned was independent of
breath test results and yoked to the average voucher earnings in the first
10 subjects in the escalating incentives condition. All participants were
asked to try to refrain from smoking during the study, and the average
amounts of vouchers earned were similar across the three conditions.
Results showed that participants in the escalating voucher amounts condition were less likely to resume smoking after achieving an initial period of
abstinence (e.g., three negative breath tests in a row) than those in the
fixed voucher amount condition and control condition. Thus, reinforcer
magnitudes that escalate in value over occurrences of abstinence are more
effective than those that do not escalate.

The magnitude of the reinforcement available also directly impacts CM's
effects. Stitzer and Bigelow (1983, 1984) found that abstinence increased
as a function of the magnitude of the reinforcement available, ranging
from $0 up to $12 per day. Silverman et al. (1999) found that cocaine-
dependent methadone patients who did not respond to standard voucher
amounts achieved abstinence if the amount of vouchers available increased
about threefold, and Dallery, Silverman, Chutuape, Bigelow, and Stitzer
(2001) noted a direct relationship between voucher amounts and abstinence in cocaine-abusing methadone patients as well.

Prize-Based Contingency Management

Although effective in reducing drug use when appropriate behavioral parameters are included, voucher-based CM interventions have not been widely adopted by community drug treatment programs, in part because they are too costly for many programs to implement. Patients in the voucher-based CM studies described thus far in this chapter could earn up to $1200 in vouchers if all submitted urine specimens tested negative for cocaine (Higgins et al., 1991, 1993, 1994; Silverman, Higgins, et al., 1996).

To address the issue of cost, we (e.g., Petry, Martin, Cooney, & Kranzler, 2000) developed a prize-based CM intervention that provides tangible reinforcement on a variable ratio schedule. Patients in prize-based CM who provide evidence of abstinence earn the opportunity to draw slips of paper, and the number of slips drawn increases with successive abstinence. In the typical prize CM program, patients draw slips from a bowl of 500. Half the slips have encouraging messages but do not result in prizes, and half the slips result in a prize. There are typically three prize magnitudes: "small" (worth about $1: patients' choice of toiletries, bus tokens, fast-food gift certificates, etc.), "large" (worth about $20: patients' choice of portable CD players, telephones, pot and pan sets, etc.), and "jumbo" (worth about $100: DVD player, television, or stereo). With this system, there is always an opportunity to earn something of high value, but overall earnings are modest on average. Patients draw from the prize bowl once their urine samples test negative, and prizes are kept on site so they can be provided immediately on winning. This prize CM system provides tangible rewards on an intermittent schedule, the schedule that produces the highest rate of response and greatest resistance to extinction (Nevin & Grace, 2000). Further, by not reinforcing every negative sample with a tangible reinforcer, prize-based CM has the potential to produce similar behavioral outcomes to voucher CM at a lower cost.

In the initial study of prize-based CM, Petry et al. (2000) randomly assigned 42 alcohol-dependent men participating in a Veterans Affairs outpatient substance abuse treatment program to standard care or standard care plus prize CM. All participants submitted breathalyzer samples at each daily visit to the treatment program, and those in the CM group who tested negative for alcohol earned the opportunity to draw for prizes. Patients who received CM in addition to standard care were significantly more likely than those receiving standard care alone to remain in treatment for the 8 weeks of the study (84% vs. 22%) and to remain abstinent from alcohol for the duration of the study (69% vs. 39%). Individuals who received CM compared with those who got standard care alone were less likely to relapse to heavy alcohol use by the end of the study (26% vs. 61%). The average value of prizes earned by each participant in the CM condition was $200.

A direct comparison of voucher- and prize-based CM interventions for cocaine- abusing patients found both CM treatments to be superior to standard care without CM. Petry, Alessi, Marx, Austin, & Tardiff (2005) randomized 142 patients to a prize CM condition, a voucher CM condition or standard care. Both CM conditions significantly enhanced treatment retention and durations of abstinence achieved, and although not significantly different, a trend toward greater retention was noted in the prize CM group relative to the voucher CM group. Patients in prize CM, voucher CM, and standard care groups remained in treatment for 9.3 ± 3.7 weeks, 8.2 ± 3.8 weeks, and 5.5 ± 3.6 weeks, respectively. Patients receiving prize CM achieved an average of 7.8 ± 4.2 weeks of abstinence compared with 7.0 ± 4.2 weeks for those in voucher CM, and 4.6 ± 3.4 weeks for those receiving standard care. Further, 45% of patients randomized to the prize CM condition achieved 12 weeks of continuous abstinence, compared with 28% of those receiving voucher CM, and 8% of those receiving standard care. Similar results with respect to abstinence were achieved in a parallel study (Petry, Alessi, Hanson, & Sierra, 2007) conducted among cocaine-abusing methadone maintenance patients, when the arranged prize reinforcement was about one-half ($300) that of voucher reinforcement ($585).

Given that prize CM with an average of about $300 in prizes was efficacious in reducing cocaine use, we also examined the extent to which prize magnitudes could be further reduced and still impact drug use. Petry et al. (2004) randomized 120 cocaine abusers to one of three conditions: standard care, standard care with CM with an average maximum of $240 in prizes, or standard care with CM with an average maximum of $80 in prizes. In the CM conditions, the probability of winning prizes was identical among groups, but the majority of prizes won in the $80 condition were of a lower value ($0.33, $5, and $100 prizes) than those in the usual prize condition ($1, $20, and $100 prizes). Longest duration of continuous abstinence (in weeks) was greater in the $240 CM condition compared to the standard treatment control condition, without significant differences between the $80 CM condition and standard care condition. Further, when only patients who submitted a cocaine-positive sample at baseline were included in analyses, longest duration of continuous abstinence was significantly greater in the $240 CM condition compared to the $80 CM condition as well as the standard care condition, with mean weeks abstinence being 3.6 ± 3.6, 1.5 ± 2.7, and 0.5 ± 1.2, respectively. Reducing the cost of prize-based CM by decreasing the value of prizes decreased the efficacy of the procedure, similar to the effects noted with voucher CM reviewed earlier, and these effects may be especially relevant for patients who present to treatment still abusing substances.

Based on its positive results when at least $240 in reinforcement is available, prize-based CM was selected by the National Institute on Drug Abuse Clinical Trials Network (CTN) to be integrated in community-based treatment clinics throughout the country (Petry, Peirce, et al., 2005; Peirce et al., 2006). In the largest study of CM to date over 800 stimulant abusers were recruited from 12 community clinics, which were located primarily in urban settings, but suburban and rural settings were represented as well. The duration of the study was 12 weeks, and patients were randomly assigned to one of two treatment conditions: standard care or standard care plus prize CM, with average maximal expected earnings of about $400 in prizes.

Patients from psychosocial clinics who were randomized to CM plus standard care were more likely than patients randomized to standard care alone to remain in treatment for the entire 12 weeks of the study (49% vs. 35%). The longest duration of continuous abstinence was significantly greater in the CM compared to the standard care patients (8.6 ± 9.2 weeks vs. 5.2 ± 6.9 weeks), and CM patients were more likely than standard care patients to achieve 4 (40% vs. 21%), 8 (26% vs. 12%), or 12 (19% vs. 5%) weeks of continuous stimulant abstinence.

A parallel study (Peirce et al., 2006) was conducted at six community-based methadone maintenance settings as part of the CTN. Participants randomized to CM plus standard care were nearly twice as likely to submit negative samples during the 12-week treatment period compared to participants in standard care only (54% vs. 38%). Similar to the Petry, Peirce, et al. (2005) study results, CM participants obtained longer durations of continuous abstinence compared to standard care participants (3 weeks vs.

1 week), and CM participants were more likely than standard care participants to achieve more than 4 (24% vs. 9%), 8 (17% vs. 2%), and 12 (6%
vs. 1%) weeks of continuous abstinence.

Together, these CTN and other studies demonstrate that prize CM is
efficacious in reducing stimulant use. Although much of the research on
CM interventions has focused on its effects reducing cocaine use, CM is
also efficacious in affecting other substance use. CM is efficacious in
decreasing use of methamphetamine (Roll et al., 2006), opioids (Bickel,
Amass, Higgins, Badger, & Esch, 1997; Kidorf & Stitzer, 1996; Preston,
Umbricht, & Epstein, 2000; Silverman, Wong, et al., 1996), alcohol (Petry
et al., 2000; Miller, 1975), marijuana (Budney, Higgins, Radonovich, &
Novy, 2000; Budney, Moore, Rocha, & Higgins, 2006), and nicotine
(Donatelle, Prows, Champeau, & Hudson, 2000; Roll et al., 1996; Shoptaw
et al., 2002). Thus, CM is a highly generalizable intervention. Two independent meta-analyses of randomized studies of CM conclude that CM is
efficacious in facilitating drug abstinence (Lussier et al., 2006; Prendergast,
Podus, Finney, Greenwell, & Roll, 2006). A recent review and meta-analysis
of psychosocial interventions find CM to be the most efficacious intervention for substance use disorders (Dutra et al., 2008).

Failure to Implement CM in Practice

Despite evidence of its efficacy, CM has rarely been implemented in
community-based treatment settings. A survey of clinicians in state-funded
substance abuse treatment facilities found that 48% had no familiarity at
all with CM, and only 9% reported any practical experience with it (McGovern, Fox, Xie, & Drake, 2004). Clearly, costs are one impediment to the use
of CM in practice settings, and even with prize CM, costs may be considered prohibitive.

Using data from the two CTN studies, we estimated incremental cost-
effectiveness ratios of CM compared to standard care. Resource utilization
(e.g., number and duration of counseling sessions, urine and breath tests,
draw sessions, and value of prizes) and outcomes (longest duration of
abstinence) were obtained, and unit costs of services were estimated via
surveys from the 14 clinics. The incremental cost to lengthen abstinence
by 1 week was $258 in psychosocial (Olmstead, Sindelar, & Petry, 2007)
and $141 in methadone clinics (Sindelar, Olmstead, & Peirce, 2007). Thus,

compared to standard care, CM had higher costs, but it also resulted in substantially better outcomes. We (Sindelar, Elbel, & Petry, 2007) also evaluated incremental cost effectiveness of CM in the study in which different magnitudes of prize CM were evaluated (Petry et al., 2004). Outcome data were used in combination with unit cost data on services accessed and costs for maintaining and administering CM. The usual-magnitude ($1, $20, and $100 prizes) CM condition produced outcomes at a lower per-unit cost than the low-magnitude ($0.33, $5, and $100 prizes) CM condition. The higher-cost CM weakly dominated lower-cost CM, and acceptability curves were used to illustrate uncertainty in the incremental cost-effectiveness ratios. These findings suggest that increasing upfront costs can be more cost effective overall, and they pave the way for expansion of CM interventions in practice settings.

Moreover, costs of CM, which can be associated with dramatic reductions in drug use, may be small in contrast to those associated with continued drug use. These include societal costs associated with emergency room visits, inpatient stays, or medical care for an individual who contracts HIV (Drucker, 1986; Holder & Blose, 1991), and recent data suggest that prize CM is efficacious in decreasing risky behaviors that transmit infectious diseases (Hanson, Alessi, & Petry, 2008; Petry, Weinstock, Alessi, Lewis, & Dieckhaus, 2010). CM interventions may also save money in reduced criminal justice system costs, reduced public assistance payments, and increased productivity (a negative cost). By retaining patients in treatment with effective services and reducing drug use, immediate costs for ancillary services and long-term costs for other in- or outpatient substance abuse treatment, medical treatment, and criminal justice system involvement may be reduced substantially. Although more research on the cost effectiveness and cost benefits of CM is needed to confirm and extend these findings, objections beyond those associated with costs are commonly voiced about the use of CM in practice.

For example, Kirby, Benishek, Dugosh, and Kerwin (2006) surveyed 383 substance abuse counselors, supervisors, and their medical/clinical support staff working in five different states. Over three-quarters of the respondents indicated they would consider including "social incentives" in their program (e.g., praise or recognition from the counselor or therapy group), but far fewer were interested in adding tangible incentives. Although costs were cited as one obstacle, other objections were also raised. Prominent among these was that over half the respondents felt that tangible incentives do not address the underlying issues of addiction. Another common objection to CM was that tangible incentives were seen as "bribes" that could "damage" the treatment process. No evidence exists that CM impedes the treatment process, and studies investigating motivation to change drug use reveal no differential changes between those receiving CM and standard care interventions (Budney et al., 2000; Ledgerwood & Petry, 2006; Litt, Kadden, Kabela-Cormier, & Petry, 2008).

Clinicians have also expressed concern that patients will sell the items purchased with their vouchers or won in the prize system and use the proceeds to buy more drugs. There is no evidence to support this contention, and instead the CM system is designed to prevent such behaviors. If patients were to purchase and use drugs with reinforcement earnings, the voucher amount or number of prize draws available would reset back to the originally low level at the next scheduled testing session (Petry, 2000).

Another commonly voiced objection to CM is that drug use will be reinstated when reinforcers are removed. Some within-person reversal design studies demonstrate that once positive reinforcement for abstinence is discontinued, drug use returns to baseline levels (Corby, Roll, Ledgerwood, & Schuster, 2000; Robles et al., 2000; Roll et al., 1996). However, these findings are usually limited to non-treatment-seeking individuals, such as smokers who do not desire to quit smoking, or to interventions that are very brief (1 week) in duration. Many of these studies were designed as laboratory interventions investigating specific reinforcement parameters and their impact on behaviors, without expectations of engendering long-term effects. When CM is applied to treatment-seeking methadone patients, for example, it generally maintains some benefits even after reinforcers are removed (Iguchi, Belding, Morral, Lamb, & Husband, 1997; Kosten, Poling, & Oliveto, 2003; Petry & Martin, 2002; Petry, Martin, & Simcic, 2005; Petry et al., 2007).

Furthermore, a large body of research with CM now demonstrates that abstinence achieved during treatment is highly predictive of posttreatment abstinence. Higgins, Wong, Badger, Ogden, and Dantona (2000) found that a strong predictor of abstinence 1 year after CM ended was the longest duration of continuous abstinence achieved during treatment. Similarly, with prize CM, Petry et al. (Petry, Alessi, et al., 2005; Petry, Martin, et al.,

2005; Petry et al., 2006, 2007) reported that longest duration of abstinence achieved during treatment is highly and consistently predictive of abstinence post-CM treatment. Interestingly, such objections about the enduring nature of treatment are rarely raised about other interventions, including pharmacotherapies, applied to substance-abusing and other populations.

McLellan, O'Brien, Lewis, and Kleber (2000) argue that no intervention should be held to unrealistic standards of engendering complete and long-term abstinence in substance-abusing populations. Rather, models used in other life-long behaviorally related disorders, such as diabetes, hypertension, obesity, and asthma, should be considered. In treating these diseases, one starts with an intervention in intensity that matches the severity of the presenting symptoms. Supplemental treatment, such as CM, should be added until beneficial effects are achieved (e.g., ALLHAT, 2002). If the presenting problem dissipates, the intensity or types of treatments administered can be reduced, but symptoms are monitored, and treatments adjusted accordingly, on a long-term basis.

Although a multitude of objections are commonly raised about CM when applied to substance-abusing populations, behavioral interventions similar to CM are used in other clinical and nonclinical settings, with substantially fewer concerns. For example, CM is based on basic behavioral therapies widely utilized in mental retardation, autism, and conduct-disordered youth (e.g., Eyeberg, Nelson, & Boggs, 2008; Matson & Boisjoli, 2009). Similar techniques have benefits for improving medication adherence (Burkhart, Rayens, Oakley, Abshire, & Zhang, 2007; Haug & Sorensen, 2006; Haug, Sorensen, Gruber, Lollo, & Roth, 2006; Post, Cruz, & Harman, 2006; Rosen et al., 2007; Roth, Brunette, & Green, 2005; Sorensen et al., 2007), enhancing engagement in medical care, including mammography testing (Bailey, Delva, Gretebeck, Siefert, & Ismail, 2005; Stoner et al., 1998) and immunizations (Birkhead et al., 1995; Hoekstra et al., 1998; Lieber, Colden, & Colon, 2003), and improving healthy behaviors such as exercise (Epstein, Smith, Vara, & Rodefer, 1991; Jason & Brackshaw, 1999; Weinstock, Barry, & Petry, 2008) and weight loss (Jeffrey, Wing, Thorson, & Burton, 1998; Nunn, Newton, & Faucher, 1992; Stalonas, Johnson, & Christ, 1978; Volpp et al., 2008). Concerns about "bribery," intrinsic motivation, or long-term effects are rarely, if ever, voiced in relation to these other conditions.

In part, criticisms raised about CM in substance abuse treatment settings seem to relate to a bias against substance abusers. Much substance abuse is illegal. Substance abusers may be considered undeserving of "special treatment," and some argue that society should not be "paying drug abusers to do what they should do anyway." Given the demonstrated benefits of CM techniques in reducing drug use and the lack of more effective interventions (Dutra et al., 2008), such sentiments imply that individuals with substance use disorders are in some way unworthy of treatment interventions with established efficacy.

These issues highlight concerns about responsibility from several perspectives—responsibility of the individuals with substance use disorders and responsibility of health care providers and of society more generally. Some argue that substance abusers are responsible for their drug-using behavior and as such should not receive additional reinforcers for what they ought to be doing anyway (i.e., abstaining). On the other hand, diseases and some psychiatric disorders in particular are characterized at least in part by diminished capacities. In actuality CM interventions may challenge and strengthen existing capacities for self-control; patients may learn how better to exert self-control over drug-using behaviors as the reinforcers associated with *not* using increase and those associated with poor control decrease. In fact, in the study of Silverman, Higgins, et al. (1996), 61% of patients receiving CM reported they used "willpower" to stop or reduce their cocaine use compared with only 27% receiving standard care. Thus, CM interventions may garner willpower and self-control, but further research is necessary to uncover mechanisms of CM's actions.

In terms of responsibilities of health care professionals and society, the Institute of Medicine (1998) reported on a longstanding disconnect between interventions with evidence basis and those utilized in practice. McGlynn et al. (2003) reviewed records from 6000 patients to ascertain the quality of care received for 30 illnesses. Although patients suffering from many disorders failed to receive appropriate standards of care, substance-abusing patients were the least likely to receive recommended care—only 11% of the time. These data suggest that substance abuse treatment programs are not held to the same standards as other areas of medicine with respect to implementing evidence-based practices. Meaningful changes in care delivery are unlikely to occur until financial, and perhaps legal, pressures mandate improvements in standards of care for substance-abusing populations.

Politics and ideology will clearly impact the expansion or failure to implement CM in practice. Nevertheless, data on the efficacy of CM, and the orderly nature in which substance-using and abstinence behaviors respond to behavioral principles, clearly indicate that substance use is a behavior that is under environmental control. On the other hand, blaming substance abusers for their failures to abstain may be tantamount to blaming individuals with high blood pressure for not getting their blood pressure under control. Genes and environment interact to propagate both disorders, and just as those with hypertension should benefit from the most effective interventions available, so should substance abusers.

Acknowledgments

Work described in this report and preparation of this chapter was supported by National Institutes of Health Grants P30-DA023918, R01-DA022739, R01-DA027615, R01-DA021567, R01-DA024667, R21-DA021836, R01-DA13444, R01-DA016855, R01-DA018883, R01-DA14618, R01-MH60417, P50-DA09241, P60-AA03510, T32-AA07290, and M01-RR06192.

References

ALLHAT Officers and Coordinators for the ALLHAT Collaborative Research Group. (2002). Major outcomes in moderately hypercholesterolemic, hypertensive patients randomized to pravastatin vs. usual care: the Antihypertensive and Lipid-Lowering Treatment to Prevent Heart Attack Trial. *Journal of the American Medical Association, 288*, 2998–3007.

Bailey, T. M., Delva, J., Gretebeck, K., Siefert, K., & Ismail, A. (2005). A systematic review of mammography educational interventions for low-income women. *American Journal of Health Promotion, 20*, 96–107.

Bickel, W. K., Amass, L., Higgins, S. T., Badger, G. J., & Esch, R. A. (1997). Effects of adding behavioral treatment to opioid detoxification with buprenorphine. *Journal of Consulting and Clinical Psychology, 65*, 803–810.

Birkhead, G. S., LeBaron, C., Parsons, P., Grabau, J. C., Maes, E., Barr-Gale, L., et al. (1995). The immunization of children enrolled in the Special Supplemental Food

Program for Women, Infants, and Children (WIC). The impact of different strategies. *Journal of the American Medical Association, 274,* 312–316.

Budney, A. J., Higgins, S. T., Radonovich, K. J., & Novy, P. L. (2000). Adding voucher-based incentives to coping skills and motivational enhancement improves outcomes during treatment for marijuana dependence. *Journal of Consulting and Clinical Psychology, 68,* 1051–1061.

Budney, A. J., Moore, B. A., Rocha, H. L., & Higgins, S. T. (2006). Clinical trial of abstinence-based vouchers and cognitive-behavioral therapy for cannabis dependence. *Journal of Consulting and Clinical Psychology, 74,* 307–316.

Burkhart, P. V., Rayens, M. K., Oakley, M. G., Abshire, D. A., & Zhang, M. (2007). Testing an intervention to promote children's adherence to asthma self-management. *Journal of Nursing Scholarship, 39,* 133–140.

Corby, E. A., Roll, J. M., Ledgerwood, D. M., & Schuster, C. R. (2000). Contingency management interventions for treating the substance abuse of adolescents: A feasibility study. *Experimental and Clinical Psychopharmacology, 8,* 371–376.

Dallery, J., Silverman, K., Chutuape, M. A., Bigelow, G. E., & Stitzer, M. L. (2001). Voucher-based reinforcement of opiate plus cocaine abstinence in treatment-resistant methadone patients: effects of reinforcer magnitude. *Experimental and Clinical Psychopharmacology, 9,* 317–325.

Donatelle, R. J., Prows, S. L., Champeau, D., & Hudson, D. (2000). Randomized controlled trials using social support and financial incentives for high risk pregnant smokers: significant other supporter (SOS) program. *Tobacco Control, 9* (Suppl. 3), 67–69.

Drucker, E. (1986). AIDS and addiction in New York City. *American Journal of Drug and Alcohol Abuse, 12,* 165–181.

Dutra, L., Stathopoulou, G., Basden, S. L., Leyro, T. M., Powers, M. B., & Otto, M. W. (2008). A meta-analytic review of psychosocial interventions for substance use disorders. *American Journal of Psychiatry, 165,* 179–187.

Epstein, L. H., Smith, J. A., Vara, L. S., & Rodefer, J. S. (1991). Behavioral economic analysis of activity choice in obese children. *Health Psychology, 10,* 311–316.

Eyeberg, S. M., Nelson, M. M., & Boggs, S. R. (2008). Evidence-based psychosocial treatments for children and adolescents with disruptive behavior. *Journal of Clinical Child and Adolescent Psychology, 37,* 215–237.

Ferster, C. B., & Skinner, B. F. (1957). *Schedules of reinforcement.* New York: Appleton-Century Crofts.

Hanson, T., Alessi, S. M., & Petry, N. M. (2008). Contingency management reduces drug-related human immunodeficiency virus risk behaviors in cocaine-abusing methadone patients. *Addiction (Abingdon, England)*, *103*, 1187–1197.

Haug, N. A., & Sorensen, J. L. (2006). Contingency management interventions for HIV-related behaviors. *Current HIV/AIDS Reports*, *3*, 154–159.

Haug, N. A., Sorensen, J. L., Gruber, V. A., Lollo, N., & Roth, G. (2006). HAART adherence strategies for methadone clients who are HIV-positive: A treatment manual for implementing contingency management and medication coaching. *Behavior Modification*, *30*, 752–781.

Higgins, S. T., Budney, A. J., Bickel, W. K., Badger, G. J., Foerg, F. E., & Ogden, D. (1995). Outpatient behavioral treatment for cocaine dependence: One-year outcomes. *Experimental and Clinical Psychopharmacology*, *3*, 205–212.

Higgins, S. T., Budney, A. J., Bickel, W. K., Foerg, F. E., Donham, R., & Badger, G. J. (1994). Incentives improve outcome in outpatient behavioral treatment of cocaine dependence. *Archives of General Psychiatry*, *51*, 568–576.

Higgins, S. T., Budney, A. J., Bickel, W. K., Hughes, J. R., Foerg, F., & Badger, G. (1993). Achieving cocaine abstinence with a behavioral approach. *American Journal of Psychiatry*, *150*, 763–769.

Higgins, S. T., Delaney, D. D., Budney, A. J., & Bickel, W. K. (1991). A behavioral approach to achieving initial cocaine abstinence. *American Journal of Psychiatry*, *148*, 1218–1224.

Higgins, S. T., Wong, C. J., Badger, G. J., Ogden, D. E. H., & Dantona, R. A. (2000). Contingent reinforcement increases cocaine abstinence during outpatient treatment and 1 year of follow-up. *Journal of Consulting and Clinical Psychology*, *68*, 64–72.

Hoekstra, E. J., LeBaron, C. W., Megaloeconomou, Y., Guerrero, H., Byers, C., Johnson-Partlow, T., et al. (1998). Impact of a large-scale immunization initiative in the Special Supplemental Nutrition Program for Women, Infants, and Children (WIC). *Journal of the American Medical Association*, *280*, 1143–1147.

Holder, H. D., & Blose, J. O. (1991). Typical patterns and cost of alcoholism treatment across a variety of populations and providers. *Alcoholism, Clinical and Experimental Research*, *15*, 190–195.

Hunt, G. M., & Azrin, N. H. (1973). A community-reinforcement approach to alcoholism. *Behaviour Research and Therapy*, *11*, 91–104.

Iguchi, M. Y., Belding, M. A., Morral, A., Lamb, R., & Husband, S. D. (1997). Reinforcing operants other than abstinence in drug abuse treatment: An effective alternative for reducing drug use. *Journal of Consulting and Clinical Psychology*, *65*, 421–428.

Institute of Medicine. (1998). *Bridging the gap between practice and research: forging partnerships with community-based drug and alcohol treatment.* Washington, DC: National Academy Press.

Jason, L. A., & Brackshaw, E. (1999). Access to TV contingent on physical activity: effects of reducing TV-viewing and body-weight. *Journal of Behavior Therapy and Experimental Psychiatry, 30,* 145–151.

Jeffrey, R. W., Wing, R. R., Thorson, C., & Burton, L. R. (1998). Use of personal trainers and financial incentives to increase exercise in a behavioral weight loss program. *Journal of Consulting and Clinical Psychology, 66,* 777–783.

Johanson, C. E., Balster, R. L., & Bonese, K. (1976). Self-administration of psychomotor stimulant drugs: the effects of unlimited access. *Pharmacology, Biochemistry, and Behavior, 4,* 45–51.

Kidorf, M., & Stitzer, M. L. (1996). Contingent use of take-homes and split dosing to reduce illicit drug use of methadone patients. *Behavior Therapy, 27,* 41–51.

Kirby, K. C., Benishek, L. A., Dugosh, K. L., & Kerwin, M. E. (2006). Substance abuse providers' beliefs and objections regarding contingency management: implications for dissemination. *Drug and Alcohol Dependence, 85,* 19–27.

Kosten, T., Poling, J., & Oliveto, A. (2003). Effects of reducing contingency management values on heroin and cocaine use for buprenorphine- and desipramine-treated patients. *Addiction (Abingdon, England), 5,* 665–671.

Ledgerwood, D. M., & Petry, N. M. (2006). Does contingency management affect motivation to change substance use? *Drug and Alcohol Dependence, 83,* 65–72.

Lieber, M. T., Colden, F. Y., & Colon, A. L. (2003). Childhood immunizations: a parent education and incentive program. *Journal of Pediatric Health Care, 17,* 240–244.

Litt, M. D., Kadden, R. M., Kabela-Cormier, E., & Petry, N. M. (2008). Coping skills training and contingency management for marijuana dependence: exploring mechanisms of behavior change. *Addiction (Abingdon, England), 103,* 638–648.

Lussier, J. P., Heil, S. H., Mongeon, J. A., Badger, G. J., & Higgins, S. T. (2006). A meta-analysis of voucher-based reinforcement therapy for substance use disorders. *Addiction (Abingdon, England), 101,* 192–203.

Matson, J. L., & Boisjoli, J. A. (2009). The token economy for children with intellectual disability and/or autism: a review. *Research in Developmental Disabilities, 30,* 240–248.

McGlynn, E. A., Asch, S. M., Adams, I., Keesey, J., Hicks, J., DeChristofano, A., et al. (2003). The quality of health care delivered to adults in the US. *New England Journal of Medicine, 348,* 2635–2645.

McGovern, M. P., Fox, T. S., Xie, H., & Drake, R. E. (2004). A survey of clinical practices and readiness to adopt evidence-based practices: dissemination research in an addiction treatment system. *Journal of Substance Abuse Treatment, 26,* 305–312.

McLellan, A. T., O'Brien, C. P., Lewis, D., & Kleber, H. D. (2000). Drug dependence, a chronic medical illness: implications for treatment, insurance, and outcomes evaluation. *Journal of the American Medical Association, 284,* 1689–1695.

Miller, P. M. (1975). A behavioral intervention program for chronic drunkenness offenders. *Archives of General Psychiatry, 32,* 915–918.

Nevin, J. A., & Grace, R. C. (2000). Behavioral momentum and the Law of Effect. *Behavioral and Brain Sciences, 23,* 73–130.

Nunn, R. G., Newton, K. S., & Faucher, P. (1992). 2.5 years follow-up of weight and body mass index values in the Weight Control for Life! program: a descriptive analysis. *Addictive Behaviors, 17,* 579–585.

Olmstead, T. A., Sindelar, J., & Petry, N. M. (2007). Cost-effectiveness of prize-based incentives for stimulant abusers in outpatient psychosocial treatment programs. *Drug and Alcohol Dependence, 87,* 175–182.

Peirce, J. M., Petry, N. M., Stitzer, M. L., Blaine, J., Kellogg, S., Satterfield, F., et al. (2006). Effects of lower-cost incentives on stimulant abstinence in methadone maintenance treatment: A National Drug Abuse Treatment Clinical Trials Network study. *Archives of General Psychiatry, 63,* 201–208.

Petry, N. M. (2000). A comprehensive guide to the application of contingency management procedures in clinical settings. *Drug and Alcohol Dependence, 58,* 9–25.

Petry, N. M., Alessi, S. M., Marx, J., Austin, M., & Tardiff, M. (2005). Vouchers versus prizes: contingency management treatment of substance abusers in community settings. *Journal of Consulting and Clinical Psychology, 73,* 1005–1014.

Petry, N. M., Alessi, S. M., Carroll, K. M., Hanson, T., MacKinnon, S., Rounsaville, B., et al. (2006). Contingency management treatments: reinforcing abstinence versus adherence with goal-related activities. *Journal of Consulting and Clinical Psychology, 74,* 592–601.

Petry, N. M., Alessi, S. M., Hanson, T., & Sierra, S. (2007). Randomized trial of contingent prizes versus vouchers in cocaine-using methadone patients. *Journal of Consulting and Clinical Psychology, 75,* 983–991.

Petry, N. M., & Martin, B. (2002). Low-cost contingency management for treating cocaine- and opioid-abusing methadone patients. *Journal of Consulting and Clinical Psychology, 70,* 398–405.

Petry, N. M., Martin, B., Cooney, J. L., & Kranzler, H. R. (2000). Give them prizes and they will come: contingency management for the treatment of alcohol dependence. *Journal of Consulting and Clinical Psychology, 68*, 250–257.

Petry, N. M., Martin, B., & Simcic, F. (2005). Prize reinforcement contingency management for cocaine dependence: integration with group therapy in a methadone clinic. *Journal of Consulting and Clinical Psychology, 73*, 354–359.

Petry, N. M., Peirce, J. M., Stitzer, M. L., Blaine, J., Roll, J. M., Cohen, A., et al. (2005). Effect of prize-based incentives on outcomes in stimulant abusers in outpatient psychosocial treatment programs: A National Drug Abuse Treatment Clinical Trials Network study. *Archives of General Psychiatry, 62*, 1148–1156.

Petry, N. M., Tedford, J., Austin, M., Nich, C., Carroll, K. M., & Rounsaville, B. J. (2004). Prize reinforcement contingency management for treating cocaine abusers: how low can we go, and with whom? *Addiction (Abingdon, England), 99*, 349–360.

Petry, N. M., Weinstock, J., Alessi, S. M., Lewis, M., & Dieckhaus, K. (2010). Group-based randomized trial of contingencies for health and abstinence in HIV patients. *Journal of Consulting and Clinical Psychology, 78*, 89–97.

Post, E. P., Cruz, M., & Harman, J. (2006). Incentive payments for attendance at appointments for depression among low-income African Americans. *Psychiatric Services (Washington, D.C.), 57*, 414–416.

Prendergast, M., Podus, D., Finney, J., Greenwell, L., & Roll, J. (2006). Contingency management for treatment of substance use disorders: a meta-analysis. *Addiction (Abingdon, England), 101*, 1546–1560.

Preston, K. L., Umbricht, A., & Epstein, D. H. (2000). Methadone dose increase and abstinence reinforcement for treatment of continued heroin use during methadone maintenance. *Archives of General Psychiatry, 57*, 395–404.

Robles, E., Silverman, K., Preston, K. L., Cone, E. J., Katz, E., Bigelow, G. E., et al. (2000). The brief abstinence test: voucher-based reinforcement of cocaine abstinence. *Drug and Alcohol Dependence, 58*, 205–212.

Roll, J. M., Higgins, S. T., & Badger, G. J. (1996). An experimental comparison of three different schedules of reinforcement of drug abstinence using cigarette smoking as an exemplar. *Journal of Applied Behavior Analysis, 29*, 495–505.

Roll, J. M., Reilly, M. P., & Johanson, C. E. (2000). The influence of exchange delays on cigarette versus money choice: a laboratory analog of voucher-based reinforcement therapy. *Experimental and Clinical Psychopharmacology, 8*, 366–370.

Roll, J. M., Petry, N. M., Stitzer, M. L., Brecht, M. L., Peirce, J. M., McCann, M. J., et al. (2006). Contingency management for the treatment of methamphetamine use disorders. *American Journal of Psychiatry, 163*, 1993–1999.

Rosen, M. I., Dieckhaus, K., McMahon, T. J., Valdes, B., Petry, N. M., Cramer, J., et al. (2007). Improved adherence with contingency management. *AIDS Patient Care and STDs, 21,* 30–40.

Roth, R. M., Brunette, M. F., & Green, A. I. (2005). Treatment of substance use disorders in schizophrenia: A unifying neurobiological mechanism? *Current Psychiatry Reports, 7,* 283–291.

Shoptaw, S., Rotheram-Fuller, E., Yang, X., Frosch, D., Nahom, D., Jarvik, M. E., et al. (2002). Smoking cessation in methadone maintenance. *Addiction (Abingdon, England), 97,* 1317–1328.

Silverman, K., Chutuape, M. A., Bigelow, G. E., & Stitzer, M. L. (1999). Voucher-based reinforcement of cocaine abstinence in treatment-resistant methadone patients: effects of reinforcement magnitude. *Psychopharmacology, 146,* 128–138.

Silverman, K., Higgins, S. T., Brooner, R. K., Montoya, I. D., Cone, E. J., Schuster, C. R., et al. (1996). Sustained cocaine abstinence in methadone maintenance patients through voucher-based reinforcement therapy. *Archives of General Psychiatry, 53,* 409–415.

Silverman, K., Wong, C. J., Higgins, S. T., Brooner, R. K., Montoya, I. D., Contoreggi, C., et al. (1996). Increasing opiate abstinence through voucher-based reinforcement therapy. *Drug and Alcohol Dependence, 41,* 157–165.

Sindelar, J., Elbel, B., & Petry, N. M. (2007). What do we get for our money? Cost-effectiveness of adding contingency management. *Addiction (Abingdon, England), 102,* 309–316.

Sindelar, J. L., Olmstead, T. A., & Peirce, J. M. (2007). Cost-effectiveness of prize-based contingency management in methadone maintenance treatment programs. *Addiction (Abingdon, England), 102,* 1463–1471.

Skinner, B. F. (1974). *About behaviorism.* Oxford: Knopf.

Sorensen, J. L., Haug, N. A., Delucchi, K. L., Gruber, V., Kletter, E., Batki, S. L., et al. (2007). Voucher reinforcement improves medication adherence in HIV-positive methadone patients: a randomized trial. *Drug and Alcohol Dependence, 88,* 54–63.

Stalonas, P. M., Jr., Johnson, W. G., & Christ, M. (1978). Behavior modification for obesity: the evaluation of exercise, contingency management, and program adherence. *Journal of Consulting and Clinical Psychology, 46,* 463–469.

Stitzer, M. L., & Bigelow, G. E. (1983). Contingent payment for carbon monoxide reduction: effects of pay amount. *Behavior Therapy, 14,* 647–656.

Stitzer, M. L., & Bigelow, G. E. (1984). Contingent reinforcement for carbon monoxide reduction: within-subjects effects of pay amounts. *Journal of Applied Behavior Analysis, 17,* 477–483.

Stoner, T. J., Dowd, B., Carr, W. P., Maldonado, G., Church, T. R., & Mandel, J. (1998). Do vouchers improve breast cancer screening rates? Results from a randomized trial. *Health Services Research, 33,* 11–28.

Volpp, K. G., John, L. K., Troxel, A. B., Norton, L., Fassbender, J., & Loewenstein, G. (2008). Financial incentive-based approaches for weight loss: A randomized trial. *Journal of the American Medical Association, 300,* 2631–2637.

Weinstock, J., Barry, D., & Petry, N. M. (2008). Exercise-related activities are associated with positive outcome in contingency management treatment for substance use disorders. *Addictive Behaviors, 33,* 1072–1075.

10 Addiction, Paradox, and the Good I Would

Richard Garrett

To paraphrase Shakespeare, Addictions come, not as single spies, but as whole battalions (Hamlet, act 4, scene 5). I can truthfully say that I am a food addict, but it is also true that my addictions came in clusters or battalions and not as single spies. Immanuel Kant said that it was David Hume who awakened him from his "dogmatic slumbers." But in my case, it was an awareness of my food addiction and my struggles with it that awakened me from my own dogmatic slumbers. An interesting fact about addictions is that they are, in many respects, unique to the individual: each person has his own set of *addiction-fingerprints* so to speak. For each person has a unique combination of genetic makeup and familial and cultural context as well as a unique personal history. Yet, like fingerprints, addictions or addiction clusters have certain commonalities in their origins, in their patterns, and in their consequences. It is primarily these commonalities that I will be addressing, even when I am describing my own personal struggle. Because I am an addict who knows that he is an addict, as I shall explain throughout this chapter (and especially in later sections), this recognition of my addiction and, especially, my struggle with it have provided me with a window that enables me to see myself, others, and life itself with a greater clarity, depth, and compassion. It is in this sense that my addiction has awakened me from my dogmatic slumbers.

In this chapter, I discuss the course and nature of addiction by charting the following: I begin by *looking backward* at some earlier parts of my personal history of addiction. Next, I briefly describe some of *the terrible personal costs of this addiction*. After that, in preparation for what follows, I elaborate on *the paradoxical character of addiction*. I then explain some of my *strategies for controlling addiction*. Finally, I consider the greater *wisdom* that can be derived from our struggles with our addictions.

Looking Back

My personal history and possibly also my personal genetic profile make it
quite unsurprising that my addictions center around food issues. So this
will be a good place to begin. In order to examine the way in which I
became addicted to food, it will be useful to distinguish weight problems
from eating problems. For it is quite possible to have an eating problem
without having a weight problem (which was the case with me and my
siblings in early life), and it is also quite possible to have a weight problem,
without having an eating problem. Regarding the latter, a friend of mine,
who is seriously overweight, recently described his daily diet to me. He
explained to me that he has an unusually low rate of metabolism and that
he takes a medicine for a serious asthmatic condition that further compromises his metabolism. If what he says about his daily diet is accurate, then
he should be very slender (if not unhealthily thin) rather than 60 or 70
pounds overweight. Generally, however, the two problems go together,
and, almost without exception, an individual's eating problem is the
conspicuous and obvious cause of that person's weight problem.

Nonetheless, since I had eating problems long before I had weight
problems, for the sake of clarity, it is useful to distinguish between
eating problems and weight problems. Neither I nor my five siblings had
weight problems while we were growing up. However, I think that all of
us had some eating problems even while we were children, and, in any
case, I certainly did. Two family stories illustrate the problematic nature of
my eating behavior. The first story involved little boxes of candy given out
each Christmas by the local fire company and also by our Sunday school.
As I recall, each box weighed a quarter of a pound. Consequently, my three
older brothers and I received eight boxes of this candy adding up to a grand
total of two pounds. I was only six years old at the time, but I managed
to eat not only all of my candy but a considerable amount of my three
older brothers' candy as well.

According to the second story, even though I was younger at the time
(only five years old), my performance was even more telling. In this case,
it had to do with cookie dough. Each year at Christmas time, my mother
would make an enormous batter of raw cookie dough that was composed
mostly of butter, sugar, and flour, with various spices and flavorings. I
developed a sweet tooth for the raw cookie dough, which she kept in the

refrigerator. So, one day, I launched several raids on the raw cookie dough. However, during one of these raids, I met with an obstacle: Mrs. Snook (an elderly housekeeper who stood no more than 4 feet, 10 inches) was standing guard in front of the refrigerator between me and the cookie dough. Nonetheless, I was so determined to get to the cookie dough that I pulled her hair and chased her away. This is not the end of the story: Later that day, I had terrible stomach cramps, was taken to see Dr. Good (the family physician) and, on his recommendation, I was rushed to the hospital where it was discovered, not surprisingly, that my stomach was filled with undigested raw cookie dough. And here is the most important part of the story: No sooner had they pumped my stomach, relieving my pain, but I was complaining to my mother that I was "hungry."

Even though, as I said, I was not at all overweight as a child, my issues around food started very early on. I can only guess at some of the early factors that played a role, but my obsession with food was very likely about more than just food. My mother told me that I was the only one of the six siblings who never went through a "fussy period," a time when each of my siblings was very particular about what and how much he or she ate (a phenomenon that caused problems for my mother). My mother always stated this fact in very positive tones, so that I felt quite proud of myself over this "accomplishment." It was a way that I, as the fourth child of six, was able to stand out, if not quite be outstanding. Another source of pride came from my mother's telling me that I was very placid and peaceful as a very young child and was very easy to deal with: indeed, she found that whenever I was upset as a baby, she could always soothe me by feeding me. Unwittingly, she was teaching me to turn to food when I was upset. I don't at all blame her, considering she had three older boys to deal with, and at the time she had no idea that she was helping me to associate food with being loved and comforted when I was upset. Moreover, it is worth noting that food could not similarly be used to effectively soothe my siblings, which suggests to me that I was very likely hardwired with a tendency to be highly reinforced by food, not unlike alcoholics, who similarly seem to be hardwired to find alcohol reinforcing.

Although, as far as my siblings and I go, I was the leader of the pack when it comes to food addiction, quite clearly each one of my siblings had/has an addiction to food as well. This is evident from the fact that before any of us reached our late 20s, we all started to have weight problems. By the time we were 35, every one of us was a good 10 to 25 pounds overweight, and the problems around weight worsened over the years and have haunted us throughout our adult lives.

Two factors stand out rather conspicuously. The first has to do with my family culture. Like many families, especially large, rural families, mealtime was family time, a time when some of our fondest moments occurred and when we were all gathered and interacted as a single unit. There was, moreover, an emphasis on food and hearty appetites, and the enjoyment of food was perceived as healthy and "manly," a concept of no small importance in a family of five boys and a baby sister who, very understandably, loved the rough-and-tumble of boys. Ours was, one might say, a very "masculine" culture, and indeed all of us, including my sister, were excellent athletes, which brings me to the second factor. All of the boys played football and also participated in at least two other sports besides. My brother Roger, who was All-American honorable mention in football, also held the shot put record at Cornell for more than three decades. Our devotion to athletics is significant in two different ways. First, because we were so active as children, athletically during the school year and in physically very demanding jobs during the summers, this explains why, in spite of our preoccupation with food, we were not overweight as children and young adults. Second, athletes in those days, especially football players, like our family, associated large appetites with strength and manliness. I can recall that when I played football in college, without exception the team always had an elaborate steak dinner the night before every game.

It is worth mentioning that the family-athletic culture surrounding my father, who was one of 10 siblings, was very similar. He was voted the outstanding college pitcher in the East when he played baseball at Rutgers University, and one of his brothers was a professional basketball player, while another brother was an All-American football player. It is also worth noting that my uncles loved gatherings with food and similarly had weight problems. This is significant because they were, in many respects, models for us. In later years as my weight problem developed, for quite a long time I did not perceive it as a truly serious problem but, rather, simply as something that naturally and inevitably happens to athletes, especially football players, as they age.

This "ho-hum" attitude toward being overweight came to an abrupt halt when, in the late summer of 1993, I was diagnosed with diabetes, something that I knew about because my father had had diabetes, developed heart problems, and died of heart failure in 1980. Moreover, my younger brother who is a physician advised me that if I lost weight and exercised faithfully, there was a very good chance of controlling my blood sugars and possibly even avoiding the need for any kind of medicine. I took this advice very seriously but did not relish the restrictions it entailed on the quality and quantity of food that I could now eat. In fact, I can recall feeling somewhat depressed, as I accompanied my wife and my two daughters to a Ben & Jerry's ice cream parlor, at the thought that I was not supposed to eat ice cream for the rest of my life. Furthermore, at the time, I was terribly overweight: 270 pounds, a good 60 pounds heavier than my playing weight over 30 years earlier when I was playing college football and was at an ideal weight. Moreover, considering my age, my loss of muscle tissue, and the fact that I was diabetic made me realize that I was presently probably 75 pounds over my present ideal weight. The thought of having to lose 75 pounds was something like being told that I had to climb Mount Everest by myself, without any training, and without any mountain-climbing equipment. "Impossible" I thought! Yet, it was a matter of losing that weight or very possibly not surviving even a decade longer. So I knew that I had to try, and I did.

I tried, but, at first, my success was insufficient and only temporary. But this changed when I discovered a 12-step program for food addicts (known as Food Addicts in Recovery Anonymous). What I learned from the Food Addicts in Recovery Anonymous community was not only a lifesaver, a way to lose weight and keep it off, but a whole new way of looking at my eating problem, seeing it as an *addiction*, which is to say as behavior that lay outside the domain of my rational control and that reflects problems that are not only of a psychological nature but of a spiritual and moral nature as well. This awareness reawakened my interest in Buddha's Eightfold Path, which I had studied diligently throughout the 1970s, during the years that I taught inmates at Norfolk and Walpole state prisons here in Massachusetts. For it occurred to me that what we today call an addiction is essentially the same phenomenon that Buddha called "attachment." This return to my study of Buddha's Eightfold Path helped me to understand the deeper aspects of my addiction. What I learned in Food Addicts, moreover, was very parallel to Buddha's teachings. In any case, I have found it convenient to simplify matters and to explore addiction primarily within the framework of the Eightfold Path. Before I do so, however, it will be useful to consider very briefly and very generally some basic costs of having an addiction and after that to say something about the puzzling or paradoxical nature of addictions.

Unholy Feasts: The Price of Admission

To say that it is *rational* to choose to have an addiction is like saying that it is *rational* to spend your life savings on a penny's worth of chocolate. I would like very briefly to say something here about the high cost of addiction.

I am sure that most of you are aware of the physical health costs of addiction to alcohol, drug, and cigarettes. No doubt, moreover, some of you are addicted to food. If you cannot seem to win "the battle of the bulge," then you very likely have an addiction to food, and if you are aware of this then you know that you are at terrible physical risk. These physical health costs are quite serious, but, believe it or not, there is an even greater cost to be paid for any addiction. Whether it is an addiction to some kind of physical substance or to something else (e.g., to power, to glory, to work, to a very unhealthy relationship, to sex, to money, or to anything else), the real price to be paid for an addiction is nothing less than the price of your very soul: addiction is a Faustian bargain. For it entangles the individual in a web of delusion, lies, deceits, and fantasies and thereby prevents the person from being real, from being a whole human being, or even coming close to realizing his or her true potential to live a truly good life. I will put meat on these bare bones throughout this chapter, especially toward the end.

The Paradox: What Is Voluntary Is Not Voluntary

In a very real sense, addictive behavior is both voluntary and not voluntary. However, what we have here is not an out and out contradiction but a paradox. Moreover, this paradox is readily resolvable by simply distinguishing between two senses in which we might speak of someone's behavior as being voluntary. On the one hand, following B. F. Skinner, we can legitimately think of addictive behavior as being voluntary as follows: for Skinner, the divide between voluntary and involuntary behavior is simply the divide between *operant behavior* and *respondent behavior* (Skinner, 1953, 45–140 and 227–241). Operant behavior is behavior that produces consequences and that is made more likely by their recurrence if those consequences are rewarding in some way. It is very clear that addictive behavior is reinforced or rewarded in this way, as, for example, when the food addict overeats, for very clearly there is some kind of reward, pleasure, comfort, or escape that results from his eating that extra serving of roast beef or slice of pie. In contrast, respondent behavior is, one might say, slavishly tied to some antecedent stimulus. If you flash a light in someone's eyes, the person's eye pupil will contract, whereas if you darken the room, the eye pupil will dilate, and there is nothing that the person can do to prevent this from happening no matter what consequences will follow or not follow the contraction or dilation of the eye pupils. You could hold a gun to the person's head, for example, and tell him that you will shoot him if his eye pupils contract. No matter. When the light is shined into his eyes, his pupils will contract. In contrast, if you followed a food addict around all day, held a gun to her head and threatened to kill her if she goes off her diet even slightly, she would never go off her diet. So very clearly there is a real sense in which the person's behavior is consequence sensitive or voluntary.

On the other hand, if we distinguish between behavior that is voluntary in Skinner's sense and behavior that is rationally voluntary, the addict's behavior is not voluntary. As an addict, I know this too well. Indeed, the very first step in 12-step programs (see Alcoholics Anonymous, 1976) is for the individual to admit that he is "powerless" to control his addiction. What is going on here is not that the individual addictive behavior is insensitive to all consequences. Rather, addictive behavior is not sufficiently controlled by the really *good* and *important* consequences that would follow from abstention. Instead, relatively unimportant consequences such as experiencing some momentary pleasure or comfort has too much control. Thus, the addict's reason tells him that what he is about to do will have the most terrible consequences over time and that the benefits he will receive are not even close to the cost he will pay. No matter! Reason becomes impotent at such moments. Hence, we may say that, although the addict's behavior is voluntary in the sense that it is a function of its reinforcing consequences, it is not *rationally voluntary*; i.e., the best of reasons cannot compete with the imminent pleasure, comfort, and/or escape they are expecting to experience.

Doing the Good I *Would* by Doing the Good I *Can*

In Romans 7:19, St. Paul says ". . . the good that I would, I do not: but the evil which I would not, that I do." This is of course the very paradox just spoken of where the good I would do is what our reason tells us to do, while the evil I would not do is what our reason tells us not to do. Plato and Aristotle called this the problem of "moral weakness." What we want, of course, is to bring our addictive behavior under the control of reason. That is the addict's problem in the nutshell. To accomplish this, *the addict must discover behaviors already under reason's control that can bring the uncontrollable undesirable behaviors under reason's control.* Suppose, for purposes of illustration, that you could not control your tendency to smoke, but that by simply wearing a "patch" that is chemically treated, you become nauseated every time you attempted to smoke and that this entirely suffices to bring your smoking career to an end. Putting the patch on is behavior that presently lies within the control of reason, and that behavior in turn brings your presently uncontrollable habit of smoking under the control of your best reasoning.

Here I want to discuss some of the things that we *can* do in order to bring our addictions under our control. For reasons that I hope will become obvious, it will be convenient to discuss what can be done within the framework of Buddha's Eightfold Path.

Although my primary focus in this section will be on Buddha's Eightfold Path, I will mix in a fair helping of Aristotle with Buddha because Buddha's central notion of the Middle Way and Aristotle's central notion of the Golden Mean are parallel notions, and I find that much of what Aristotle says about the Golden Mean can be very illuminating. There are differences between Buddha and Aristotle to be sure. Nonetheless, when it comes to understanding the Middle Way (Rahula, 1959, 57–64) on the one hand and the Golden Mean (McKeon, 1941: *Nicomachean Ethics, Book II,* ch. 6–9) on the other, these differences are relatively secondary and unimportant. What is important is that Buddha and Aristotle discovered the vital truth that extremes, both extreme excesses and extreme deficiencies (in emotions, desires, and behavior) are undesirable (i.e., are contrary to what is in our true interest). Having discovered this basic truth about ourselves, we should not be surprised that there are many parallels in Buddha's and Aristotle's moral reckoning. This is especially helpful because, as we shall see, there are times when Aristotle provides us with more guidelines in interpreting certain matters of practical importance.

In order to understand the Eightfold Path (Bodhi, 1984, 12–14), it will be helpful to organize the eight steps into the traditional three groups as follows:

A. The Wisdom Group: (1) Right Understanding and (2) Right Intentions.

B. The Moral Group: (3) Right Speech, (4) Right Action, and (5) Right Livelihood.

C. The Concentration Group: (6) Right Effort, (7) Right Mindfulness, and (8) Right Concentration.

We may then consider each of the eight steps in greater detail.

The Wisdom Group

We may begin by noting that, although the final, liberating wisdom comes at the end of the path, The Wisdom Group (Bodhi, 1984, 14–44) is listed first. This is because there are three different levels of wisdom: (1) There is the initial wisdom, which motivates the individual to undertake the Eightfold Path in the first place and so comes before everything else. (2) There is the intermediate wisdom, which gradually unfolds and develops and guides the individual as he progresses along the Path. (3) Finally, there is the liberating wisdom, which is the ultimate reason for pursuing the Eightfold Path. At this point of the discussion, I focus primarily on the initial wisdom that motivates individuals to pursue the Eightfold Path.

If you are aware of having an addiction or any dysfunctional behavior that is causing great suffering for you and for others but that you cannot control, then you are blessed. The blessing lies not in having the addiction or dysfunctional behavior but in having the awareness of it. This awareness can help you to understand Buddha's Four Noble Truths. First of all, although you may currently be powerless to control your addiction, as noted above, your addiction is clearly consequence-sensitive or voluntary behavior and therefore behavior that is being reinforced in various ways, for example, through certain pleasures or, even more importantly, because it offers you comfort and a temporary escape from things that are deeply painful and troubling. If you follow the addiction trail with enough patience and care, it will lead you to get in touch with an underlying despair, a sense of the meaninglessness and emptiness of life in general. If you have gotten that far in your understanding of your addiction, then you can appreciate Buddha's First Noble Truth. For Buddha's First Noble Truth says that life is suffering or *dukkha,* and this is best understood as saying that there is a deep despair underlying human life (Bodhi, 1984, 1–7).

If this were the end of the story and the only truth that Buddha had to tell us, then he certainly would rightly be called a pessimist. But Buddha offers a diagnosis of our despair. The clue is this: just ask yourself who is it that is momentarily reinforced by your addictive or dysfunctional behavior. Very clearly, the answer has to be "No one but me!" This means that our addictions are all about us, our temporary pleasures, our temporary comforts, and our temporary escapes. So being addicted is a form of self-preoccupation, a symptom of a basically self-centered mode of being in the world. This leads us to be able to appreciate Buddha's Second Noble Truth: The cause of our despair or *dukkha* is our selfish striving or *tanha* (Bodhi, 1984, 7–9).

Now, The Third Noble Truth (Bodhi, 1984, 9–11) makes it very clear that Buddha is not a pessimist. For Buddha tells us that there is a path that we can follow that will liberate us from our self-centered existence, which is the very cause of our despair. I argue below that, ultimately, to be liberated in this way is to master the art of living according to the Golden Rule. For now, let us simply think of the remedy for despair as the process of having compassion for all living things and liberating ourselves from the shackles of selfish striving.

Finally, the Buddha's Eightfold Path may be seen as a comprehensive program of mental and behavioral modification by means of which we can transform ourselves from self-centered creatures into truly loving beings. This is Buddha's Fourth Noble Truth (Bodhi, 1984, 11).

To understand these Four Noble Truths in a way that motivates and equips the individual to pursue the Eightfold Path (or its equivalent) is to have Right Understanding. Moreover, so far as all of your intentions or goals are consistent with the Four Noble Truths, they are Right Intentions. So far as you have such Right Understanding and Right Intentions, you have attained first-level wisdom.

The Moral Group

The Moral Group (Bodhi, 1984, 45–66) entails Right Speech, Right Action, and Right Livelihood. What we do and say and the way that we make our living may or may not lead us to the ultimate goal of living a truly good life. This is obvious in the case of our actions and our livelihood. After all, stealing from people, bullying them, or becoming a hired killer will hardly make for becoming a decent person and living a truly good life. Nor is what you say unimportant. For, on the one hand, what we say to others and to ourselves can be untruthful, unhelpful, unhealthy, hurtful, harmful, and even lethal, whereas, on the other hand, what we say to others and to ourselves can be truthful, uplifting, upbuilding, enlightening, empowering, and even life-saving.

The Concentration Group

If the Wisdom Group is concerned with Right Understanding and Right Intentions and the Moral Group is concerned with Right Action , Right Speech and Right Livelihood; the Concentration Group (Bodhi, 1984, 45–66) concerns building a bridge between the Wisdom Group and the Moral Group. For it is one thing to have Right Understanding and Right Intentions in the abstract, and it is quite another to concretely retain them with sufficient clarity and firmness in our daily lives when we face concrete situations that in some way seriously tempt, upset, or threaten us. So here is where we face our addictions head on.

As I plainly stated at the very beginning of this chapter, I am a food addict. So, when I am presented with delicious food and everyone is merrily eating and talking away, I very strongly want to join in on the fun. Or, again, if, after a very stressful day, I am alone and tired and worried about the future, I have a very powerful inclination to numb out before the television with my favorite comfort food. (No doubt my mother's use of food to soothe me when I was a baby is playing a potent role here.) Because I am a food addict, it is difficult not to regularly give into such desires even when I have had sufficient food and even though my rational mind tells me that I am paying much too dearly for such behavior. I say that overeating is soul destroying because, when I overeat, my mind fogs out, so that my thinking and judgment are impaired, I become more irritable and impatient, I am more inclined to behave in various inappropriate, irrational, and self-centered ways, and my energy and zest for meaningful activities as well as my ability to behave in a morally desirable and fruitful way are all seriously compromised.

All addictive behaviors are, in one way or another, self-centered and soul destroying, ultimately reinforcing and deepening our despair. What I need to do is to find a way of changing a downward spiral into an upward spiral. That is where the sixth step, Right Effort comes into play. Right Effort is a matter of starting to become more conscious of just what I am doing and just what is going on inside of my head—talking to myself much as a good football coach might address his team at halftime. Furthermore, just as Right Effort for an athlete means training, practicing, and conditioning his or her mind and body before Saturday's game, so too, Right Effort for an addict means training, practicing, and conditioning one's mind and body for the trials and temptations that the addict must face daily.

If I am an addict, moreover, my opponents are not another team or something or someone else out there in the world but, rather, the unwholesome states of mind right within my self. Three of these are particularly notable: desire, ill will, and delusion. My allies or teammates are the wholesome mental states that I can cultivate, such as compassion for those who suffer, loving kindness for every being or creature that desires to be happy, equanimity, diligence, energy, inquiry and careful observation, and reflection. What I need to do is to do whatever will reduce or eliminate the unwholesome states and cultivate and strengthen those that are wholesome. Not surprisingly, we can find a counterpart to all of this in Aristotle (McKeon, 1941, *Nicomachean Ethics, Book V,* ch. 1–14). Where Buddha speaks of cultivating wholesome states and eliminating unwholesome states, Aristotle speaks of cultivating the various virtues and eliminating the various vices. Accordingly, Right Effort, for Aristotle, amounts to giving the very highest priority in one's life to the cultivation of the various virtues and the elimination of the various vices. Consequently, it will be useful to consider in some detail just what this entails.

The principles of the Middle Way as well as the Golden Mean are applied to all emotional states and their resulting actions. Fear is an example. It is possible to have too little fear (which is foolhardiness) as well as an excess of fear (which is called cowardliness). Thus, on the one hand, if a person drives through Waltham at 90 miles an hour, such a deficiency of fear for people's safety is foolhardiness. On the other hand, if a person cannot stand up for him- or herself or another when it is in his or her true self-interest or in the true interest of another, such excessive fear is cowardly. But, if a teenager refuses to show that he is "brave" by driving 90 miles an hour in spite of the ridicule of peers, this is courage. Furthermore, if a person stands up for herself or for another even though it is dangerous to do so, then, if this is in accord with her true interest and/or the true interest of another, this is also a demonstration of courage (McKeon, 1941: *Nicomachean Ethics, Book III,* ch. 6–9). Note that the Golden Mean (or the Middle Way) between two extremes is not a simple mathematical midpoint. Rather, it entails good judgment about what is truly in the interests of the parties affected by the actions in question. I will have much more to say about this in the discussion below.

Aristotle observes that the more we practice acting in accord with the Golden Mean, the more natural it becomes, until it finally becomes *second nature,* which is to say something we do unthinkingly and automatically. Indeed, Aristotle notes that when we instill such a disposition to behave in accord with the Golden Mean (or the Middle Way) in ourselves, there is a certain pleasure or pleasantness that accompanies such behavior (McKeon, 1941: *Nicomachean Ethics, Book II,* ch. 3). So far as we accomplish this, we have what Buddha calls wholesome states and Aristotle calls virtue. Applying this to my eating addiction, so far as I have mastered my desires around food and it becomes second nature to prefer healthy eating, I may be said to have the virtue of temperance (McKeon, 1941: *Nicomachean Ethics, Book III,* ch. 10–12).

When I became a member of the Food Addicts community, joining that community was something that I could do and reasonably saw that I should do after the very first meeting. The members of the 12-step program taught me how it is possible to do the good I *would* by doing the good that I *can.* Moreover, what is true of my eating addiction is equally true of all addictions. It is a matter of discovering the many things that we *can* do to get our addictions under our rational control. *Right Effort* entails doing whatever we *can* do in order to do all of those good things that we rationally *would do* but irrationally *do not do* and to stop doing those things that we rationally *would not do* but irrationally *do* anyway.

It is especially here that the seventh step, Right Mindfulness, comes in to play. Right Mindfulness is essentially a matter of observing *without interpretation* whatever is happening inside my mind and outside it in the situations I am in from moment to moment. It is *living in the moment,* which is the very opposite of living for the moment. To live for the moment is to cling to comfortable, pleasant, or pleasurable experiences (when it is not in our true interest or in the true interest of others to do so) while, at the same time, attempting to escape all painful or unpleasant experiences (that either cannot really be escaped or that it would be in our true interest to face up to). In contrast, Right Mindfulness or *living in the moment*, entails paying attention to our unwholesome desires and emotions in response to the various situations confronting us. To be sure, we will have unwholesome feelings and unwholesome desires, but, by being aware of them, stepping back from them, and understanding and carefully evaluating them, we can experience them without them taking control of us. It is a matter of having such desires and feelings, rather than such desires and feelings having us, and thereby leading us to behave in ways that are unwholesome. In this way, we can begin to examine such unwholesome states and, by examining them, begin to liberate ourselves from them. The more that we practice Right Mindfulness, the more it becomes second nature to us, and the more we become capable of acting in ways that are in our true interest and in the true interest of others.

This brings us to the third member of the Concentration Group, which is itself called Right Concentration. The goal of Right Concentration is twofold in ways that are related. On the one hand, Right Concentration practices and exercises are aimed at what may be described as serenity, which is roughly an advanced state in which the individual is free (or relatively free) of all unwholesome states and thereby experiences a certain undisturbed, mental-spiritual peace.[1] On the other hand, achieving this goal is related to the second goal, which consists of achieving a deeper understanding of oneself, others, and life as these things are experienced daily in one's life.

Some Buddhists think of third-level wisdom as that wisdom that is so penetrating and so liberating that the individual will cease to partake of the cycle of reincarnation, that the person will not return to this world. Taken literally, this is an extraordinarily controversial idea, no less controversial than the claim made by many Jews, Christians, and Muslims that there is an afterlife or, for that matter, the atheist's claim that this world is all there is. Such claims all belong to the realm of faith, a realm where it is reasonable to expect reasonable people to disagree with us no matter what we believe. Another metaphysical notion, seemingly inconsistent with the first, is Buddha's doctrine of no-soul or no-self. Whether there is third-level wisdom in this *metaphysical* sense is something that need not concern us, at least not so far as we focus on our life here on Earth. In the next paragraphs I shall in fact suggest a kind of third-level, practical wisdom that does not concern itself with such metaphysical questions and that is quite consistent with nearly all of Buddha's other teachings and with Aristotle's practical philosophy as well.

Third Level Wisdom: The Mean between Deficient and Excessive Self-Love

Rabbi Hillel, of ancient times, made the following statement: "If I am not for myself, who will be for me? And if I am for myself [alone], what am I? And if not now, when?" It is reasonable to interpret Hillel as saying that to completely fail to love yourself would be one extreme (the extreme of a deficiency of self-love), whereas to love only yourself would be the other extreme (the extreme of having an excess of self-love). If, as is extremely likely, this is what Hillel meant by his words, then Buddha and Aristotle would agree. But in exactly what *way* should we love ourselves and others? Moreover, to what *extent*, or in exactly what *proportion*, should we love others and love ourselves? Hillel's statement leaves these two questions unanswered.

Yet, loving ourselves and loving others in the right way and to the right extent, I argue, is the moral basis for everything else that we do. Accordingly, finding the right way and the right extent or proportion we should love ourselves and love others is the key to finding the Golden Mean (i.e., the Middle Path) between any two extremes of excess or of deficiency with respect to anything whatever and so of correctly judging the moral rightness or moral wrongness of any action, practice, rule, law, institution, or system. So, it is the key to understanding just what way of living constitutes a truly good life. I begin by first discussing *in exactly what way we should love ourselves and others*. After that I consider *in exactly what proportion we should love ourselves and others*.

Let us begin with the observation that the kind of love we are talking about must be, on the one hand, a kind of love that we can have for both ourselves and for others, and, on the other hand, it must be a love that is thoroughly rational (since it needs to set the standard for everything else). What I call *caring love* satisfies both of these conditions, since we can care about both ourselves and others and since caring love, in the sense to be specified, is always a good thing so long as it is kept within its proper boundaries. We can define *caring love* as follows: to have caring love for someone is to desire and seek whatever is in that person's true interest.

Note that *what someone is truly interested in* and *what is in someone's true interest* can be quite different things: thus, the king might be truly interested in drinking the wine that has been placed before him, while, at the same time, it would not be in his true interest to drink that wine, if someone has poisoned it. To have *caring love* for someone (ourself or another) is to desire and seek what is in that person's true interest, not what the person happens to be truly interested in. All good parents understand and deeply appreciate the importance of this distinction. Yet it is a distinction that applies across the board to everyone, including the case where the beloved happens to be ourselves. Only the truth about what is in our best interest can really set us free. Keeping this vital distinction in mind, let us consider caring love first as it applies to loving ourselves and afterward as it applies to loving others.

It is *unconditionally* rational for me to desire and to seek what is in my true interest so long as I do so within the proper boundaries, that is, according to the proper proportion (to be discussed below).[2] The crucial point I wish to make here is that self-love in the sense specified above is *unconditionally* rational. For, how could it ever be rational (or in accord with the best of reasons) for me to not desire or to deliberately not seek what is in my true interest (so long as I stay within the boundaries set by what is morally right)? Under what conditions would it be rational for me to count what is in my true interest as being of no importance? What would constitute a good reason for not desiring and not seeking what is in my true interest (within the boundaries set by morality)? If, then, we grant that it is indeed unconditionally rational for me to desire and to seek what is in my true interest, then it is no less true that it is unconditionally rational for you to desire and to seek what is in your true interest as well. It also follows that I will rationally desire that you do not act contrary to what is in my true interest and that you indeed also desire and seek what is in my true interest, at least so far as it is consistent with what is in your true interest. But, as it is with me, so again, it is with you: You naturally and rationally desire me to reciprocate; that is, you rationally and naturally desire that I do nothing that is inconsistent with your true interest and that I, likewise, desire and seek what is in your true interest (at least so far as it is consistent with what is in my true interest). And what is true of you and of me is no less true of everyone else. So, it follows that every one of us desires that everyone else act in ways that are consistent with what is in our true interest. It further follows that there is no way to achieve a *rational harmony* in the world unless we respect one another in these ways.

This leads us to the second question: How important can we consider what is in our own true interest in proportion to what is in another's true interest? Should we count what is in our own true interest as being more important than or less important than what is in another's true interest? In other words, what boundaries need to be placed around each person's self-love? I see no way that I can rationally count what is in my true interest as being any *less* important than what is in anyone else's true interest. Yet if I cannot rationally do such a thing, then neither can you or anyone else. So, each of us must count *what is in our true interest and what is in the true interest of each and every other person* as being equally important if we are going to achieve a *universally rational harmony* (i.e., a way of harmonizing our lives that each and every person can rationally accept).

The basic principle that we have arrived at immediately above may be expressed as follows: *The mean between an excess of self-love and a deficiency of self-love is to count what is in our own true interest and what is in the true interest of each and every other person as equally important.* A second way of stating this principle is to simply say that *we should love our neighbor as we love ourselves.* This is of course what is called the Golden Rule. Because the Golden Rule is, as we have seen, really a principle and not a rule, I hereafter refer to it as the Golden Principle.

It is interesting to note that although the Golden Principle was first beautifully and succinctly stated in Leviticus (19:18), presumably by Moses, Moses never elaborates on the Golden Rule and never provides us with clear indications of what it means to love others as we love ourselves or exactly how this encompasses all of our duties to all persons. So, it is not at all clear that Moses understood that the Golden Rule, rightly interpreted, may be said to be the supreme principle of all morality. Jesus, on the other hand, appears to have understood the Golden Rule (or Golden Principle) and to have assigned it to its proper place as the supreme foundation of all morality. This is evident in Matthew (22:34–40) and elsewhere, where Jesus states that our whole duty to God is to love God with all our heart and mind and soul and that *our whole duty to other persons is to love them as we love ourselves.* I have spent the last five decades studying and reflecting on the Golden Rule and I have looked for illumination from every source I could find (including such luminaries as Immanuel Kant and John Stuart Mill and many other philosophers and scholars interested in interpreting the Golden Rule) and, in the end, I have found no better guidelines for understanding the Golden Rule than the sayings of Jesus in the New Testament. It is worth noting that, on the basis of various comments ascribed to him, Rabbi Hillel likewise seems to have understood The Golden Principle and also clearly seems to have taken it to be the fundamental principle of Jewish moral law. According to one story, for example, in response to a challenge by a Gentile to explain the entire Torah while standing on one foot, Hillel replied "What is hateful to you, do not do to your fellow: this is the whole of Torah; the rest is commentary; go and learn." Although this way of stating the principle only tells us what we should not do (and not what we should do as well), other statements made by Rabbi Hillel elsewhere rather clearly indicate he may well have had a deeper understanding of the principle than the last quote might suggest.

Loving people as we love ourselves means taking them as we find them as opposed to how we might want them to be. This is beautifully and touchingly illustrated in a recent PBS documentary titled *The Emotional Life*. In the first of three episodes, we encounter a troubled family in which the parents are learning how to help an adopted child who, as a result of 2 years of neglect and lack of love and nurturing, is unable to return their affection and love them in the way children generally and naturally do when lovingly nurtured in their early years. Asked about the ordeal of raising such a child, the father wisely and lovingly comments that he is not able to be the father he wanted to be (meaning a father enjoying a healthy interactive, reciprocally loving relationship with his son) and that he is finding that, instead, he must be the father that his son needs him to be (meaning a father who does what is in the true interest of his son without necessarily expecting love in return). This father shows that he clearly understands that it is important for us to be there for others, to love them in the fundamental sense of desiring and seeking what is in their true interest without necessarily expecting them to do the same in return. This is the very essence of what it means to be a good parent. Indeed, it is the very essence of being a good husband, wife, sibling, son, daughter, friend, and, across the board, in being a good and decent person in any relationship that we have with anyone, including casual acquaintances, colleagues, complete strangers, and even those who despise us, those who only intend us ill, and those who in no sense desire or seek what is in our true interest.

Such love for our "enemies" is clearly required by the Golden Principle. After all, to love others as we love ourselves is likewise to love others unconditionally, even those who mean us ill and who do truly wicked things. For it is entirely rational for me to continue to love myself in spite of my wicked ways, since to love myself (to seek what is in my true interest) is, among other things, to desire and seek to put an end to my wicked ways. Similarly, to love our enemies in the same unconditional way that we love ourselves is always to seek what is in their true interest, and this includes putting an end to their harmful and wicked ways. So, to love all others as ourselves is by no means to be a doormat.

Thus, the Golden Rule or Golden Principle applies to all of our human "neighbors" in the sense of all persons with whom we have a relationship or simply encounter along life's path. But, its scope reaches far beyond that. For it equally applies to our "neighbors" in the sense of each and every person who is affected by our choices and actions, including persons on the other side of the globe whom we do not know at all as well as those who are our so-called enemies in war and those who perform the most despicable acts. They too deserve our unconditional love, our unconditional concern with what is in their true interest, even when they engage in the most terrible actions. This means that, so far as we can, we need to do our part in helping to design our own communities, our own nation, and all nations according to the Golden Principle (and by whatever means are available to us, including the politicians, laws, and institutions that we support).

Again, as noted above, this does not entail being a doormat. Rather, it entails resisting those of ill will as lovingly as the circumstances permit. Gandhi insisted that he never encountered a situation where nonviolent resistance would not have been effective and where force, therefore, was needed. However, Gandhi also said that forceful resistance is preferable to no resistance, if we are confronted with a situation that renders nonviolent resistance impossible. I believe that, although Gandhi disputed the matter, World War II was clearly a situation where force became necessary. In any case, if there is no other way to resist those who would do terrible harm to the innocent, then loving them not only includes deadly force but requires it (Merton, 1964, 24–34). After all, it cannot really be in anyone's true interest to allow evil to take over the world. Moreover, better I be dead than that I be permitted to commit some horrible crime against my fellow human beings. Willfully, wrongfully, and selfishly taking the life of another, and not dying, is the worst thing that can happen to a person. It is best for everyone to nonviolently contain violence. But, if that is not possible, the next best thing is to violently contain violence.

To even come close to being someone loving others as we love ourselves, as Jesus, Buddha, Gandhi, and others have noted, is an arduous task and requires nothing less than a radical transformation of ourselves in the deepest and most basic parts. But, it is humanly possible (as the examples of Jesus, Buddha, Gandhi, Martin Luther King Jr., and others teach us) if we are willing to wrestle with our many demons, our many addictions and many dysfunctional behaviors, and, above all else, with our powerful tendency to self-centeredly attach more importance to what is in our true interest over what is in the true interest of others. So long as we do not face our demons and subdue them, they will undermine our best intentions and distort our best thinking in ways that make it impossible to really love others as we love ourselves.

To understand our need to subdue our demons, to understand that their ultimate source is our powerful tendency to be excessively self-loving, and to understand the suffering we thereby bring upon ourselves and others is to understand Buddha's First and Second Noble Truths at the third level. Moreover, to understand Buddha's Third and Fourth Noble Truths is to understand the universal nature of our selfish striving and our many unwholesome states (or vices) as well as to understand how to cope with our unwholesome states (or vices) and to understand how to cultivate wholesome states (or virtues). But we cannot do it alone: We need the help of supporting communities, of qualified therapists and other professionals as well as supporting friends and family, along with the best that science, philosophy, literature, and religion have to offer. Any path (be it Buddha's Noble Eightfold Path, some 12-step program, some wonderful therapist, some therapy group, or some very loving religious community) will do. So long as it works. The crucial thing is that the practice in question enables us to realize our full potential to love others as we love ourselves. This, above all else, is what I am calling Third-Level Wisdom.

The matter can be stated as follows: *We possess Third-Level Wisdom so far as we possess an understanding of ourselves, of others, and of life that enables us to love ourselves in the sense of doing what is in our own true interest, and we love all others in that very same way.* It is the possession of such wisdom that enables us to live truly good and meaningful lives. It is worth noting, however, that our Third-Level Wisdom is necessarily incomplete, a work forever in progress. For our understanding of these matters can always be modified, deepened, and enriched as we go through life. It is this deeper understanding of myself, of others, and of life that I came to through my struggles with addiction and what I have been alluding to when I spoke of my addiction awakening me from my dogmatic slumbers. It is in this sense that I can truthfully say that my addiction or, more accurately, my awareness of and subsequent struggle with my addiction, has been a blessing.

Notes

1. As an aside, I should mention that for many Buddhists the relevant practices and exercises concern some variety of meditation. However, my experience, as a theist, has led me to believe that prayer, rightly done can accomplish everything that meditation accomplishes. This has not only been my first hand experience, but something that I have observed in the prayer practices of those who participate in 12 Step Programs.

2. It is worth noting that the idea of loving ourselves *unconditionally* is George Graham's highly fruitful way of interpreting the second defining property of love discussed by Harry Frankfurt in his book, *The Reasons of Love* (Frankfurt, 2004, 79–82).

References

Alcoholics Anonymous. (1976). New York: Alcoholics Anonymous World Services, Inc.

Bible. (1611). *The Authorized King James Version (KJV)*. Oxford: Oxford University Press.

Bodhi, B. (1984). *The Noble Eightfold Path*. Kandy, Sri Lanka: Buddhist Publication Society.

Frankfurt, H. G. (2004). *The reasons of love.* Princeton, NJ: Princeton University Press.

McKeon, R. (Ed.). (1941). *The basic works of Aristotle: Nicomachean ethics.* New York: Oxford University Press.

Merton, T. (Ed.), (1964). *Gandhi on non-violence.* New York: New Directions Publishing Corporation.

Rahula, W. (1959). *What the Buddha taught.* New York: Grove Press.

Skinner, B. F. (1953). *Science and human behavior.* New York: The Free Press.

11 What Is It Like to Be an Addict?

Owen Flanagan

Public Speaking about Private Matters

They say that people fear public speaking more than death. The origin of this chapter involved surviving death barely, and living to speak about matters that I wish I didn't know about, specifically about what it is like to be an addict. There was nothing in my autobiography, certainly not in the story of my formative years, say the first 18 years of my life, that would have foretold that my future, 40 years later, would involve my giving a talk with this title, "What Is it Like to Be an Addict?" to a distinguished professional society, the "Society for Philosophy and Psychology." But here I was at the University of Pennsylvania in June, 2008 at SPP's annual meeting speaking about the phenomenology of my addiction, speaking about what it had been like for me to be an addict and to live in—or should I say, to live as—the sick hollow vessel that was myself at the end. At the end, my self was knit only of the cloth of shame and desperation, my *Dasein*'s maximally reflective pose was as a bare pair of foggy eyes catching glimpses of a lonely detached racing heart in a bowl of thin gruel that was me.

The occasion where I was to express such thoughts out loud was a panel on "Addiction & Responsibility" with several major theorists of addiction and I, the addict, as commentator. The organizers who had asked me to speak were two dear old friends who knew of my struggles. The audience for the most part did not. I thanked the chair of the session who had introduced me and then opened a PowerPoint slide that looked like this:

WHAT IS IT LIKE TO BE AN ADDICT?

Owen Flanagan

This slide brought the audience of 150 or so—mostly philosophers and psychologists—many of whom I knew professionally, most of whom knew me through my scholarly work—to sit up and pay attention. My last major address to the Society had taken place over a decade earlier in Nashville, Tennessee when I gave my presidential address "Dreams, the Spandrels of Sleep," and where several years later, coincidentally, I went into rehab. The audience seemed significantly more attentive, or perhaps it was attentive in a different way, than the audiences who attend the type of talk that I normally give—talks with titles like "The Really Hard Problem: Meaning in the Material World," "Atheism and the Meaning(s) of Life," "Is Morality Modular?" "Is Wittgenstein a Non-Naturalist?" Perhaps this wasn't so, and I was simply especially sensitive to my audience's gaze, aware that I was about to engage in a form of self-disclosure that frightened me, which I knew would arouse thoughts and feelings and judgments—and gossip— about me over which I had no control. And to what end? It was not and is not clear. Perhaps it will help someone—an addict or a victim of an addict. Perhaps it will help deepen our understanding of a bewildering phenom- enon, which has this structure: I wanted not to use, I expressed to myself, my loved ones, and to mental health professionals a sincere desire not to use, and I used. Again and again. P & ~P. What is it like to live the sort of performative inconsistency that is an addict's lot? What does the agency of the addict feel like to the addict in active addiction? The answers to these questions have some relevance to questions of whether an addict is acting, as opposed to being merely the locus of a series of happenings, a passive node in some unfolding, and whether and how terms such as "voluntary" and "responsible" apply to (which of) his feelings, thoughts, and actions.

Two Molecules and Me

The occasion of my talk and now for writing this chapter was not of course the first time I had taken a reflective, critical pose toward my addiction, toward myself as addict. I had done this almost every day during my years of active addiction. But then it was mostly in the form of "how is this— fucking—possible?" where the possibility question was not a calm Kantian, transcendental pose but the desperate one of a dying man utterly bewil- dered by his pathetic impotence in the face of ethanol. I was addicted to a molecule $CH_3–CH_2–OH$, which looks like this (figure 11.1):

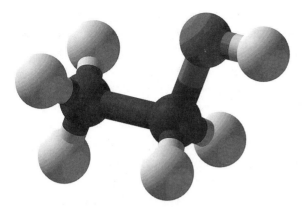

Figure 11.1

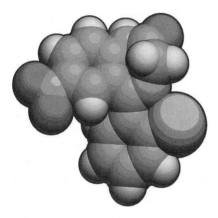

Figure 11.2

I was also a drug addict. I was addicted to this molecule (figure 11.2), which comes as a Rx with the name clonazepam, and which—along with valium, lorazepam, and Xanax of the family benzodiazepines—I used longer and more regularly, every day for 20 years, than alcohol, from which I took many breaks, once for 7 years. My psychiatrist says I abused clonazepam because it says on the bottle "Do Not Drink" while using this drug. I claim 50% compliance since I did not "Drive Farm Machinery," which was also prohibited.

A proper phenomenology of alcohol preference among normal drinkers would want to distinguish among preferences based on taste, aroma, texture, whether the drink accompanies food or not, and so on. Alcoholics also have such preferences, but for the addict preferences for beer versus wine versus vodka are superficial because every alcoholic will reveal that he prefers the molecule over how it is presented or housed or flavored. There are some exceptions: not all alcoholics will drink mouthwash or perfume, but many will. But with other drugs the situation is different. A clonazepam addict like me will, if there is no clonazepam around, seek any benzo he can find to "eat" (this is the way we speak) but might be indifferent to pot or cocaine or heroin or oxycodone. The point is that with alcohol there is one molecule that the addict seeks, preferences among kinds that turn on cost, taste preferences, and dosing options will reveal themselves when the molecule is available in several delivery systems. But for other drugs, there are often strong preferences within (clonazepam over lorazepam) and across category (opioids and benzos) based on the different effects of different molecules. A complete phenomenology of addiction would need "what it is like" reports on, among other things, $Addict_{alcohol}$ and $Addict_{benzodiazepines}$ and $Addict_{opiate}$, where $Addict_{benzodiazepines}$ and $Addict_{opiate}$ would branch into separate phenomenologies for $Addict_{Xanax,\ lorazepam,\ clonazepam}$ and $Addict_{morphine,\ codeine,\ heroin}$. The reason is that there are phenomenological differences in how these drugs seem to different people, as well as whether and how they seem is pleasant or not.

Here is the kind of phenomenology I have in mind. By the early 1990s I had been on benzodiazepines for about a decade, and I was, like every good addict, a kind of "People's Pharmacy" when it came to subtle differences among drugs in the class. For me, as well as for many (but not all) others, each benzo had a different phenomenological feel as well as some different effects. I loved Xanax but it made me very sleepy. Lorazepam and Valium produce a very pleasant, airy, spacy feel, but they also produced a certain forgetfulness. I was not introduced to clonazepam, my favorite, until 1994. Besides its pleasant calming effects (all benzos have that effect on me)—it made me feel "not scared," as all drugs I like do—it also eliminated immediately feelings of claustrophobia and acrophobia that I had never mentioned to anyone or sought treatment for. But all three effects, the feeling of calm and not scared-ness, which I always sought from benzos and got, as well as the completely gratuitous feelings of not feeling crowded in closed spaces and not bothered by heights, were very welcomed. The point for now is this: different molecule, different effect. Or better, if there is a different experienced effect, a phenomenological difference between drugs, presume that there is a physical difference.

Anti-Eudaimonics

Aristotle says, and I agree, that everyone seeks *eudaimonia*, to flourish, to find meaning and fulfillment, to be happy. It therefore seems utterly bewildering that a person could come to want and need molecules such as these to the point that he would chose them regularly over money, health, friends, even love, knowing that they defeat all prospects for *eudaimonia*? But I did that. Almost all addicts report doing that. I reported once to fellow addicts that I had the thought on the day of the birth of my firstborn that this was the most amazing day in my life for a host of reasons including the experience of that incredibly precious feeling of unconditional love, *and* at the same time I thought that this event and those feelings were inconvenient because they were interfering with my drinking. Every addict in the room understood this; they had been there.

What it is like to be an addict is like being someone who needs molecules such as these (although without having any desire for the molecules as the molecules they are, or as we philosophers say, not for the molecules under that description, but for the molecules because of what they do), more than all the things that wise persons have ever thought have existential importance, that matter, that might produce *eudaimonia*—the desire to flourish, the will to meaning. It is impossibly perplexing. It happens. It happened to me. One way it can seem to the addict is that the addict comes to need what he doesn't really, in one sense, want. But since one ought to want what one needs, one wants what one doesn't want. Imagine Sisyphus on the hedonic treadmill, Sisyphus as a hamster destined to eternally chase its own tail and for no other end than that is what he must do. That is what addiction feels like. There is a brave and heroic *"must"* where one stands up for something of great value; the "must" of addiction is not like that. But it is more like a "must" than it is like a "can" or "might" since it has qualities of inevitability.

The title of my talk, and thus of this chapter, is, of course, a riff on Thomas Nagel's 1974 classic "What Is It Like to Be a Bat?" (in Nagel, 1979).

Nagel has us reflect on how we gain entry, if we do, into what it is like to be a bat. And he puts the difficulty in these terms: imagine that you possess a complete theory of what makes bats tick, a complete neurocomputational-cognitive-behavioral account of the life of bats. Would you know what it is like to be a bat? Nagel says "no," and I agree. All known objective scientific accounts of the life of bats are compatible with there being nothing it is like to be a bat. This is a problem because we are confident that there is something it is like to be a bat. The bats, alas, cannot speak to us and tell us what it is like to be them. Furthermore even if the bats could speak, they would be speaking about experiences we humans do not have. Blind people have some experience with sonar, but they do not know what it is like to have sonar mosquito detectors that can be activated in high-speed flight the way bats do.

So it is with being an addict. There is something it is like to be an addict, or what is different, to be addicted, to be "high," to be sick "coming down," to be addicted to booze, versus being addicted to benzodiazepines, specifically to clonazepam, the name of my generic pharmaceutical lover. But we are members of the same species, and we are language users, so there are prospects for mutual understanding in the case of addiction. So let me tell you a bit about what it was like at the beginning and at the end, two vignettes that reveal what it seemed like, what it felt like to me the boy who had hard cider, and then what it felt like at the end, to be the man who was dying, who wanted to die, except for the fact that if you are dead, you can't use, and I had lost all sense of what not using meant, what it could be like for me to not use.

The Beginning: Feeling Safe

There were only a couple of drinking episodes of significance in high school nothing very interesting or memorable. What was memorable, or seems in retrospect significant, was my first, more-than-a-sip-from-Dad's-drink, drink. It occurred in eighth grade in the early 1960s. I was 12. Johnny E. was the smartest kid in my elementary grammar school. His parents, both born in Germany, worked in New York City, a half-hour commute. Despite his parents' absenteeism, which was unusual in those days, Johnny's house was not a party house. But there were memorable things we, really just he and I, did there together. I loved talking to Johnny about the world, especially about the Nazis and about apartheid in South Africa. We were both curious about the horrors of the adult world and fancied ourselves liberators in a new, improved world in which there would be no anti-Semitism, no racism. Johnny's father had a workroom that contained two things of great interest: a few black and white photos of naked women, and a small wooden keg that contained hard apple cider. On one memorable fall afternoon, Johnny and I did a viewing of the (to me) both sexy and creepy (1950s German housewives) nudes, which we had done before, and then for the first time, had a drink of the hard cider. Well, I did. I assume Johnny did too. But I don't remember what he did that day at all. What I remember and remember vividly is the mile or so walk home to 16 Woods End Road along Hartsdale Avenue, especially the feeling(s) I had as I walked past the farm stand on the corner of Secor Road and Hartsdale Avenue. I can still see the farm standing off to my right, and smell the autumn leaves, see the particular light and hue of that late fall afternoon sky. *I felt release from being scared and anxious*. It was good. I did not know, I would not have known to say if asked at the time, that I was a scared and anxious type. Perhaps I did not know until that medicinal moment what it was like not to be scared and anxious. It is too long ago to say. However, it seems that at that moment on the corner of Secor Road and Hartsdale Avenue a certain eighth-grade boy was released for a little time from a certain inchoate fear and anxiety. I loved this first drink. It calmed my soul. But I did not immediately go back for more.

My first experience with benzos, my other drug of choice (DOC), 20 years later produced a similar safe-haven feeling. Neither pot, which I liked a lot, nor opiates, which I never developed a taste for, had any effects on me that related to reducing fear, a fear of nothing in particular. But both alcohol and benzos did produce some sort of safe feeling. It is hard to describe, but it is less like feeling objectively safe, because the ship has finally made it to port or because the fierce animals have left the campsite. I normally felt safe in those ways. I was brave enough, braver than most, in those kinds of situations. It was more of an existential anxiety involving not feeling safe in my own skin—being scared *simpliciter*. Ludwig Wittgenstein, the most overrated philosopher of the 20th century but an extremely interesting person, thought that the "feeling of [absolute] safety" was transcendentally precious and that its description, the description of the gift it would be if one could experience it, put us up against the limits of language. That sounds like my experience, like the feeling I chased with the molecules that I liked most.

Not all addicts chase the particular transcendentally precious feeling of safety. Some of the feelings they report chasing are less a relief like mine than a full-on hedonic enhancement or blast. All heroin addicts speak of a hedonically extraordinary "seeming." But I have never gone there. Whereof one cannot speak there is, or ought to be, silence. The point is that I have explained the common feeling that my two drugs produced. But addicts get addicted to substances (and processes) that produce heterogeneous kinds of good feelings.

The End

Travel was a problem. Or *me* traveling was a problem. Either way this was a problem, because I traveled a lot. I was sipping espresso in a café in Nice and started a conversation with an Australian disk jockey and a beautiful Tunisian woman—to whom I deeded a precious Van Gogh fountain pen later that night. There were then two lost days in Nice. Such things—new friends and lost days—were normal if I went back out. I always seemed to go "back out." At that time, but not now, the anticipatory dread that I would go back out was a constant companion. I had tried so many ways to stop and always failed. I had very little confidence. It was always just a matter of time. Knowing this felt worse than knowing that I would die or even imagining that my own death would be very painful. Much worse. Dying is natural; enacting my spiritual death seemed necessary, inevitable, but thoroughly unnatural. Shameful.

Although my drinking career began more or less normally, it ended in a grave repetitive soul sickness, in a near (very) near-death experience. My last days of the last time were similar to previous "last times," but a bit more ominous and inescapable. If I was awake, I was drinking (and taking my pills). Sleeping involved becoming unconscious from drinking, and waking was coming to because I needed to drink, akin to the way normal sleep can be interrupted by needing to pee—not at all like waking up to meet a new day. I would come to around 6:15 a.m., swearing that yesterday was the very last time. This was convenient because I was always out of booze by morning. So I would self-announce "I will not drink today, perhaps never again, but certainly not today." "Today, please let today be the first day of my new sober life." I'd boil water, grind the coffee for the

French press. I'd pace, drink a cup of coffee, and try to hold to my terrified resolve. But by 6:56—every time, failsafe, I'd be in my car, arriving at the BP station—which meant beer to me; only incidentally and in an emergency did BP have to do with gas, petrol, fuel. At 7 a.m. sharp I'd gather four or five 16-ounce bottles of Heineken, hold their cold wet balm to my breast, put them down on the counter only long enough to be scanned, paid for, and placed in the brown paper that would conceal their wet preciousness from the police or my loved ones who might interfere with my insanity. By the last months, I did not care, not at all—I even sought the sad consolation that the sweet kind souls who sold me my morning brew provided, knowing as they did how pathetic, how wretched, how lost I was. I guzzled one beer in the car. Car cranking, BP, a beer can's gaseous earnestness—like Pavlov's dogs, when these co-occur, Owen is off, juiced. And then gone. The second beer I sipped in an addict's sort of way over perhaps the next 4 or 5 minutes. It, the second beer, was usually finished by the time I pulled back up to the house, the house on whose concrete porch I now spent most conscious, awake, time drinking, wanting to die. But afraid to die. When you're dead you can't use. I lived to use and to die. The desire to live was not winning the battle over death. The overwhelming need—the pathological, unstoppable—need to use, was. Living was just a necessary condition of using. The third and the fourth morning beers were ingested more slowly than the first two. I knew that this was not a breakfast of champions. Not at all. But I was hardly a champion. Perhaps I had been once. But now I was a pathetic loser. Ashamed and alone.

Even at the end there was some control that came in the form of maintenance so that I could minimally do my job. Very minimally. After class I could drink vodka, which I preferred to beer. This pathetically degraded self-control was pretty much all the control I had left and then only sometimes. I was very sick, but not with a flu. I was—all the empirical evidence suggested—in a pathetic losing battle with the economy of my desires run amok, sometimes fighting off overwhelming craving for my drug, other times knowing, in some sense of "know," that my relationships with genuinely good people, my work, my life could, indeed, *would* be lost if I choose to use. And I'd still choose to use. Well, I'd use. That much was clear.

My morning fix did temporarily suppress the self-loathing that was my constant morning companion. It mitigated briefly, maybe for 30 seconds or a minute, the inglorious shame of being the pathetic wretched being I was, that I had become. And although it may seem hard to believe, I loved that half-minute, that minute, in which I was briefly, ever so briefly, saved from my self-loathing. Then I would enter into numbness—until the next morning when the cycle would repeat itself.

I was a wretched, worsening train wreck of a person—a whirling dervish, contaminating, possibly ruining, the lives of my loved ones. What if they weren't strong enough to escape the harm? This was always the worst thought. And it was my constant tortuous companion if I was awake and not using, which by the end was not often. This was self-caused torture and self-degradation, but possibly also the ruination of those I loved the most—my own private waterboarding. My sole, occasional consolation was the thought, the hopeful thought, that although I was most certainly a wretch, that I was merely like a pesky mosquito in the lives of my loved ones, an incredibly annoying inconvenience but no big thing from the point of view of their larger lives that would soon, it seemed, be able to go on (eventually I hoped happily) without me. If people survive a train wreck or a hurricane, they normally go on and are OK. So I hoped that the chaos I created was ephemeral. Certainly this was so from the point of view of the universe. My existence and my plight were of exactly zero cosmic importance. But if the world—for some inexplicable reason—was just, then my loved ones would survive and flourish despite the maddening toxin I had been. This worry about my loved ones was the psychically most difficult thing. I have said about all I can say. Those thoughts were and still are terrifying, and this despite the fact that my three precious ones love me and are doing well and faring well.

The story about the beginning and the end of my drinking career seems to have a simple experiential logical structure: I found some substance that alleviated a certain kind of inchoate fear. I liked that substance, or better, I liked its effect; I used it. Eventually it produced a much worse dreadfulness than the fear it initially provided relief from. But by then I couldn't find my way to stop. *Huis Clos.*

Phenomenology

I am trying to stick close to the "what it is like" issues and to make minimal and uncontroversial surmises about that which lies beyond the "seemings" (surmises such as that in my case my drugs of choice produced an anxiety or fear-reduction effect at the start; and thus I call the fear that I was released from "inchoate" fear partly because it felt that way but also to avoid projecting back content to that fear from the perspective of the way things "seem" to me now). Happily now for me, the task is memorial, not one I can any longer speak about as today's reality. Still, it is vivid. My life, according to professionals in the addiction field and many friends, depends on keeping it that way. Once an addict, always an addict (I am not sure this is so, but I will to believe it in a William Jamesean sort of way since it seems either useful or harmless). I am speaking about the subjective life of this addict, but I am a token of a type, an instance of a kind, actually two kinds, for as I have said I was addicted to both alcohol and prescription drugs. And although there are many particularities of my story, the phenomenology is shared by many fellow addicts. Because I talk to fellow addicts as often as I talk to students and colleagues, I allow myself to make some claims about addicts generally, to speak as heterophenomenologist, to speak with some authority about what it is like for fellow addicts. I should say: not all addicts speak about the effect they first liked, and then chased in my way, as a safe-haven effect. The initial appeals, the effects that are found pleasant, are multifarious. Some people love the effects of hallucinogens, which to me are exciting and interesting but do not produce feelings of safety. What is universal is that the effect that is initially sought and for a time gained is eventually defeated by using. By that point there seems to be no exit.

I am trying to steer away from two kinds of objective questions, questions of causation and questions of constitution. Edmund Husserl, an important phenomenologist, said that in doing phenomenology one ought to bracket out certain distracting assumptions, for example, the assumption that the mind's job is solely to reliably track an external world that is "given." Consider what I have said and will go on to say as involving an attempt to "bracket" out questions of causation and constitution, so that the experience of addiction can be reseen and reexperienced by myself and conveyed to you the reader. First, I am trying to resist saying anything about causation, for example, about what caused me to become an addict and thus something of an authority on "what it is like" to be one, or even more generally about what causes some people to become addicts or what causes people who are "in remission" as my doctor calls it, to go into remission if and when they do. There are theories about such matters.

I said at the start that there was nothing in my autobiography up to my late teens that would have led me to see that I would become an addict and live to speak and write about it. That is compatible with there being truths about me—perhaps they are revealed in what I said about my first experiences with alcohol and benzos and the feeling of safety, of fear reduction that came with those drugs—that might have positioned an objective observer with a good theory to predict that I would become an addict, possibly antecedent to my birth. Seven out of eight members of my family of origin became addicts (the four still alive are all in "remission"). Autobiographically I did not see addiction in my future. A biographer, especially perhaps a scientific biographer, not being I, having access to information I did not have (or, what is different, do not have) might have seen my addiction coming. When I do speak here of antecedents or consequences of my addiction, please take me to be speaking in a Humean voice—about conjunctions that may or may not be causal. The diachronic story I tell is committed to a certain temporal order, the one thing after another order. I remain agnostic about whether it matches the causal order.

The second set of objective questions I will remain unopinionated about are those about synchronic constitution, facts for example that pertain to the bodily states (neural or wider) that realize, for example, the overwhelming desire to use or those times in which it seems possible—always short— to abstain. Addicts talk about addiction as involving two components: "mental obsession"— you are always thinking about where, when, and how you will next use, or continue using, even while seeming on task—and "physical compulsion," the car turns into the liquor store, you do not; the drinking is done, it must be, but in some sense it is not me, despite an overpowering awareness that I need to use and am about to use (again).

I have a theory of mind that I call *subjective realism* or *neurophysicalism* that says there is such a basis for such mental states, that every subjective state has a brain state or wide body state that realizes it as the mental state it is. But I, of course, with my addiction, as with my mental life generally, am in zero first-personal touch with what those neural states are, even where they are. I, like everyone, am attached to myself as experiencer only.

Addiction: First-Person and Third-Person

"What Is It Like to Be a Bat?" is both a clear and vivid statement of the philosophical problem of other minds and a set of reflections on the problem of whether and how the subjective and objective points of view contribute to our understanding of creatures with conscious minds. Regarding the problem of other minds, Nagel writes:

> No matter how the form may vary, the fact that an organism has conscious experience *at all* means, basically, that there is something that it is like to *be* that organism—something it is like *for* that organism . . . . fundamentally an organism has mental states if and only if there is something there is like to *be* that organism—something it is like *for* that organism. (Nagel, 1979, 166)

Strictly speaking, my mental states are experienced as mental states, or as the mental states they are, only by me, and so for you, and for each and every individual who has a self-enclosed nervous system. The access of others, even loved ones, to what I think, feel, believe, and so on, comes from my speech, my body language, as these are understood by being embedded in a frame, a background that holds information about my past, our common culture, and so on. I have views about what it is like to be you, but I never have your experiences. We share each other's experiences, but we do not have them.

Reflection on the problem of other minds leads some to worries about solipsism and to skepticism that we can never know another. Despite wanting sometimes to know exactly what it is like to be another, to have the experiences of another, to "get inside the other's head," as we say, there are limits. Indeed, Mother Nature would have been a pathetic engineer if she had left us confused about whose experiences we were having, if experiences just swarmed into heads like radio waves. We get along understanding each other through the common resources of very similar bodies, shared culture, and language.

There are actually three kinds of knowledge I might possess about your mind but that I presumably do not experience exactly as you do because I am not you. There are "knowing-thats"—you know that certain states of affairs happened because *you* were there, I was not; "knowing-hows"—you know how to water ski, I do not; and there is "knowing what it is like to be _____"—say, poor, a woman, a heroin addict, or an octogenarian, that I have no experience of.

Many people in North America at least—but not everyone in Thailand or Taiwan, especially not women—know what it is like to get drunk, and many know what it is like to be high on marijuana or valium-like drugs (benzodiazepines). Being an addict is nothing like being drunk or high. This may seem surprising because an addict's life does involve normally getting drunk or high. But being an addict is not like being drunk or high all the time even though it involves a lot of being drunk or high. What it is like to be an addict involves both more and less than being drunk or high all the time. It involves more than this because addiction involves constant self-loathing that being drunk needn't involve. And it involves less than being wasted all the time because much of the activity of middle and late addiction involves maintenance dosing. Maintenance dosing seems necessary (the best of a set of undesirable strategies) when one has a body that will seize (and feels as if it will seize) if, as in my case, alcohol is not in the bloodstream most of the time (alcohol withdrawal is not as painful as heroin withdrawal, but it is much more dangerous because of a much higher likelihood that one will seize to death). Also it is common-place if not universal that one is addicted to a drug that no longer produces the effects it once did, which might have once been pleasant, but which now produces an indifferent effect or even an unpleasant one, but one that is absolutely required. Addicts chase "a good buzz," but rarely experience one once they have become addicts.

Are there any universal aspects of addictive phenomenology? Call the conception of addiction as involving mental obsession and physical compulsion, addiction-1. Addiction-1 is the most common way that addicts I know express their common experience as addicts, and this across every kind of substance addiction. Let addiction-2 refer to the syndrome composed of addiction-1 (mental obsession and physical compulsion) plus characteristic situations, feelings, and behaviors associated with use, for example, various kinds of cues, preparatory rituals, behaviors, outcomes, and so on, what we might call "the addict's lifestyle."

Every addict-1 is also an addict-2, but the two aspects can be marked off in phenomenological space, and it can be useful to do so. Addiction-1, I am inclined to say, is invariant, but addiction-2 varies across individuals, often even more across communities of users depending on their drug of choice—one can always get beer in a crack house but not normally the other way around.

If this is so, then we are gaining some texture for a phenomenology of addiction. But so far we have no knowledge of what in the person or in the person and the world explains why the phenomenology is as it is. This requires that we take up the third personal perspective of objective science.

In addition, to providing a vivid reminder of the lack of transparency of every person's mind to every other person, some might say of the opacity of every mind to every other mind, Nagel also aims to teach something about how understanding of persons from different perspectives interlocks or fails to interlock to yield a unified picture of some psychological phenomenon. Nagel writes that:

The subjective character of experience is not captured by any of the familiar, recently devised reductive analyses of the mental . . . . [T]his bears directly on the mind-body problem. For if the facts of experience—facts about what it is like *for* the experiencing organism—are accessible only from one point of view, then it is a mystery how the true character of experiences could be revealed in the physical operation of that organism. (Nagel, 1979, 172)

This is relevant in the present case, and for the present volume, in the following way. As for addiction, as for every other kind of mental disorder, there are theories, for example, about the causes of anxiety, depression, schizophrenia, amnesia, bipolar disorder, postpartum depression, as well as the various kinds of addiction. There are also theories about the (usual) way(s) people with these disorders think, process information, and behave. There are theories about the psychology of addiction, functional theories about causes and effects, and neurobiological theories about changes in the neurochemistry of persons in the grip of addiction. But these theories notoriously do not capture what it is like to be a token of the type. The solution here is to distinguish two kinds of "capture" that once done secures an ineliminable place for phenomenology: There is a sense of "capture" by which we mean to explain causally why something happens or what it is constitutively. Objective, third-person science aspires to do this kind—or these two kinds—of capturing, and it does so well. The other sense of "capture" means to experience first-personally. Because subjective realism is true of creatures that have experiences (humans and many other animals), only the creature itself can capture its experiences in this second way, where one actually has the experience. The reason is fully consistent with a robust naturalism. Only the individual organism is situated to *have* its own experiences. The situation is puzzling, not mysterious.

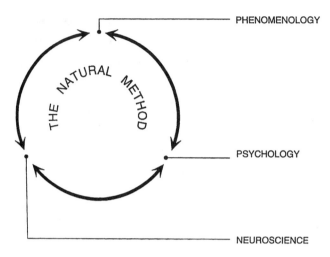

Figure 11.3
The natural method. Adapted from Flanagan (1995, 9).

My work in the philosophy of mind and specifically my battle with my mysterian friends involves recommending what I call "the natural method" to understand any mental phenomena, at least any mental phenomena that involve conscious awareness. Approach the phenomena from three perspectives at once, beginning with the phenomenological—what the mental state type seems like at first-person level of awareness. Then examine the phenomenology in light of theories at the psychological and neuro-scientific levels (figure 11.3).

So take first-person reports such as the sort I have been offering and see what, if any, illumination is created for that subjective picture by the objective picture and vice versa.

Consider George Ainslie's and George Koob's theories about addiction. Ainslie's view (Ainslie, 2001) is that alcoholism and cocaine addiction as well as pathological gambling and overeating have the same underlying structure, and thus, they can be explained by the same functional law, a law that involves hyperbolic discounting and intertemporal bargaining, which possibly can be expressed as one law, call it "the law of addictive gravity." Roughly, the addict overrates near rewards and underrates far costs, and before he realizes that he is hooked, he is hooked. By the time that the person realizes what he is doing, it is too late.

Recently, there have been theories about which part of the brain causes the reward-punishment mechanism to go awry. In the memorable phrase of some of Ainslie's colleagues, when things go awry it is because there has been a "midbrain mutiny." Whereas the theory of hyperbolic discounting explains the process of addiction psychologically, in terms of principles of operant conditioning and schedules of reinforcement (the "law of addictive gravity" is a variation of Herrnstein's "matching law"), the suggestion that the midbrain is involved in the inexorable process of addiction gestures in the direction of neuroscience. The need to go down to this level is obvious. Whereas hyperbolic discounting provides a unified theory for many addictions, possibly all, it leaves unexplained why some people get addicted to substances (cocaine, opiates, benzos, and ethanol) and others to processes (gambling, sex, overeating, and exercise).

George Koob's theory (Kuhn & Koob, 2010) is that each substance that is addictive works differently in the brain, although these differences may or may not show up at either the phenomenological or psychological level. For example, alcohol causes the release of dopamine and opioid peptides. Opioid peptides produce effects similar to real opiates, which explains some of the pleasant feeling associated with drinking. Cocaine, meanwhile, produces mostly dopamine release, which is also very pleasant. What happens with addiction is that the reward system reaches a state in which it changes its regulation from a homeostatic one to an allostatic one, which is where the system goes from a standard equilibrium or set point to having a variable, unpredictable set point. The evidence suggests that the midbrain-basal forebrain areas (where "the midbrain mutiny" occurs) are implicated in the positive reinforcing effects of drugs of abuse and also in the negative reinforcement associated with drug addiction. The extended amygdala in the basal forebrain that contains parts of the nucleus accumbens and amygdala and neurotransmitters such as dopamine, opioid peptides, serotonin, GABA, and glutamate are all doing important but different work depending on the drug. Sorted out in a precise way for different molecules, we explain common features of drug withdrawal such as dysphoria, depression, irritability and anxiety, and dysregulation of brain reward systems. What the system has to do to get you addicted and to get you to quit involves the same system(s) now working for different ends. The same neurochemical systems implicated in the acute reinforcing effects of drugs of abuse need to be recruited in withdrawal and abstinence.

Once we have a phenomenology, a psychology, and a neurobiology of addiction in place, or better—as we are putting these things in place—we can (and do) ask whether they are consistent or not. When I proposed the "natural method," I was often asked which is trump. My answer remains the same: no level of analysis is trump. Look at the weight of evidence and see how different claims stack up one against another. Suppose that the neuroscience of addiction revealed that all substance addictions involve exactly the same neural processes. I would say keep looking because the recognizable differences in phenomenological feelings produced by different drugs are robust among the people who use them.

It is commonplace in the philosophy of mind to say that a true, complete, neuropsychological account of addiction, to stick with the present example, expressed in the most precise mathematical and scientific language would not, and could not conceivably, capture what it is like, really like, deep down inside, to be an addict. The problem is a general one. The objective scientific idiom simply does not capture what it is like first-person experientially for the creature whose behavior is being explained. The right general theory about the causes and effects of schizophrenia, alcoholism, or cocaine addiction will not tell you one bit about what it is like to be me, the addict, nor will it tell you what it feels like to be high or coming down, sick and desperate. I can use words to get you to the vicinity of what it is like to be an end-state user, but I know that being in the grip the way I was (knock wood) is unimaginable unless you have been there.

This is true for reasons I explained above. There are two distinct senses in which experience can be captured. The first-person phenomenology and the objective science have different jobs. They *capture* one and the same phenomenon—in our case the *Dasein* of addiction, from different perspectives, with different epistemic access conditions. The first personal has limited access to the third personal (I can see myself behaving but have no access to what implements my feelings, thoughts, and the like); the third personal has no first personal access, which is different from having no third personal access to the first personal. But they all are trying to understand the same thing: the addict, how he, a person, became one, and what is going on inside him now that explains why he feels as he does and is as he is.

What I call the *expanded natural method* recommends going wider than the natural method as the phenomena in question and the explanatory

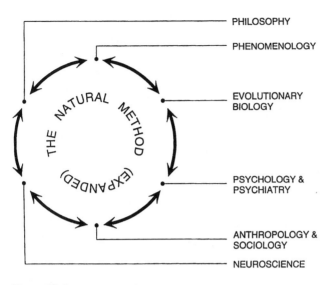

Figure 11.4
The natural method, expanded. Adapted from Flanagan (1995, 9).

questions about the phenomena expand. Thus, if one wants to understand addiction widely, one will need the expanded method to examine, for example, the social, cultural, gender, and economic facts that are highly relevant to addiction, to the who, what, where, when, and how of addiction in a culture, at a time (figure 11.4).

The usual method for gaining traction of the "what it is like to be-ness" of some mental disorder is metaphorical. There are multiple metaphors that try to help us, who are not tokens of the relevant type, understand what it is like, what it is like mentally, to be in a manic state or to be OCD, even what it is like to be schizophrenic. Two of my favorite books in the genre are William Styron's *Darkness Visible* (Styron, 1992), the best memoir I have ever read on the phenomenology of severe immobilizing depression, and Kay-Redfield Jamison's account of her life as bipolar, *An Unquiet Mind* (Jamison, 1995). Interestingly, Styron's story begins, that is, his depression begins, when he gives up his true love, alcohol. His book is about his life as depressive, not about his earlier, indeed, next adjacent, life as alcoholic. And Redfield-Jamison has lots to say about her own drinking career, a common accompaniment of bipolar disorder. But neither book focuses on the phenomenology of addiction. Caroline Knapp's *Drinking: A Love Story* (Knapp, 1996) is an eloquent memoir of alcoholism. One special contribution of her story is to reveal how much more any addiction involves than just love for certain molecules, even if molecules are in fact the thing that has the strongest grip, and that explains many of the phenomenological features of addiction. There is also nostalgia for "the days of wine and roses," perhaps; for the music, the sex, the glasses, the ice, the smells, the tastes, the needles, the crack pipes—"the whatever there is" or "whatever there was"—that is associated with the good times, and which, according to good, old-fashioned regimens of classical and operant conditioning, gets a grip in the economy of desire along with the dangerous molecules. A full account of addiction will require the sort of narrow phenomenology I have provided here, plus a social and cultural phenomenology, a "romantics of addiction," plus of course a sociology, economics, and anthropology of addiction to track the who, what, and where of different kinds of addiction.

The good news is that we can and should shift back and forth across narrow or individual phenomenology and wide or social phenomenology depending on our explanatory concerns. The same is true about moving between levels, the levels that tell us about the ways things seem and those that tell us about the causal and constitutive fields in which the "seemings" are embedded.

Control and Responsibility

I start with a declaration. If you want philosophical wisdom on volition and agency read Aristotle's *Nicomachean Ethics*, John Dewey, and Daniel Dennett. Do not get sucked into that philosophical black hole, which is the literature on free will and determinism. There is no such thing as metaphysical freedom of the will. It is a silly idea invented to support religious regimes of eternal reward and punishment. What the law and morality need and use is a continuum idea of the voluntary, involuntary, and nonvoluntary (Aristotle, 1999, book III, ch. 1). For that read Aristotle. Then STOP!

If you are tempted to get near the philosophical black hole, Dewey and Dennett might save you. Dewey (1922) says (I paraphrase from memory): What men and women have fought for in the name of "freedom" has never been metaphysical freedom of the will, it has always been freedom from oppression, political freedom—freedom (I add) from coercive, oppressive situations of myriad sorts that keep individuals and groups from doing what they want, and what their reasonable, considered judgments rightly see would be good or better than things are now. From Dennett (1984) we get a robust empirically informed picture of how such freedom is possible in a material world.

OK, so free will is not being discussed. There is no such thing. Assuming I have not lost you to the black hole, I ask: How do addicts think about agency, control, and responsibility? How did my agency seem at various stages of my addiction?

In rooms of addicts in recovery the favored simile is that addiction is like type 2 diabetes. Sometimes the analogy to cancer is used. But diabetes type 2 is favored. The idea as I understand it is this: the addict, like the type 2 diabetic, once had, enacted, or was sick with a disease in which he was a participant. Type 1 diabetes involves being born without the capacity to produce insulin, whereas type 2 involves faulty insulin metabolism associated with poor diet, exercise, etc. Type 1 diabetes, certain kinds of colon and breast cancer involve no agent participation; whereas lung cancer, skin cancer, and type 2 diabetes do involve some authorial control.

If one has started to exhibit signs of type 2 diabetes one can exercise and eat better. If one has started to get skin cancer one can use sunscreen, stay out of the sun, and get checked regularly by the dermatologist. If one is an addict, one can stop using and in that way put the obsession and constant craving into hibernation or remission or some such. I consciously craved alcohol for 4 months after I stopped using, and for 3 years a craving would occur at least weekly. What I did and what most of my fellow addicts do is to create a zone of control between your self and the substance that will bring you down, that will make you sick once again, possibly, producing a "sickness unto death." The zone of control is between oneself and the first drink or drug. If you take the first drink or drug, then the drink or drug is in control and you may not be able to stop. Possibly not ever. I have many addict friends who have died after going back out, sometimes after many years in recovery.

Now this way of speaking in so far as it expresses the way things seem is not theoretically innocent. Indeed, a topic about which I have said nothing but that deserves mentioning is that neither phenomenology nor introspection is something a language user does as a theoretical virgin. It is possible that addicts might sit around saying they experienced themselves as moral slime who brought great calamity on themselves and their loved ones because they used their free will badly and thus that they deserve to burn in hell for all eternity. That view is out there. Every addict in our culture has experienced her agency that way. It is a common trope.

In rooms of addicts it has proved useful generally not to speak this way. Every addict I know speaks as if he or she, having abstained for a while (several weeks at least), through acute withdrawal and a bit beyond (which has a "what it is like to be-ness" that varies from drug to drug and is always very unpleasant), is in the process of resecuring a zone of control. The zone of control is a narrow band between the agent and the first drink or pill or needle. After that, the first one, the drinks take the drinks, the pills take the pills. This is the way we speak. I leave it to others to judge whether there is wisdom in this way of speaking and thinking.

It did prove useful in my case. I knew I had a problem for a long time. But I found the idea of complete abstention from alcohol inconceivable, terrifying. Again and again, over many years, I tried to drink in moderation (all alcoholics do). But in my case I actually thought—in some sense of "actually thought"—that my main problem was a dosing problem. I believed that my problems occurred somewhere after a pint of vodka and before a quart, or between 8 and 15 beers, or between 1½ and 3 bottles of wine. I cognitively resisted accepting that my problem was with the first drink or with my relationship to a certain molecule with which I had an allostatic relation, one that meant that I could never, ever find a dosing equilibrium.

As for the person who is still using and trying to stop, we addicts assume something like this: You the addict want to stop (either because you feel wretched or because you are about to lose everything or usually both). You are motivated to stop. You think, all things considered, that it is best for you and others that you stop. But you are not *yet* at the point where you can reliably negotiate the wee zone of control between yourself and the first drink or drug. Normally there are two favored options. Sit with fellow addicts, talk and let them help you not use and/or go into rehab where the same thing will happen, that is, a social group will help you overcome your own seeming powerlessness (in rehab there will be drugs, usually benzos to get you through—benzos are used even to get you off benzos).

Addicts speak about themselves as if they are and were responsible in all the normal ways other people speak about such matters. Addicts think they are responsible for what they do. However, it has proved useful for addicts to admit that they are *powerless* over ____, where ____ is the addict's drug of choice or list of DOCs. Why is this useful? First, it seems true. The mental obsession and physical compulsion that mark addiction-1 involve severely diminished control over thinking and action with respect to ____. Second, the repetitive P & ~P, performative inconsistency that *is* his life is acknowledged by the addict, as well as everyone else, to be against his or her (and their) best interests. This makes the behavior a paradigm case of irrational behavior. Normally, reasons for action that pass all things considered evaluation find their way onto the motivational circuits as causes. This does not happen normally in cases of addiction (compare: nuclear reactions are abnormal physical operations, but we can and have figured out how to start and stop them). Third, the addict is interested in control, specifically in self-control, but he is having trouble leveraging that control. Regaining control in early recovery is dedicated to establishing that very small zone of control between the addict and that first drink or drug. It is a trick that works.

There is much more that could be said about control and responsibility. I will finish with this question and a comment. Does "disease" seem like the right description of addiction to me as an addict? Not really. If "disease" is useful, then type 2 diabetes is perhaps a better simile than cancer or the flu—illnesses where agency matters little. But the idea that addiction is a disease or illness seems less useful in describing "what it is/was like" for me than to say that my being, my whole being, physically, psychologically, and relationally was disordered, in disarray. My being was not coordinated with my best judgments about what and how and who I wanted to be. My reasons and desires were not in harmony with each other. And I couldn't get a grip; I couldn't—despite my desires—find a way to regain order and harmony and integration. I couldn't find the right way out or in. I wasn't sure which direction even—out or in—was the right way to seek escape or reintegration. But with help I made my way to the clearer and better place I live in now. There was help from the wise parts of myself as well as from loved ones who still saw a space for a better, less-disordered self, and who kept trying over the years to articulate its possibility. Indeed, it was often the bare phenomenological possibility of feeling and being better that kept the hope alive. And there was help from the community of addicts, as well as in my case from mental health professionals, psychologists, psychiatrists, and psychopharmacologists.

There came a time in my life as an addict where, try as I might, I couldn't find a way to leverage my own powers of agency against myself. It felt that way. *Huis clos*. P & ~P. I was—as I said—a performative inconsistency, miserable and desperate. And now I am not. What happened is that others, some, including myself, who cared for me personally, and some professionals with the sort of knowledge that comes from both humane wisdom and science, helped me gain some control over my agency that I acting alone had either lost or couldn't find. The solution was social.

References

Ainslie, G. (2001). *Breakdown of Will*. Cambridge: Cambridge University Press.

Aristotle. (1999). Irwin, T. (Trans.), *Nicomachean ethics*. Indianapolis, IN: Hackett Publishing Company.

Dennett, D. (1984). *Elbow room: the varieties of free will worth wanting*. Cambridge, MA: MIT Press.

Dewey, J. (1922). *Human nature and conduct: an introduction to social psychology*. New York: H. Holt.

Flanagan, O. (1995). Deconstructing dreams: the spandrels of sleep. *Journal of Philosophy*, *92*, 5–28.

Jamison, K. (1995). *An unquiet mind*. New York: A.A. Knopf.

Knapp, C. (1996). *Drinking: a love story*. New York: Dial Press.

Kuhn, C., & Koob, G. (2010). *Advances in the neuroscience of addiction*. Oxford: Taylor & Francis, Inc.

Nagel, T. (1979). What is it like to be a bat? In *Mortal questions* (pp. 165–180). London: Cambridge University Press.

Styron, W. (1992). *Darkness visible: a memoir of madness*. New York: Vintage Books.

About the Authors

George Ainslie studies impulsiveness and self-control as intertemporal conflict within individuals (picoeconomics). He is the author of *Picoeconomics: The Strategic Interaction of Successive Motivational States within the Person* (Cambridge University Press, 1992) and *Breakdown of Will* (Cambridge University Press, 2001), and he has published widely in the psychological, psychiatric, philosophical, and legal literature. He is a research psychiatrist at the Department of Veterans Affairs Medical Center, Coatesville, PA.

Sheila M. Alessi earned her doctorate in psychology from Wayne State University in 2000, after which she completed a National Institute on Drug Abuse Postdoctoral Research Fellowship in the Human Behavioral Pharmacology Laboratory at the University of Vermont. Dr. Alessi is currently an assistant professor of medicine in the Calhoun Cardiology Center at the University of Connecticut Health Center. She conducts research on substance use disorders with an emphasis on cigarette smoking, and her work is funded by the National Institute on Drug Abuse and the Donaghue Foundation.

Kent C. Berridge is James Olds Professor of Psychology and Neuroscience at the University of Michigan. Research in his laboratory seeks answers to questions such as: How is pleasure generated in the brain? And how do the neural and psychological bases for wanting a reward relate to those for liking the same reward?

Louis C. Charland is a philosopher who specializes in the philosophy of emotion and the history and philosophy of psychiatry. He is currently associate professor with tenure in the Department of Philosophy at the

University of Western Ontario in Canada, where he also holds appointments in the Department of Psychiatry in the Faculty of Medicine and the School of Health Studies in the Faculty of Health Sciences. Previous appointments include various teaching, research, and policy positions at McGill University's Faculty of Medicine, the Toronto Hospital for Sick Children, and the Ontario Premier's Council on Health Strategy. Current research includes work on decisional capacity and anorexia, a book on the role of the passions in 19th century moral treatment, and the psychopathology of affectivity.

Owen Flanagan is James B. Duke Professor of Philosophy at Duke University, Durham NC. He is the author of *The Really Hard Problem: Meaning in a Material World* (MIT Press, 2007).

Richard Garrett is a professor of philosophy at Bentley University, where he teaches courses in ethics, metaphysics, and the theory of knowledge. He has published widely in the field of ethics, theory of knowledge, and metaphysics as well as in related fields such as the philosophy of language and the philosophy of mind. His deepest, most enduring and compelling interests are in ethics and especially in practical wisdom.

George Graham is a professor of philosophy and neuroscience at Georgia State University, having served on the faculties of the University of Alabama at Birmingham (UAB) and at Wake Forest University. He is a past president of the Society for Philosophy and Psychology. He works on issues in philosophy of mind and philosophical psychopathology. His most recent book is *The Disordered Mind* (Routledge, 2010).

Neil Levy is head of neuroethics at the Florey Neuroscience Institutes, Melbourne, Australia, and Director of Research at the Oxford Centre for Neuroethics. He is the author of five books, including, most recently, *Neuroethics: Challenges for the 21st Century* (Cambridge University Press, 2007).

Stephen J. Morse, J.D., Ph.D., is Ferdinand Wakeman Hubbell Professor of Law and Professor of Psychology and Law in Psychiatry at the University of Pennsylvania. He has written extensively about the relation of social science, psychiatry, and neuroscience to criminal responsibility, including the responsibility of addicts, and to criminal law theory more generally.

Nancy M. Petry earned a Ph.D. in psychology from Harvard University in 1994. She joined the faculty of the University of Connecticut Health

Center in 1996, and she is presently professor of medicine in the Calhoun Cardiology Center. Dr. Petry conducts research on the treatment of addictive disorders, ranging from substance use disorders to pathological gambling. Her work is funded by the National Institute on Drug Abuse, the National Institute of Mental Health, and the National Institute on Alcohol Abuse and Alcoholism.

Jeffrey Poland currently teaches in the Department of History, Philosophy, and the Social Sciences at the Rhode Island School of Design and in the Science and Society Program at Brown University. He is the author of *Physicalism: The Philosophical Foundations* (Oxford University Press, 1994) and a co-author (with William Spaulding and Mary Sullivan) of *Treatment and Rehabilitation of Severe Mental Illness* (Guilford, 2003). In addition to clinical experience in inpatient psychiatric rehabilitation, he has also held academic positions at Colgate University and the University of Nebraska-Lincoln.

Nancy Nyquist Potter is professor of philosophy at the University of Louisville. Her published books include *How Can I Be Trusted? A Virtue Theory of Trustworthiness*, and *Mapping the Edges and the In-Between: A Critical Analysis of Borderline Personality Disorder*. She has published articles in the field of philosophy and psychiatry in journals ranging from *Philosophy, Psychiatry, & Psychology* to *Journal of Personality Disorders*, and *Current Opinion in Psychiatry* to *Harvard Review of Psychiatry*. She serves on local hospital ethics committees and is president of the Association for the Advancement of Philosophy and Psychiatry.

Carla J. Rash earned a Ph.D. in psychology from Louisiana State University in 2007. She is currently completing a National Institute of Alcohol Abuse and Alcoholism–funded postdoctoral fellowship in the Department of Psychiatry at the University of Connecticut Health Center. Her research interests focus on factors affecting treatment outcome and relapse in addictive disorders.

Terry E. Robinson is Elliot S. Valenstein Professor of Behavioral Neuroscience and professor in the Psychology Department and Neuroscience Program, at the University of Michigan. Research in his laboratory concerns neural and psychological mechanisms of drug sensitization and addiction and the nature of individual differences related to the susceptibility to addiction.

Gideon Yaffe is associate professor of philosophy and law at the University of Southern California. Among other topics, he writes about responsibility, particularly criminal responsibility, and the conditions that undermine it. His published works include articles such as "Recent Work on Addiction and Responsible Agency" (*Philosophy and Public Affairs,* 2002) and books such as *Attempts* (Oxford University Press, 2010).

Index